MAKING PIECE

MAKING PIECE

A Memoir of
Love, Loss
and Pie

Beth M. Howard

ISBN-13: 978-0-373-89257-0
MAKING PIECE
Copyright © 2012 by Beth M. Howard

Library of Congress Cataloging-in-Publication Data
Howard, Beth M.
Making piece : a memoir of love, loss and pie / Beth M. Howard.
p. cm.
ISBN-13: 978-0-373-89257-0
ISBN-10: 0-373-89257-8
1. Howard, Beth M. 2. Journalists--United States--Biography.
3. Bakers--United States--Biography. 4. Widows--United States--
Biography. 5. Consolation. 6. Bereavement. I. Title.
PN4874.H685A3 2012
664'.752092--dc23
[B]
2011029012

www.Harlequin.com

Printed in U.S.A.

For Marcus Iken
Liebe meines Lebens

They say spirits read everything.
I say you didn't just *read* this book,
you helped me *write* it. Please consider it
a love letter and apology to you ... until
we meet again and I can tell you in person.

"Strange is our situation here upon earth. Each of us comes for a short visit, not knowing why, yet sometimes seeming to a divine purpose. From the standpoint of daily life, however, there is one thing we do know: That we are here for the sake of others . . . for the countless unknown souls with whose fate we are connected by a bond of sympathy. Many times a day, I realize how much my outer and inner life is built upon the labors of people, both living and dead, and how earnestly I must exert myself in order to give in return as much as I have received."

~Albert Einstein

"We must have pie.
Stress cannot exist in the presence of a pie."

~David Mamet

I blame pie. If it wasn't for banana cream pie, I never would have been born. If my mom hadn't made my dad that pie, the one with the creamy vanilla pudding, loaded with sliced bananas and covered in a mound of whipped cream, the one that prompted him to propose to her, I wouldn't be here. Think about it. The anatomical shape of bananas. The pudding so luscious and moist. The cream on top as soft as a pillow on which to lie down and inspire certain sensuous acts. My parents were virgins and intended to stay that way until they exchanged vows at the altar. That pie made wedding plans urgent. If it wasn't for that pie, they may never have gotten married and had kids, had me.

If I had never been born, I never would have learned to make pie; not just banana cream, but apple and strawberry-rhubarb and chocolate cream and peach crumble and many others. If I had never been born, I never would have grown up to become a writer and gotten that job at the dot com that paid so well, but stressed me

out so much that I quit to become a full-time pie baker in Malibu.
If I hadn't gotten that baking job, I never would have made pies
for Barbra Streisand and Steven Spielberg, and I never would have
taken time off to go on that road trip, the one where I ended up
at Crater Lake National Park and met Marcus Iken that night in
the hotel lobby.

If I had never met Marcus, never fallen in love with him and
his almond-shaped green eyes, exotic German-British accent
and those odd-yet-elegant leather hiking boots that laced up at
the sides, I never would have invited him to join me at my friends'
wedding in Tuscany. And thus, I never would have taken the train
from Italy to his apartment in Stuttgart, Germany, carrying that
pie I baked him, the apple one heaped high with fruit, drowning
in its own juices and radiating the seductive scent of cinnamon,
the one that made him realize I was like no woman he'd ever met
before and that he couldn't live without me—the pie that prompted
him to propose to me.

If it wasn't for pie, I never would have been born. I never
would have married Marcus and moved to Germany, to Oregon
and then to Mexico with him. If I had never married him, I would
not have been the one listed as the emergency contact, the
one who got The Phone Call that day. I never would have learned
how a call from a medical examiner can mean only one thing,
how harsh the word would sound in my ears—"Deceased,"
he'd said—and how that word would haunt me, change my life,
change me.

If I had never been born, I never would have known what it feels
like to lose Marcus, never known what his sexy, athletic body, the
body I had made love to hundreds of times, looked like lying in a
casket, cold, hard, lifeless, eventually cremated, his ashes buried,
never to be seen again.

If only my mom hadn't made my dad that banana cream pie. Fuck pie.

♥♥♥

I am a pie baker and I live in the American Gothic House. Yes, *the* American Gothic House, the one in the iconic Grant Wood painting of the couple holding the pitchfork. It is the second most famous white house in the U.S.A., second only to the White House. Yes, *the* White House in Washington, D.C. The American Gothic House is nowhere near Washington, D.C. It is located in rural Southeastern Iowa in a sleepy, former railroad town called Eldon (pop. 928), and while the house is indeed white, it is decidedly smaller and humbler than the presidential one. Because it is famous and old—old as in "built in 1881" old—it is listed on the National Register of Historic Places. But one doesn't need documentation or a plaque by the front door to know the age of this house. The slanted, worn, wide-plank floorboards, the rectangular shape of the nail heads handcrafted by blacksmiths and the cracks in the front door that let in the winter drafts speak for its many years of weathering a hardscrabble life on the windswept prairie.

Living in a tourist attraction (which *must* be where the expression "living in a fishbowl" comes from) takes a special person. And since I live here, I guess that makes me special in that I can handle the daily foot traffic tromping across my front porch, I accept how strangers, unable to restrain their curiosity, peer into my windows, and I politely offer to snap the occasional photo of a couple striking the prerequisite pose in front of the Gothic window.

Out of the hundred-plus places I've ever lived, this is the first and only one where I signed a lease requiring that the "tenant shall treat the public in a friendly manner." And mostly I am friendly. Except when I've had too many faces pressed up against the glass in my kitchen window. In which case, the white cotton curtain gets yanked across their hungry eyes, and I retreat to the most private room in the house: ironically, the upstairs bedroom, the one immediately behind the house's main feature, the Gothic window.

Legend has it that this window—and the matching one on the opposite end of the second floor—was purchased via mail order from Sears Roebuck. The triangular shape of the paned glass attracted Grant Wood's attention when he visited Eldon in 1930. He found it incongruous, if not pretentious, that such a simple white wooden farmhouse would be adorned with such an ornate, if not religious, window. Wood was so intrigued, he drew a sketch of the front of the house, returned to his art studio in Cedar Rapids, convinced his sister and his dentist to pose as the spinster daughter and dour father to represent the stoic, roll-up-your-sleeves-and-just-do-it, Midwest stereotype, painted the three individual elements onto one canvas, and the rest, as they say, is history. The house—and its window—is so famous that it attracts over 10,000 visitors a year to its remote Iowa location.

It is behind this window and its lace curtain that I sleep, dream, read, cry, snuggle with my two small dogs and escape the peering eyes of passersby. The lease also states "tenant agrees to maintain South Window curtains similar to those featured in Grant Wood's *American Gothic* painting." This is no problem, as the lace curtains came with the house. In the upstairs bedroom window, the showcase one, I simply hung white sheers over the lace curtain, which maintains the original appearance for the tourists' photo opportunity, but adds a layer of privacy from the outside world, and keeps at bay the blazing Iowa sun, which rises around seven each morning over the neighbor's soybean field.

On the weekends, when the weather is good, I sell pies out on the lawn of the house. I can't say if this has ever been done before at the American Gothic House. Out of the many families that have lived here—the Dibbles, the Joneses, the Smiths—mine are certainly not the first pies to be baked inside. That would be impossible, seeing as Iowa is the pie capital of America, where pies are a way of life, baked into the fabric of Midwestern existence. Eldon, Iowa, is full of pie bakers. (I know this because I've sampled Arlene Kildow's coconut cream pie. It would win first prize at the Iowa State Fair if she would enter. And Janice Chickering's apple pie, which I haven't tried yet, must be delicious because it wins every local pie contest.) But setting up a pie table right outside the famous house, as if it were an Amish farm stand or a Girl Scout bake sale? That might be a first.

I didn't move into the American Gothic House to sell pies. Moving into the American Gothic House wasn't in my plans at all. In fact, until that hot, humid, late August day that I happened upon the road sign for the house, I didn't even know of its existence. I will tell you how and why I came to live here, how I became known as "America's Pie Lady," how I became adopted by the mayor and other residents of Eldon, and most important of all, how my grief began to ease and my heart eventually began to heal. I will tell you all that and more. But I have to begin further back in time.

You will find my story is a lot like pie, a strawberry-rhubarb pie. It's bitter. It's messy. It's got some sweetness, too. Sometimes the ingredients get added in the wrong order, but it has substance, it will warm your insides and, even though it isn't perfect, it still turns out okay in the end.

I killed my husband. I asked for a divorce, and seven hours before he was to sign the divorce papers, he died. It was my fault. If I hadn't rushed him into it, I would have had time to change my mind, and I didn't want to change my mind again. I was sure this time. I wasn't good at being a wife and I was tired. Marcus and I still loved each other, still desired each other, we were still best friends. But in spite of best intentions, after six years, our marriage had become like overworked pie dough. It was tough, difficult to handle and the only option I could see was to throw it out and start over.

I was a free-spirited California girl, trying to mix with a workaholic German automotive executive. Too often, it had seemed like an exercise in futility, like trying to whip meringue in a greasy bowl where, with even the slightest presence of oil, turning the beaters up to a higher speed still can't accomplish the necessary lightness of being. We needed to throw out the dough, I insisted.

Chuck the egg whites, and wash out our bowls so we might fill them again. I was impatient and impulsive, overly confident that there was something, someone better out there for me. I was also mad at him. He worked too much. All I wanted was more of his time, more of him. Asking for a divorce was my cry for attention. And since I couldn't get his attention, couldn't get the marriage to work, couldn't get the goddamn metaphorical pie dough to roll, I was determined to start over. It was my fault. He died because of me. I killed him.

August 19, 2009, Terlingua, Texas

I wasn't even halfway through my morning walk with the dogs, but the sun had already risen high above the mesa of the Chisos Mountains. We should have left earlier, but every morning started with the same dilemma. Make coffee or walk the dogs first? I loved savoring my café latte on the front porch, taking that first half hour to shake off sleep and greet the day. But the window of dog-walking time was short, so the dogs always won. It never failed to amaze me how fast the sun rises in this West Texas frontier, how quickly a summer desert morning could transition from tolerable to intolerable, how a ball of fire that was welcome at first light so quickly became the enemy to be avoided, something from which to seek escape.

Other than the dogs' needs, the heat made no difference to me, as I had made a commitment to staying inside no matter what the weather. My plan was to spend the summer in my rented miner's cabin, chain myself to my computer and bang out a completed draft of my memoir about how I quit a lucrative web-producer job to become a pie baker to the stars in Malibu. How I used pies as if they were Cinderella's slipper to find a husband, and finally did fall in love and get married, to Marcus. The book was going to be a lighthearted tale of romance, adventure and pie baking. It was supposed to have a happy ending.

As I scanned the path for rattlesnakes while Jack ran ahead on the dirt road that stretched for miles through the empty, uninhabited expanse, the only thing visible on the horizon was the heat, a thermal curtain rising up from the ground, waving like tall grass in the breeze. I looked for my second dog, Daisy, the other half of Team Terrier, as I affectionately called my four-legged companions, but her light hair was the exact blond color of the desert floor, so she was much harder to spot between the scruffy patches of sagebrush.

I had gotten into a routine of jogging in the mornings, but on this day I wasn't feeling very strong. In fact, it wasn't the sun baking me to a crisp or the sweat running down the back of my legs that made me want to cut the walk short. It was my heart. It was racing, even though I was walking slowly—so slowly my gait was barely a shuffle. This was not normal for me. I have the strong heart and slow pulse of a professional bike racer, so much so that I often get surprised looks from doctors when probing me with their stethoscopes.

Something was wrong with me. Was I having a heart attack? I needed to get home before I collapsed and became breakfast for the vultures who were already circling overhead. I called for my dogs, who reluctantly gave up on their bunny chase to come back to me. I looked at my digital Timex watch before I turned around. It was 8:36 a.m. Central time.

I made it back to my miner's shack, a hundred-year-old cabin made of stacked rocks chinked with mud. It was primitive but stylish, rustic but elegant, clean and sparsely furnished with just the right touches of safari chic. Decorated by my landlord, Betty, a transplant from Austin, who lived next door, the cabin's style was *Real Simple* meets *Progressive Rancher*. The place had running water with a basic kitchen, but the shower was in a separate wing, which could be reached only by going outside. And the toilet? The toilet was an outhouse, a twenty-five-yard walk from the house. While I loved this simple living by day, I wouldn't go near the outhouse at night for fear of walking the gauntlet of snakes and tarantulas.

With the dogs safely back in the house—no one was going to get left outside to fry in the ungodly heat—I flopped down on my bed. My heart continued to race like a stuck accelerator, and I lay there, alone, holding my body still, thinking about how this was so unusual, so intense, so unlike any sensation I had ever experienced. I remember wondering if I was going to die. Would death come so early in my life? Really? I had just turned forty-seven, I had the heart of a bike racer, I was just out for an easy morning walk with my dogs, and now this? This was how and where it was going to end? I closed my eyes and tried to stay calm. I wasn't afraid of death. I just didn't think I was ready for it. Besides, if I died, who would take care of my dogs?

My BlackBerry in its rubber red casing sat next to my pillow. It rang and I glanced at the screen to see who was calling. "Unknown" was all it said. Marcus called me daily and he was the only person I knew whose number was "Unknown." We were living apart because of his corporate job that had transferred him yet again, this time back to Stuttgart, Germany, where I had lived with him before but I'd refused to live there again. Marcus wasn't in Germany now. He was in Portland, Oregon, taking a three-week vacation that was originally supposed to include coming to see me in Texas. But then I told him not to come. Oh, and then, after telling him not to come, I added, "As long as you're going to be in the States, this would be a convenient time for us to get a divorce."

I didn't want a divorce. I just wanted him to stop working at his job so much and work more at our marriage. I wanted him to spend less energy at his office so he would have some left for me when he got home. I still loved him, we still talked every single day, and I always, always, always took his calls. Especially ever since we'd had the conversation where I let it slip that there had been a few times when I hadn't picked up the phone when he called.

"Only when I'm writing and trying to concentrate," I assured him. His feelings were so hurt I never had the heart to ignore a call from him again. But with my heart racing, my muscles weak and now my head aching badly, I didn't feel up to talking to him or to anybody, so I let the call go to voice mail. It was just over two hours since I'd returned from my walk.

Twenty minutes later, I figured that if perhaps I wasn't going to die, I should at least get my ass out of bed and go see a doctor. Terlingua, a ghost town with a population of 200, didn't have a doctor per se, but there was a physician's assistant at a local resort who might be able to diagnose what was wrong. Before I called him, I checked my voice mail.

The message wasn't from Marcus.

If I could turn back the clock, if I could hit the reset button, if I could change the course of history and the unfolding of events, I would. I'd gladly sell my soul to go back in time to a date three and a half months earlier, the first week of May 2009—May 5, to be precise, our final day together—and start over from there. I was in Portland for a reunion with Marcus, who was about to begin a new one-year contract in Germany. It was the same day I got laid off from the job I had in Los Angeles, the one that I used as my excuse to leave Mexico, where Marcus had been posted for the past ten months. I had tried to be a good wife by following him to Mexico, after having followed him to Germany for almost three years and then to Portland for nearly two.

"Good wife" wasn't a role that came naturally to me and I lasted five months with Marcus in Mexico, where I spent too many long and lonely days in our house on the pecan farm before I reached my breaking point. So I took a position as U.S. Director for a London-based speakers' bureau, for which I would book famous people for public-speaking gigs at a rate of 120 grand for one hour of their time. The height of a tanking economy ensured I wouldn't succeed, not when company meetings were the first budget items to get cut. No meetings, no guest speakers. Thus, six months later, the phone call from my boss in London with news of my termination came as no surprise. I've been fired from many jobs (let's just say I'm a little too entrepreneurial in spirit to be employable) and I've never mourned the loss of anything that confined me to a cubicle in an office with sealed windows. I never looked back, because I always saw endings—fixable endings such as these, anyway—as opportunities for something new, something better. In this case, I used the free time and severance pay to travel to Texas to rent the miner's cabin for the summer so I could write about quitting one of those cubicle-confining jobs to become a pie baker.

So during this first week of May, between the ending of Marcus's Mexico assignment and the beginning of his new one-year contract in Germany, and coinciding with the termination of my L.A. job, we met up in Portland. Portland had been our home for almost two years, it's where we still had a lot of friends, a houseful of furniture in storage and where his company's North American headquarters was located. We spent four honeymoon-like days together, eating at our favorite French,

Italian and Thai cafés, getting massages, drinking lattes at the hipster coffeehouses, having dinner with other couples and holding hands a lot.

We agreed we could manage the long distance with me in L.A. and him in Germany and still keep our marriage intact. We had done it before; we could do it again. We would see each other once a month and it would be a win-win, because he could continue his steady career climb, and I could avoid being a stay-at-home nag. After one year he would either find another position back in the U.S. or find a different kind of work altogether.

Our whole existence—all seven and a half years of it—was like that. It was about international airports, romantic hellos and tearful goodbyes, about job changes and job transfers. When asked what the biggest challenge of our marriage was, he would say, "Logistics." (Though he used to say it was my lack of concern for stability, for things like health insurance and a retirement plan.) I would say the biggest obstacle was his job.

"My job provides a roof over your head," he liked to remind me. "And health insurance."

"I didn't marry you so you could be my provider," I argued. "I married you because I wanted a partner who would want to spend time together, do things together, *participate* in the marriage and not expect me to be the one to do all the housework while you go off to work like we're some 1950s couple."

"I'll pitch in more when I'm not so busy," he insisted. "And when you get a job."

This made no sense to me, as there would never be an occasion when his work didn't demand so much of his time. (In fact, it would only get worse.) And besides, as a freelancer, I wasn't really looking for a job per se. My projects, which provided decent income, came and went, but in a "feast or famine" way—not the

German way. Not the steadfast, loyal "Employee for Life" way that Germans revered.

I retaliated by applying for and getting full-time jobs. And since the only career-type work I could find was back in the U.S., I was the one being driven to the airport. This usually resulted in me getting fired and running back to my safety net, my rock, my man. I ran away, but I always came back. But once I got back, it was never long before I again faced the reality—and loneliness—of a mostly empty house and a life that was about dishes, laundry and shopping—and waiting for Marcus to come home.

His job demanded long hours, which he willingly gave, which inevitably drove me to look for something else to do. I needed to keep my brain busy, needed friends, needed to keep from getting angry with him for having moved my life halfway across the world only to feel so alone. Ironically, the only solution I could find meant living apart. It wasn't what I wanted. I just wanted more time with him. Even if he couldn't give me that time, I wanted him to at least acknowledge how his schedule was affecting our relationship, affecting me. I wanted him to apologize when he came home three hours later than he said he would be. Just a little "I'm sorry I was late" would have been enough. I wanted him to tell me he missed me when he was gone all day. But he said nothing. Instead, he accepted—or at least tolerated—the situation in stoic silence.

And so it went. I felt hurt, I left, I returned for happy, passion-filled reunions, the loneliness gradually set in and the cycle started all over again. It was a pattern we couldn't seem to break.

At the end of our long weekend, Marcus drove me to the Portland airport so I could return to L.A.; he was flying to Germany the next day. I stood there in his arms, at the curbside drop-off, on a rare rainless Pacific Northwest morning, while the engine of his rented Subaru Forester idled.

Marcus's brown hair was flattened under a tight wool cap, making his high cheekbones look even more pronounced and his almond-shaped green eyes appear even deeper. He wore a brown fleece pullover and Diesel jeans with clogs. He was secure in himself and, being European, his range of style went miles beyond an American baseball hat and sneakers. Clogs had become his signature footwear. They suited him in that ruggedly handsome way, though he could as easily transform from rugged to pure elegance and sophistication when dressed for work in his hand-tailored wool suits.

My head rested against his broad chest and I felt his breath on my neck. I breathed in his clean scent and felt his soft lips on my skin as his arms pulled me closer. "Have a safe trip, my love," he said, in the British-German accent that I never tired of. The way he talked was so soothing, even when speaking his mother tongue, that more than once I made him read to me from a German washing-machine manual or DVD-player instruction book just to hear his sexy voice.

"And you have a safe flight to Germany," I replied. "Let's Skype later." We parted with a tender kiss, our mouths touching lightly in a sort of half French kiss, until I felt self-conscious about people in the cars behind us watching and pulled away. He stayed by the car and waved until I disappeared through the revolving door. I looked back through the glass window and watched him get into his rented Subaru.

And that's the last time I ever saw him alive.

CHAPTER

2

Three and a half months later on August 19, 2009, in Terlingua, Texas, I thought I was dying of a heart attack. I didn't answer my phone because I didn't have the energy to lift my head off the pillow. At 11:05 a.m., I finally checked my voice mail.

The message was from a man named Tom Chapelle, who apologized for having to call, but he didn't have my address. Why would he need my address? Why would he need to come to my house? Hell, he would have a hard time getting to my house, seeing as I was a five-hour drive from the nearest airport in El Paso, a 90-minute drive from the nearest grocery store and I lived on a dirt road with a name not recognized by the post office.

In his message, Mr. Chapelle said he was a medical examiner and he was calling because I was listed as the emergency contact for a Marcus Iken. He used the article "a" as if my husband were an object. A car. A watch. A book. A husband. I clearly don't watch enough television as I didn't have the slightest clue what a medical examiner was. I scribbled down the phone number he left and my heart, which had finally slowed a little, revved right up again, double time. My hands shook as I punched the numbers into my BlackBerry.

I might not have known what a medical examiner's job was, but instinctively I knew the call wasn't good. Worst case, I was thinking Marcus might have been injured in a car accident. He was simply in the emergency room, waiting for a broken bone to be set. Or he had fallen off his bike and needed stitches in his head, and was unable to call me himself. During his vacation, he'd been riding his road bike a lot, going on thirty-mile outings. Surely it must have been something to do with his bike and he was going to recover from whatever injury he had suffered. He was going to be fine. I didn't know that the job title "medical examiner" could mean only one thing.

In May, after I lost my job and Marcus flew off to Germany and I left Los Angeles for Texas, I prepared for my twenty-hour drive from L.A. to Terlingua by going to the library to check out some books on tape. Since I arrived at the Venice Beach branch five minutes before closing, I had to be quick, which meant I wasn't able to be terribly selective. I just grabbed an armful of CDs with authors' names I recognized. Among the titles I checked out was Joan Didion's, *The Year of Magical Thinking*. I listened to it in its entirety as I drove through the tire-melting temperatures and endless shades of red-and-brown landscape, crossing Arizona and New Mexico, until I finally reached West Texas.

I couldn't stand the reader's voice, an affected British actress, who made poor old Ms. Didion sound like a spoiled snob instead of the devastated widow that she was. A widow. A grieving widow. The book was interesting, but it wasn't anything I could relate to. I hadn't lost my husband. *My* husband was young and fit. I hadn't lost anyone close to me, except for my grandparents who'd lived well into their eighties when their aged bodies finally wore out. Death was not a subject on my radar. Still, I listened and the book's opening lines stuck with me the way pie filling sticks to the bottom of an oven. "Life changes fast. Life changes in the instant. You sit down to dinner and life as you know it ends."

I stood in the living room, next to my writing desk, my hand placed on the desktop to steady myself as the medical examiner's phone rang. He picked up after two rings and I started shaking even more. "What is your relationship to Marcus?" Mr. Chapelle asked first.

"I'm his wife," I answered. And I was. Barely. I'd asked for a divorce and pushed Marcus into starting the proceedings. We were working through a mediator in Portland who was drawing up the papers. I didn't *want* a divorce. I wanted him to fight for me, for him to say, "No! You are the love of my life and I can't live without you. I want to stay married."

In my perfect world, he would have also said, "I promise to work less, worship you more and, above all, be on time." He would have said, *should* have said—oh, why didn't he say it—"My love, if you say you're going to have dinner ready at seven-thirty, by God, I'll be home at seven-thirty. I'll even come home at seven, so I can make love to you first."

Had it really come down to his long work hours and lack of punctuality? We had been married a few days shy of six years. That's six years of cold dinners and hurt feelings. Six years of moving from country to country, continent to continent. Setting up a new house with each move; taking German lessons and then Spanish lessons; making new friends; saying goodbye to those friends and then making new ones again. Six years of trying to get Marcus to acknowledge me, what I needed, how much I wanted our marriage to come first and how his work, his schedule, his priorities were wearing me down.

Before we got married, during our year-and-a-half-long courtship, the majority of time I spent with Marcus was when he was on vacation. Europeans get six weeks of holidays, which meant six weeks with Marcus in laid-back mode, Marcus wearing jeans and reading books, not donning a suit, not checking his email, not coming home late. He cooked for me. He grilled steaks and shucked oysters. He did my laundry. He washed the dishes. And he made love to me for hours. It's no wonder I wanted to marry him!

But that was on my home turf. When I moved to Germany, everything changed—Marcus changed. When he put on his suit and tie, he became a different person.

"What about me?" I pleaded time and again. "Our marriage centers only on you and your job, your promotion, your schedule. What about my career and my happiness? What about where I want to live? Why can't we pick a place we *both* want to live, a place where I can speak the language and not feel so lonely, and just move there and we can both get jobs?"

We eventually moved to Portland and that helped for the year and a half we lived there. But then Marcus, thanks to his steady corporate executive career climb, got transferred to Mexico and we were right back where we started. My unanswered questions inevitably escalated into louder cries, harsher words. "I want to be in an equal partnership. Instead I feel like you just expect me to serve you!" I shouted. "I have a life, too!"

I had a life, all right. And now he didn't.

Joan Didion's suggestion that "life changes in the instant" might have been true for her. She was physically there in the room when her husband's heart stopped and caused him to fall out of the chair and hit his head on the corner of the table on the way down.

She saw him lying on the floor, unresponsive, his head bleeding. She had proof, evidence, visual aids. She could put her fingers on his pulse and feel he didn't have one. She could blow air into his lungs and watch his chest rise. She could call 911 and watch the paramedics as they stormed into her apartment and hooked up their electrodes and squeezed their syringes. Being there, in person, absorbing the immediacy of the action, then yes, time must have felt compressed into an instant.

News—specifically bad news—when delivered over the phone causes time to take on a different dimension. With no visual cues, there is nothing for the mind to grasp but whatever is imagined— drama, gore, violence, struggle, pain—combined with fleeting, movie-clip-like flashes of memory. There is no proof. There is only the voice of a stranger on the other end of the line. Someone you don't know, don't want to know, don't want to believe. Someone in a government building 2,000 miles away. Someone who has never met your husband, who sees the man you loved only as a corpse lying on the examination table, waiting for an autopsy.

With this one phone call, life as I knew it ended.

"Your husband is deceased," he said, his voice deep and gravelly. He had the air of a military officer, serious, official, no emotion, detached. I could just picture the man sporting a crew cut, fleshy jowl, perfectly starched shirt, maybe even khaki in color, with the buttons pulling tightly across his ample belly. Deceased. The word didn't register at first. Deceased? No, that can't be. Injured is what I had expected him to say. Hurt in a car accident or from a fall off his bike, just out of surgery but recovering nicely. Not deceased. Not Marcus. Not healthy, robust, sexy, stubborn Marcus.

I would sell my soul to turn back the clock, to never get a call from a medical examiner and continue living in my happy oblivion to never even know what one was. I wish with every cell in my body to go back three and a half months earlier to May 5, the day Marcus dropped me off at the Portland airport. I wouldn't get on the plane to L.A. I would fly to Germany with him instead, and worry about getting my belongings there later. Or I would turn the clock back even earlier. Five years, five months, it doesn't matter. I'd settle for turning the clock back five hours. Maybe that way I could have saved him. I still want to save him. I still want him to be alive. Seven hours before Marcus was supposed to sign his half of the divorce papers, I killed him. I asked him for a divorce neither of us wanted and I killed him. To verify this, I asked Mr. Chapelle in a meek tone that didn't sound anything like me, "Was it suicide?" The words snuck past my vocal cords and tiptoed out of my throat, which tightened with each passing second. It was the worst thing I could have asked; I was ashamed for asking it, but I had to know.

"No," he answered quickly. "It was something with his heart."

Of course, it was his heart. I broke it. He wanted to stay married and this was his way of making that happen. This was the second time we tried to divorce, and the second time we didn't sign the papers. We were still married. And now we would be married forever. That's a hell of a way to avoid divorce.

"The divorce almost killed both of you," my sister said later. It hadn't occurred to me, but she was right. During the hour he was struggling to stay alive after collapsing from a ruptured aorta, I felt my heart about to give out, thinking I would collapse in the middle of the Chihuahua Desert. I turned to go back home at 8:36 a.m.—that was 6:36 a.m. in Portland, the exact time Marcus was pronounced dead. Is it possible we were that connected? Were our bodies functioning in unison, joined by some inexplicable force? Was I feeling what he was feeling, the struggle of his heart to keep beating? While he was hit with defibrillator paddles and receiving epinephrine injections, I was enduring my own struggle,

staggering with weakness back to my miner's cabin with my dogs—
our dogs.

I had a few hours to contemplate my death, but did he know he
was dying? The details that were parceled out over the next few
days concluded no, he could not have known. It was instant. He
felt a cramp in his neck, got out of bed, took a few steps and collapsed on the hardwood floor of a friend's house.

I imagined him having one of those out-of-body experiences,
floating above his body, looking down and seeing himself lying
unconscious on the floor, and saying, "What the fuck just happened?" This is a man who wanted to live. He had just invested
in a new MacBook Pro and an iPhone. He had a pile of new books
including *The Passion Test, What Color is Your Parachute* and *What
Should I Do With My Life?* And he had bookmarked his favorite
new website, "Zen Habits," which was all about doing less to accomplish more. After years of my incessant nagging, he was actually exploring ways to trade in his corporate life for something
more balanced. Back in Germany, he had also just bought a new
road bike, a sleek and fast-looking LaPierre, which he had shown
me via Skype. He sent me emails from his weekend bike rides in
France, Italy and even Slovenia. This was a man with a lot of life
left to live and big plans for the future. He was only getting started.

The autopsy determined he died from a hemopericardium
(blood flooding the heart sack until the heart cannot pump any
longer) due to a ruptured aorta. Marcus had a heart condition
from birth, a bicuspid aortic valve, which means he had only two
flaps to allow oxygenated blood to flow out from the aorta instead
of the normal three. Blood pumping through the aorta is under
high pressure. Having only two flaps creates a bottleneck and
puts added pressure on the aortic wall. The wall had a weakening
that eventually tore. Unless it happens when you are already in

a hospital, a ruptured aorta is always deadly. There is no grace period. The blood moves too fast. The heart suffocates. And bam! Just like that. The man you love is gone.

His German doctors had always maintained his heart condition would never be a problem. Had Marcus known how endangered his life was, he would have taken precautions. He was that kind of guy: disciplined in everything he did, especially when it came to his diet (only the highest quality, organic, wild-caught everything for him). He didn't smoke, he exercised regularly, doing yoga, biking and running, and he loved being outside in the sun breathing fresh air. This was a guy who was so health-conscious, he flossed his teeth three times a day. Who does that? No, he was not supposed to die. Not like this. Not at forty-three. Not ever.

My brain spun with centrifugal force after hanging up with Mr. Chapelle. I looked around the living room of my miner's cabin in a wild panic. My body shook with convulsions. My eyes widened with disbelief. My breathing turned to hyperventilating. I paced back and forth between the desk and the daybed. I had no idea what to do. Did I really just get a phone call telling me that Marcus was deceased? Deceased. I hate that word. What a miserable word. If only I could have taken that word and shoved it through the phone line, stuffed it back into the mouth of the man who uttered it, crammed it all the way down his throat to extinguish it so he could never say it. If he couldn't say it, then it couldn't be true.

My first call was to our divorce mediator in Portland. "He's in a meeting," his secretary said.

"It's urgent," I told her. She must have heard the panic in my voice—high-pitched, sharp and forceful. She put me through.

"Marcus won't be coming in for his one-o'clock appointment. He died," I blurted out. "He's dead. He had a ruptured aorta." And then my composure crumbled. "I don't know what to do! I don't

know what to do! I don't know what to do! I don't know what to
do!" I kept repeating myself, practically screaming in hysterics,
as I entered into full-blown panic. To say it out loud to someone
else, to acknowledge that which I desperately did not want to be
true, made it just a little more real. Was it really true?

I could detect Michael's shock in spite of his attempt to calm
me. He was a Catholic-turned-Zen Buddhist, which he had told us
when we interviewed and subsequently hired him to help negoti-
ate our separation. Marcus was in Portland and thus met with him
in person several times. I was only connected by conference calls
and had never seen him, but based on his gentle voice, relaxed
manner of speech and his respect for Marcus's and my determination to remain amicable, he seemed nice—for a former litigation
lawyer. He had changed his career to mediation because it seemed,
well, less litigious. "Take a breath," he said. "Settle down. You're
going to be okay. Here's what you do."

He outlined the next steps for me. Someone had to instruct me,
because I couldn't think straight. I couldn't think past the image of
Marcus and his lifeless body lying in a morgue thousands of miles
away. No! I could not, would not, picture that. My mind was still
insisting he was alive. He had to be alive. This was all a mistake.
This wasn't really happening.

"Book your flight to Portland," Michael said, snapping me back
to the present. "Call his parents in Germany. And above all, take
care of yourself. You need to make sure you are okay. Do you have
someone there who can be with you?" I didn't. Betty, my landlord,
was in El Paso for a few days. I had only my dogs and I was already
scaring them. Daisy was hiding under the bed and Jack kept trying
to lick my face, something he was prone to do when he was insecure.

I wanted to fly to Portland that evening. There was a flight
available, and even with the five-hour drive to the El Paso airport,

I could have made it. But when I discussed it with Mr. Chapelle, he said there was no reason to rush. It wasn't like I needed to get there in case Marcus might take his final breath. He was already gone.

I spent the entire night awake; first tossing and turning in my bed until finally, so disturbed, so much wanting to crawl out of my skin to escape the searing pain, I moved into the living room and lay on the concrete floor in front of the fan. My forehead, pressed into the painted cement, rolled back and forth, practically wearing a groove into the hard floor as I wailed and wailed and wailed. I never heard such loud, guttural cries emitted from so deep within my core, never knew noises such as these were possible. I sounded like a dying animal, moaning like a cow hit by a car and left for dead on the road, wishing for someone to shoot it and put it out of its misery.

And I did feel like I was dying. I wanted to die. My moaning, my wailing, my cries could have been heard as far away as El Paso. But no matter how much, how long and how hard I cried, I couldn't get the pain out. This new form of agony—sizzling, burning, tearing at my heart with razor blades—was an alien being that took over my body, infiltrating every cell. I couldn't hold still. I couldn't cry hard enough. I couldn't scream loud enough. I couldn't get the emotional torture to stop.

Psychologists call it complicated grief. It was almost a relief, as much as I could fathom any inkling of relief, to learn a few months later that what I was experiencing had a name, a clinical term. I had a condition. I could be placed in a category, given a label. I could wear a sign around my neck that read "Caution: This woman is suffering from complicated grief."

Complicated grief is when someone you are close to dies and leaves you with unresolved issues, unanswered questions, unfinished business. And guilt. Lots and lots of guilt. And pain. Bottomless depths of searing pain. Complicated grief is when you ask your husband for a divorce you don't really want, and he dies seven hours before signing the papers.

I killed my husband. I was sure of it. It was my fault. I'm the one who pushed for a divorce. He didn't want it, must not have wanted it, otherwise he wouldn't have died. He was dead, we were still married, and that told me everything. Before leaving my miner's cabin for Portland, where my husband was reportedly dead, before putting my dogs in the care of my British neighbor, Ralph, I rummaged through my toiletry bag and found my wedding ring. The ring, an exact match to Marcus's, was a band of fine gold on the outside, with an inner ring of steel on the inside. The bands were connected, yet separate, and made a jingling sound when they moved against each other. We had our rings designed by a goldsmith friend of Marcus's in Germany to represent us—our strong bond balanced by our independence—and our lifestyle, the contrast of our love for both backpacking and five-star hotels.

I slid the ring back onto my finger where my white tan line had turned brown in the Texas sun, and shook my hand until I heard the familiar jingling. The gentle rattle had become a nonverbal communication between Marcus and me. We would shake our rings in each other's ears as a way to say, "I'm sorry, I still love you" after an argument, when it was too difficult or too soon to utter the words out loud. I had taken the ring off even before I asked Marcus for the divorce. I took it off because I was mad at him. Mad that I couldn't fly to Germany for my birthday in June to spend it with him. Because the auto industry was forced to make job cuts, Marcus was working two jobs and therefore he was too busy for me to visit. He started his days at 6:30 a.m. and returned home—home, which translated as a guest apartment attached to his parents' house—no earlier than 9:30 at night, night after night. He was exhausted. I could hear it in the irritable tone of his voice. I could see his fatigue when we talked via Skype. I felt bad for him, but I was also hurt.

"What about me? I'm your wife. Am I not a priority?" I continued to plead. I hadn't seen him since May. June came and went. And then there was July, a month during which he developed a chronic cough. "Don't be like Jim Henson," I chided. "You know, the guy who created The Muppets. He was sick but refused to take any time off work. It turned into pneumonia, and look what happened to him."

Marcus insisted he was fine. His doctor told him his lungs were clear, it wasn't bronchitis, gave him an asthma inhaler and sent him home. If only the doctor had checked his heart, had used ultrasound equipment to inspect his aorta, checked the thickness of its wall, had seen that there was a weakening and performed emergency surgery to put in a stent. If only.

Marcus spent his 43rd birthday on July 2—having no clue it would be his last—buying his new road bike. He still had no time for me to visit. His August vacation was coming up, so we assumed we would just wait and see each other then. I was looking forward to seeing him. I missed him. I missed his body, his shapely soccer-player thighs, his perfect, round ass. I missed his scent, or lack of scent, maybe it was just his presence I longed for. I missed spooning against his smooth skin, his chest hair tickling my back. This was the longest stretch of time we'd spent apart since we met—and, no, Skype sex doesn't count.

"Let's make a plan," I suggested.

"No," he said. "Every minute of my life is planned out for work. I don't want to make any plans right now. I'm too tired." And that was it. That was my breaking point. He didn't want to make plans for his August vacation—*our* vacation. I felt cast aside, not important enough for him to pencil me into his calendar. Work always came first. So I asked for a divorce. "You don't want to make plans? I'll make them for you. Instead of coming to Texas, you can spend the three weeks in Portland filing the papers."

He still wanted to come to Texas. He said, "I'll come there and we'll talk through our issues."

"If you come here," I replied, "we'll have a good time like we always do. We'll drink lattes and wine, we'll go hiking with Team Terrier, we'll make love and then we'll be right back to where we were."

"Yes," he said. "You're right."

Why, oh, why, *OH, WHY* didn't I let him come? Why did I have to be such a hard-nosed bitch? "But what if he would have died in Texas?" friends argued. "It's so remote, you couldn't have even called an ambulance. You would have never forgiven yourself." Forgiveness? I couldn't forgive myself for any of this. I killed my husband. It was my fault. If only I had let him come to Texas, he would still be alive.

I don't know what normal grief is like, but complicated grief? Complicated grief must be grief on steroids.

The physician's assistant of Terlingua didn't give me an appointment to check my racing heart—my heart which was also now broken, shattered beyond repair. Instead, he gave me a ride to the El Paso airport. We didn't speak for the duration of the five-hour pre-dawn drive. He left me to my silence as I stared numbly out the open window, feeling the hot Texas wind in my face. I flew from Texas to Portland into the arms of my best friend from childhood. Everyone needs a friend like Nan. Nan is the friend who, when you tell her the news—the Very Bad News that you're still having a hard time believing is true, but since Marcus didn't call the entire day after Mr. Chapelle's call, and he never went a day without at least sending an email, I was beginning to believe *could* be true—well, Nan takes charge.

"You don't have to come to Portland," I told Nan. She didn't listen. Not only did she book a flight from New York, a rental car and a Portland hotel, she made sure her flight arrived before mine, so she could scrape me off the airport floor and carry me to the car.

Marcus and I had three weddings, so it seemed fitting that we had three funerals. We first got married at a German civil service in the picturesque village of Tiefenbronn, where we signed our international marriage certificate with Marcus's parents as our witnesses. Next, we got married on a farm outside Seattle, Washington, not only to accommodate my friends and family, but also because I had been freelancing for the past year at Microsoft and therefore Seattle was my most recent U.S. base.

We saved the best for last and returned to Germany, where we took over the tiny Black Forest hamlet of Alpirsbach, booking rooms for our guests in all the charming inns, hosting dinners at cozy *Bierstubes* and walking down the aisle in a thousand-year-old cathedral, a towering beauty built of pink stone. Three weddings, three different styles, from basic to rustic to elegant. His funerals mirrored our weddings, albeit with a lot more tears—and definitely no champagne.

I didn't see his body until I had been in Portland for five days. I was still going on trust to accept that he was actually dead and hadn't instead plotted his disappearance to some tax haven where he was now living on a yacht with a supermodel. It wasn't until the day of the Portland funeral that I laid eyes on him. I had already picked out clothes for him to wear—a black linen shirt, his favorite wool bicycle jersey tied around his shoulders, Diesel jeans and his clogs. He had to wear his clogs.

And then, there on Broadway and 20th, in the understated pink-and-beige-toned parlor of the Zeller Chapel of the Roses, two hours before the Portland service was to begin, I saw him. It was him, strikingly handsome and healthy looking, even when filled with embalming fluid. It was the man I had fallen in love with, was still in love with, the man I had married, was still married to. I saw him. I talked to him, begged him to wake up. I held his hands, bluish and hard. I ran my fingers along his forehead, bruised from his collapse. I leaned down into his casket and kissed his cold lips that didn't kiss me back. Now I knew it was true. He was dead.

My tears cascaded down like Multnomah Falls and they didn't stop for ten months. They ran and ran, creating permanent puffy eyes and altering my face with so much stress old friends no longer recognized me. The tears ran the entire flight to Germany, while I sat in business class and Marcus flew in a metal box in cargo. The tears flowed all through the week I spent in Germany, from the moment his grief-stricken, ashen-faced parents picked me up at the Stuttgart airport, to when they took me to the guest apartment where Marcus's suits were hanging in the closet.

My tears kept on flowing through the German funeral, a formal and elegant church service, packed with Marcus's coworkers, accompanied by a quartet of French horns playing Dvorak's "From the New World" and presided over by the same pastor who'd married us. The tears gushed through the informal and quiet burial of Marcus's ashes, and through the final meeting at the Tiefenbronn Rathaus, the place where we had signed our marriage certificate, and where I was required to sign his death certificate.

The tears came in endless waves. They came by day, by night. My tears did not discriminate in their time or place. From

Germany, my tears followed me back to Portland, and then back to Texas, where I collected my dogs, packed up my MINI Cooper, said goodbye to Betty, goodbye to my miner's cabin, goodbye to the desert that had nurtured my creativity all summer, goodbye to life as I had known it. The tears were ever-present, ever-flowing. It was a wonder I wasn't completely dehydrated. There was only one thing that defined me now: grief. Complicated grief. Grief on steroids. It was something I was going to have to get used to.

3

What I thought was a heart attack, or a cosmic connection to Marcus as his heart struggled to keep beating and then stopped, turned out to be a hyperthyroid. I had struggled with this auto-immune condition for a few years, it was the culprit that kept me from getting pregnant, but I had finally gotten it in check. (Marcus and I had accepted that having kids wouldn't fit our lifestyle anyway. While we were in Germany, we got a dog, Jack, instead. Jack's Mexican stepsister came later when Daisy followed me home one afternoon during Marcus's assignment in Saltillo.) A simple blood test—along with the goiter in my neck that had exploded to the size of a grapefruit—indicated the hyperactivity had returned with a vengeance. My T-levels were off the charts.

Without any other purpose or sense of clarity to guide me, I let my medical problem determine where to go next. All I knew was that I couldn't stay in my miner's cabin in Texas. I spent two weeks back in Terlingua, recovering from the three weeks of funeral-related travel. Everything I had loved about the place before—the isolation, the vastness and emptiness of the desert wilderness—now threatened to consume me, and draw me further into a new world of quiet madness. I maintained just enough sanity to know I needed to be somewhere else, somewhere I could be around people. Normally I would have returned to L.A. That's where my parents and two out of my four siblings lived; it's where I had spent the bulk of my adult life, and it's where I always fled to when Marcus and I hit a rough patch. But this time, in this new, debilitating, fragile, uncertain state of being, and because I didn't have Marcus to run back to, I ran to the next closest thing: a place filled with memories of him.

Portland made sense for many reasons. First of all, I had no home anywhere else. Portland was affordable. Portland was where my trusted endocrinologist practiced and he could treat my over-active gland. Portland may have been the place where Marcus died, but it was still the place where we had lived and loved. And Portland was where our—er, *my*—furniture was stored.

Portland was where we—*I*—had friends, friends who knew both of us, knew us as a couple, friends who could lend support as I searched for meaning in life. Because so far, I couldn't find any meaning left at all. I was so down on life, so lacking in any enthusiasm to face each new day as it dawned, I couldn't even get excited about my morning coffee. Portland was where my memories of Marcus could help me feel more connected to him. In Portland, I would also attend a grief support group. I had already done my homework and found a free program. I couldn't wait to get started. I couldn't wait to stop feeling pain. Because if I continued feeling the way I was—which is to say lost, confused, angry and sad, oh, so very, very sad—I was going to be joining Marcus in the afterlife sooner rather than later. Impatient has always been my middle name. I didn't know if I could ever feel good again, but if it was possible, like I'd heard it was possible from others who had lost someone they loved, I wanted to get going.

Wanting to make things right again and demanding immediate results was ingrained in my nature. When I was eight years old, I went to horse camp, the Bortell's Bar-Rockin-B Ranch in Iowa, where my sister and I spent one full week learning to groom, saddle and ride horses. I was very excited. One of the first things our horse instructor told us was there would be an award given to anyone who fell off their horse and got back on to ride again. It was called the "Spurs Award." That sounded nice—I nodded my head approvingly—but I wasn't going to fall off my horse.

Of course, by the second day, I did fall off. I don't remember how or why I ended up on the ground—those horses must have been the world's tamest animals seeing as they were employed at a kids' camp—but what I do remember is that I wanted to win the Spurs Award. By God, I was going to get back on and ride again. From the moment I realized I was on the ground and no longer in the saddle, I brushed myself off and went running after my horse, chasing it around the arena, so I could get back on—immediately. I was determined. I was going to win that award.

I chased old Brownie until he came to a stop and, grabbing the stirrup, climbed back on, breathless and proud. At the end of the week, at the closing ceremonies for camp, when all the awards were granted—for archery, for team spirit, for cleanest cabin—I was called up to receive my award, a paper certificate with my name on it: the Spurs Award. When the horse instructor handed it to me, he commented, "When we said get back on your horse and ride again, we meant sometime before the week is over, not ten seconds after you fall off."

I wasn't that eight-year-old girl anymore. I was forty-seven and wishing I was dead, wishing I had died instead of Marcus. And yet, somewhere in between the dark cumulus clouds of grief, I still had the will to live, the determination to get back on my horse. If I was going to be forced to grieve, then I was going to face it head-on. I was going to be the best student in grief school. I was going to get straight A's. I was going to apply my usual tenacity and grit—and impatience—the way I did when I graduated early from both high school and college, and conquer my grief. I was going to run after the horse like Lance Fucking Armstrong and win the "Spurs Award for Grieving Widows."

The day of my first grief support group meeting coincided with a rare phone conversation with my mother, who had been placed on my growing roster of People to Avoid While Grieving. One thing I learned very quickly after Marcus died was the outrageous comments people are capable of making when someone you love dies. It was as if certain friends, family members and acquaintances were suffering not from the grief or shock of Marcus's death, but from verbal diarrhea. From day one, various people's mouths ran awry with inappropriate and hurtful comments—words which came out like loose stool over which they had no control. They couldn't manage to simply say, "I'm sorry for your loss." Which is all anyone should say. Period.

But, no. They said things like: "You were going to get a divorce anyway, so I don't know why you're so broken up." "The timing of his death was good; if it had been in October, it would have interfered with our party." "I don't believe in an afterlife; when he's dead, he's dead." And, oh, here's another good one: "I lost my mother last year and, believe me, it only gets harder."

Those were only a few of the gems worthy of a David Letterman Top Ten list. The less outrageous but equally insensitive comments included: "It was his time." I heard that one a lot. And "He's in a better place now." Really? You don't think he'd rather be riding his new LaPierre road bike through the Italian countryside? How do you know what place he's in and if it's better? No. Not helpful.

My mom had contributed her share of questionable commentary, and it would take me many months to turn my anger toward her into compassion, which is why I was keeping my conversations with her to a minimum. It had been only one month since Marcus's death, and I was not only angry with my crew of commentators and their unsolicited opinions, but also with myself. My own harsh words ran in my head like a heavy-metal song stuck in repeat mode. I couldn't find a quiet corner anywhere. The outside comments were bad enough, but the noisiest ones were inside my own mind.

Just a few hours before my inaugural grief support group, I called my mom to check in. I was greeted with the same innocent question that anyone would ask in any given phone call. She simply asked, "How are you?" I know, I know. It's a benign question, a conversation starter not meant to be taken literally. But I was not able to answer with the standard throwaway line, "I'm fine." I couldn't lie. Grief was like that. Grief was like truth serum that magnified each and every speck of life's minutiae. Every little thing felt so important, so urgent, so serious. If Marcus had died so suddenly, then I could, too. Anyone could. Not only that death *could* happen, but that I wanted it to come; I wished for it. My desire to keep living was diminishing with each passing day. Life became so fragile. I was fragile. I was definitely not fine.

So instead of giving the standard answer, I said, "That's just not the right question to ask." Okay, so I could have been nicer. I could have—*should have*—just lied. I didn't need to take my pain

out on my own mother. I didn't need to drag her down with me
into my Grief Pit. She was quick to lash back and her response
stung me like a scorpion bite. "Well, I just don't know what to say
to you anymore!" she snapped.

Another thing about grief is that it gives you permission to take
care of yourself in a way you never knew how to before. My animal
instincts kicked in and I recoiled into the safety of my shell. I was
a grieving widow who needed to take care of herself. So with the
sting still smarting, I did what any self-respecting, self-protecting
widow would do: I hung up on her.

I found my way to the third floor of Good Samaritan Hospital
with ten minutes to spare before the start of my first session in the
grief support group. I had been to individual therapy off and on
over the years, and I had hauled Marcus to a few sessions of marriage counseling, but I had never been to group therapy. I liked
the idea of sharing my deepest, most intimate issues in a group
setting about as much as I liked being a widow. But I was desperate
for help. And it was free. I took a seat in the circle of chairs and
waited for the two-hour session to begin. I was still upset by the
aborted phone call with my mother. Hell, I was still upset about
everything, about Marcus's death ripping my life so irreversibly
apart that I was now sitting with an assortment of strangers listening to their stories about death and dying.

One by one, going around the circle, they each took a heartfelt
turn explaining how they were coping, how they were still trying to
find meaning in life two years after their spouse was gone. What?
Two years? I could still be sitting here two years from now, trying
to get my life back together? I would rather be dead. Why couldn't
I have been the one to die? A man in his thirties, whose wife died
a year earlier of a degenerative disease, finished speaking and
then it was my turn.

"Hello, my name is Beth Howard. I just moved back to Portland after my husband, Marcus . . . " I didn't get very far before the tears bubbled out like boiled-over pie filling. In a matter of seconds, I was choking on my own spit, globs of snot running down from my nose and into my mouth. I eeked out bits of my history. "And then, as if that wasn't bad enough," I continued between heaving sobs, "I hung up on my mother today."

I was gasping for air, crying so hard, I could barely get the words out. I finally stopped talking and when I ventured a look around at a few of the faces in the circle, I was met with a round of solemn but compassionate nods. This was a knowing group who had all been there, done that, but they were all much farther along in the grieving process than me. No one else had lost it during their introduction like I had. They had all delivered their stories with composure and a detectable—an *enviable*—trace of detachment. I was a newbie. I was raw. Too raw. I didn't belong in this group. I didn't—couldn't even if I wanted to—speak again after that. Eventually, as the spotlight got turned to someone else, I was able to scale back my sobs to the normal faucet flow of tears and sat quietly for the remainder of the evening's discussion. When the session came to a close, Susan, the group facilitator, asked to see me. She led me to the far corner of the room, away from the others.

Susan was a roundish, middle-aged blonde with a quiet voice and gentle, calming energy. She was comfort in a burgundy-colored pant suit. She was a slice of warm apple pie. This grief counselor, this angel sent from heaven, looked me in the eyes—what little she could see of my eyes through my swollen eyelids—and said, "I'm worried about you. Are you going to be okay tonight? Do you have someone you can be with? Are you okay to drive home?" Oh, boy. Some angel. I was in trouble. I wanted to be the star pupil, ace the test, be cured of my sadness and depression in one, maybe two, easy sessions. The joke was on me. I wasn't going to win the Spurs Award. I was going to be committed to the psych ward.

"I'm fine," I insisted. I couldn't tell my mom I was fine, but I was in no position to give any other answer to Susan. I wasn't fine, and didn't know if, or when, I'd ever be fine, but Susan didn't know me well enough to know tonight's breakdown was normal for me—or the "new normal," as the grief books put it.

I wanted to throw those stupid, fucking grief books against the wall when they talked of this "new normal." I wanted my "old normal" back. I wanted Marcus to be alive. I wanted to turn back the clock and be a better wife, to not get mad at Marcus for working so much, to complain less and love more, to have never asked for that divorce. I didn't want to feel this way, to live in distress, walking through life in a daze, overly sensitive to some things, completely numb to others, to spend my days with a death wish. I was cognizant enough to know my "new normal" wasn't healthy. It wasn't something I could continue to live with. But after a month I had gotten somewhat accustomed to it. I was getting familiar with touching the void, plunging into the black hole of sadness. I knew what it felt like to flounder in the ocean of despair, to be pummeled by tidal waves of grief and held under in their suffocating darkness.

I wasn't afraid. I was just . . . well, okay, I might have been *borderline* suicidal. I certainly thought about it, but I wasn't going to kill myself. Not tonight anyway. My friends Alison and Thomas had dinner waiting for me and all I wanted was to get out of this hospital meeting room and back to the warmth of their home, eat a filet of grilled salmon served with pesto made from their garden, and drink a glass or three of wine while listening to Alison's infectious laugh.

I convinced Susan to let me leave, unescorted, but she wouldn't release me until I agreed to see her for private grief counseling. "Let's start with twice a week," she said. Private biweekly sessions with this cup of comfort? Yes. A thousand times, yes. It was clear that relief wouldn't come instantly. Like any college degree, it would require hard work. And time. Grief was like deep-dish pie whose filling takes longer to cook; it cannot be rushed. But with Susan— dear, sweet, life-saving Susan—relief felt a little closer at hand.

Even though my desire to be alive, along with my energy level, was at an all-time low, I still had my dogs, Jack and Daisy, and they needed to be walked and fed. I appreciated how Jack could be oblivious to my mood at times, and demand a game of stick throwing. "Keep calm and carry on," he seemed to be reminding me, like the British wartime slogan.

The dogs forced me to do just that. I couldn't let them down. I couldn't let Marcus down. The dogs were Marcus's dogs, too. He had a lot of time, love and commitment invested in these dogs. He had a lot invested in me. If I was the one who'd died and he was still alive, he wouldn't bail on life. He wouldn't wallow in self-pity. He wouldn't spend time thinking about how he would end it all. He wouldn't consider the death-wielding potential of a paring knife, my favorite pie-making tool. But I couldn't help thinking: if I were dead, I could go find Marcus, apologize to him, make love to him, make everything right. It was an attractive theory, but I had no idea if the afterlife actually works that way. There was no guarantee I'd find him, no certainty of a happy ending.

What if he didn't want me chasing after him? What if he was happy with his independence in his new life? What if he had already hooked up with some new woman—some long-haired brunette in a white chiffon dress with a halo and wings? Then what would I do? I would have left a mess behind for other people to deal with. I would have left two dogs that depended on me, loved me, loved me in spite of my frightening and confusing behavior—my "new normal."

I had responsibilities, damn it. And taxes due. Besides, I was raised with a strong Midwest work ethic. No matter how down I was, I couldn't shake the stern voices of my upbringing: "Pull yourself up by the bootstraps." "Don't get down, get busy." "If you don't have the skills, go get the skills." And, above all, "No whining." Those were some of the whip-cracking nuggets of wisdom I was spoon-fed by my parents. I credit my ability to move forward to this hardwiring of tough love. I gave my bootstraps the best tug I could muster and got busy.

This grieving business was like making pie for the first time. One needs some instruction in how to do it—consult a recipe, make a grocery list and go after the goal with gusto. To keep myself organized, I made a list. I could barely get out of bed in the mornings, let alone keep my thoughts straight, but a list gave me some framework, and reminded me that I still had some purpose. After first establishing my grief counseling schedule with Susan, I made an appointment for my thyroid treatment with Dr. Vanek. Check. Next, in between long sessions of sobbing that made going out in public or even talking on the phone problematic, I would look for a place to live.

I was staying with our friends Alison and Thomas in their three-bedroom bungalow. The house was comfortable, welcoming, but it was also where Marcus had stayed during his vacation. His suitcase, filled with his travel clothes, bike gear, books and shaving kit, was still there. His deodorant and German brand of *Zahnpasta* (toothpaste) were still in the guest-bathroom medicine cabinet.

Seeing his things exactly where he'd left them, knowing he was unaware that he would never touch them again, had initially intensified the sense of loss and, naturally, sent me spiraling into yet another bawling spree. But after the initial shock, I got used to seeing his stuff—I was having to get used to a lot of things—and over the days found some comfort in being surrounded by these pieces of him, particularly his clothes. I searched for anything that hadn't been washed—the dirtier and mustier, the better. I slept with his red plaid bathrobe pulled close to me, pressing my nose into the fabric to capture any remaining scent of him. I breathed in, long, deep inhales. I couldn't get enough of his smell, couldn't get close enough to him.

Apart from being the location of Marcus's final visit, Alison and Thomas's house was also where we had stayed during our four-day rendezvous in May. The upstairs bedroom was where we last slept together, wrapped around each other's warm, naked bodies. It was the last place we made love, the last place we would ever make love. Being in this bedroom was good and bad. Good because in that room I believed I could be connected to him. I had become a recent and voracious fan of *Ghost Whisperer,* the soon-to-be-canceled CBS-TV series starring Jennifer Love Hewitt.

Besides watching that show, I also went to the Portland library and checked out as many books as I could find about life on the "Other Side." I was convinced that if Marcus hadn't "crossed over" yet—or, "gone to the light," as they said on TV—then he might still be staying in that guest room. He would come and find me, maybe even talk to me, tell me how he was, why he died, tell me if he was angry with me and let me know if he would ever forgive me. There were signs he was there. The books all said ghosts hijack electrical appliances to get energy so they can stick around. Static on my laptop monitor, my iPod shorting out (it had never done that before), and an unusually intermittent Internet connection proved it. If he was hovering around, though, I couldn't see him. I stayed awake at night, refusing to take the sleeping pills friends insisted I use, so as not to miss him if he appeared.

But staying in this guest room was also bad in a way. My friends were incredibly generous and patient, but I couldn't stay there forever, waiting for Marcus, or his ghost, to materialize. I had already logged two weeks at their place—on the heels of Marcus staying there for almost three weeks before his abrupt and untimely departure. Not to mention, I wasn't exactly fun to be around. I'm sure my sobbing was audible throughout the house, my late-night cries echoing off the hardwood floors. I needed to be in my own space, surrounded by my own furniture, my own bedding, my candles, my dishes, my bath towels and especially my pictures—framed pictures of Marcus. So I moved to the next likeliest place he might turn up: our old house on the opposite side of town. It wasn't exactly our old house. It was the guesthouse next door to that place, and it happened to be for rent.

If Willamette Heights is Portland's best neighborhood, then Aspen Avenue is its best street. Aspen Avenue is the last street at the top of a small mountain in Portland's northwest corner, where industrial area meets city meets wilderness. The elevation provides awe-inspiring views of the snow-covered volcanoes Mount Hood and Mount St. Helens by day, and a panorama of city lights by night, a postcard-perfect scene accompanied by the sounds of the occasional blowing train horn or the clash of steel coming from the loading docks down below.

The houses are mostly hundred-year-old huge Victorians, mixed in with newer, smaller, woodsy bungalows. But the selling point wasn't the houses, the view or the proximity to the boutiques and cafés just down the hill. The draw for Marcus and me when we moved to this neighborhood two years earlier—and one of the reasons I was drawn back—was that Willamette Heights butts up against the five-thousand-acre Forest Park, a lush, dense expanse of woods with forty miles of hiking trails. Trails on which I had before, and would again, spend long hours clad in raincoat and rubber boots, hiking with Team Terrier.

The guesthouse was an A-frame studio above the detached garage belonging to the modern three-bedroom house in which Marcus and I had lived before moving to Mexico. In fact, had the guesthouse been available when we moved away, we would have rented it to keep as a home base. "It's the perfect writer's studio," Marcus had said. He must have foreseen I wouldn't last long south of the border. While the guesthouse was small (as in 400-square-feet), it was also airy with hardwood floors, white walls and high ceilings. Most important, factoring in the damp Pacific Northwest climate, it was well insulated, warm and dry. A place where I could sit by the fire and read my stack of books like, *How to Go On Living When Someone You Love Dies,* while listening to the steady rain falling on the skylights. Nestled in a stand of tall cedars, it was also very private. The one-room abode had the feel of a tree house—or, as I called it, The Grieving Sanctuary.

Of moving into the guesthouse, my German friend Joerg asked, "Are you sure that's a good idea? You will be reminded of Marcus every time you walk in and out of that house."

Joerg, who was based in Portland and had worked with Marcus, had become my go-to guy ever since I called him the day Marcus died and asked him to do the most difficult and undesirable task one could ask a friend: call Marcus's parents in Germany and tell them their son—their only child—was dead. I speak a little German, but there was no way I would have been able to provide them with a coherent explanation of what had happened, especially since I couldn't yet believe it myself.

Joerg, ever gracious and refined, complied and I was forever indebted to him. With this in mind, I was gentler in my reply than I might have been had it been anyone else asking the question. I didn't get snitty and say, "Yeah? And I'm not reminded of him every time I drive past the Legacy Emanuel Hospital? Or how about when I hear the sirens from those American Medical Response ambulances? Those frickin' ambulances are everywhere in Portland."

Instead, I told him, "This place is full of good memories, Joerg. This is where I need to be. I know it."

4

Number four on my to-do list—after Grief Counseling, Thyroid Treatment and Apartment Hunting, but before Figure out What to Do with Marcus's Stuff—was Get a Job. Not a stressful job. Not my usual PR, or web producer, or journalism career-type job, but a peaceful, part-time, nurturing kind of job. I knew just what I needed to do. Bake pie.

Eight years earlier, in 2001, I had left a grueling, lucrative web-producing job to become a minimum-wage-making pie baker. I had traded in my Banana Republic suits and high-rise office in San Francisco for an apron, overalls and a small, steamy kitchen in Malibu. Over the course of my yearlong "pie-baking sabbatical" my bank account dwindled down to nothing (try living on minimum wage in Southern California), but the joy, the friendships and the fulfillment I gained were something money couldn't buy.

I recognized that the amount of pie therapy required to recover from the blow of Marcus's death would be significantly greater than what I needed after my dot com job. But I still had faith that the healing powers of baking—the Zen-like calm induced by rolling dough, the meditative trance achieved while peeling apples, the satisfaction of seeing a pale crust turn golden brown—could once again be effective.

I hoped to recreate the restorative days of Malibu, where we had been a team of women making our various handcrafted specialties. British baker, Jane Windsor, whose wicked sense of humor and fabulous accent rivaled the deliciousness of her scones and brownies, had been the leader of the gang. We gabbed as we peeled, chopped and stirred. We had formed a small community, our own kind of support group, based around the comfort of cooking—while making comfort food. During those days, when I wasn't caught up in the plucky conversation, I got lost in my own world, transported by the process of creating edible works of art in my tiny corner of the kitchen, lulled into tranquility by the constant hum of the convection ovens.

That Malibu baking job was a salve on a fresh scar. I'd been working eighty hours a week at a cutting-edge dot com at the height of the boom, where the environment was competitive and cutthroat. In this new Internet world, the race was on to create The Next Big Thing. To go public. To have an IPO with shares valued at $200 each. To become the next millionaire under forty. I worked so much that I was eating carryout dinners in Styrofoam containers at my desk and sleeping with my cell phone next to my pillow. At least it proved I was capable of hard work.

I stayed with that San Francisco grind for over a year and a half, so it also proved I could hold a job longer than my previous record of eight months. This was saying a lot for me in normal cubicle hell conditions, but as a serial freelancer, sticking it out in *this* atmosphere, the extreme sports of workplaces . . . well, I was proud of myself. I was stretching and growing, but I was like a deer in the headlights with the daily challenges. I had to learn the language of computers, a vocabulary that increased with new terms faster than I could memorize them. And I was tasked with managing a team of young web designers who didn't want to be managed, let alone show up for work before 1:00 p.m. Yet I was as caught up in the frenzy as the next person, wanting to succeed. Who doesn't want to be a millionaire? I was also burning out faster than the cash from the company's last round of funding.

The thing that tipped me over the edge was not a matter of politics or sleep deprivation. It was philosophical. The company's oxymoronic mandate was to create more and more realistic virtual environments.

"Make the audience believe they can feel the salt water spray on their face," my bosses insisted of the sailboat event I produced. "Make them think they are on the rock face, right there with the climber," they said of the mountaineering expedition I worked on.

"It's a computer monitor, guys, not a national park," I wanted to remind them.

Then new orders came down from the chief executive officer. We were to get people to spend more time on their computers. *Stickiness* was the Word of the Day. But this was an outdoor-adventure website. And seeing as I was a journalist whose personal mission was to use my writing to motivate people to actually go outdoors and exercise as a way to empower themselves, my bosses and I had a fundamental difference of opinion. We were a mismatched couple with irreconcilable differences. So I told them to take my six-figure job and shove it.

"I'm going to go do something real, something tactile," I told them during my exit interview. "I'm going to go work with my hands. I'm going to make pie."

Why pie? Answering that is about as easy as explaining why seemingly healthy Marcus dropped dead at the age of forty-three. If only the answer was as easy as "It was his time." An answer which is about as inane as a mountain climber explaining he climbs Everest "because it's there."

But pie? Pie was practically programmed into my DNA. Pie was the reason my parents got married. My mom can still describe how it happened in detail, how she and my dad were both living in Milwaukee, Wisconsin. How my dad was studying to be a dentist and she had just graduated from nursing school. She lived with five other nurses in a one-bedroom apartment above my dad's favorite bar. My mom had considered becoming a nun, but then she met my dad—a charming, funny, handsome guy, who played an impressive game of pool downstairs and who loved banana cream pie. Six months into their courtship, she saw her window of opportunity and invited my dad over for dinner. She kicked out her roommates for the evening and prepared a romantic feast of tuna casserole, red JELL-O "salad" and a made-from-scratch banana cream pie.

My mom put her heart and her hopes into that pie. If she wasn't going to become a nun, she was going to get married—to my dad. First, she blind-baked the crust. She stirred the milk, sugar and eggs on the stovetop, cooking the vanilla custard. She sliced the ripe bananas and covered the whole lush thing with a generous portion of fresh whipped cream.

The candles burned down as the two prospective mates enjoyed their meal and, finally, after the last bite of pie had been swallowed, my dad leaned back in his chair and said to my mom, "Maureen, that was the best pie I ever had. Will you marry me?" No matter that he called her by the wrong name—her name is Marie, but his hearing was challenged even then—she said yes. The pie sealed the deal.

Pie went on to play a role in my childhood. After my parents got married, they left Wisconsin, spent two years in San Diego (where I was conceived) and eventually settled in my dad's hometown of Ottumwa, Iowa. I was born third in line out of five kids. My mom was so busy shuttling us to our piano, cello, swim, tap, ballet, gymnastics, tennis, pottery and sewing lessons, there was no time left for baking. Therefore, my first pie of record—a slice of banana cream, forever my dad's favorite—was consumed at an old-fashioned diner called Canteen Lunch in the Alley in Ottumwa.

It was on a Wednesday. I remember the day of the week, because as a dentist my dad had Wednesday afternoons off. Instead of escaping to the golf course like other medical professionals did, he picked up all five of us kids from elementary school in his little white Mustang and took us to the movie theater. We went to matinees and saw films inappropriate for our age, like *Dirty Harry* and *Taxi Driver*. We didn't care. We got to be with our dad. And eat popcorn. And get away with something we knew our mom would not approve of. She would inevitably find out.

"To-*om*," she would reprimand him when we got home, dragging out the syllables of his name. We always giggled when he got in trouble, thrilled to play a role in his game of defiance, a game I learned well and continue to play.

After the movie, he always took us to the Canteen Lunch in the Alley, a hole-in-the-wall, squatty, square-shaped, cinder-block building that, as the name implies, is situated in an alley. The Canteen, opened in the 1930s, was where my dad had developed his love for pie as a child and where nothing had changed since. Nothing. Not the speckled Formica countertop, the red vinyl-covered bar stools, the red-and white-checkered curtains or the pie safe, full of creamy and fruity homemade pies.

My dad lined up all five kids around the Canteen's horseshoe-shaped counter, each of us sitting on our own swivel stool, and we proceeded to pig out on loose-meat burgers called "Canteens." Our burgers were followed by pie. We each got our own slice. No sharing was required. My dad understood the importance of pie. He believed that no matter how stuffed our small bellies, there was always room for a whole slice of banana-cream goodness. He taught us to have reverence for this dessert, to start at the tip of the triangle with our forks and work our way back toward the crust. To let the meringue dissolve slowly on our tongues. And to moan with pleasure with each and every bite. We ate. We moaned. And we groaned from being so full.

Part of this pie initiation was also the lesson of saying thank you. We had to be reminded after the first few outings, but we eventually grasped the idea.

"Thank you, Dad," we all chimed immediately after our burger and pie feasts.

Gratitude and pie. I never could have fathomed at age seven just what a critical role the combination of these two concepts would play in my future.

By the time I was old enough to learn any baking skills, we had entered the era when modern conveniences—like packaged pudding mix and premade pie dough—were the rage. Even my Midwestern grandmothers bought into these newfangled shortcuts, as they both had full-time jobs, and didn't have time to make, let alone teach me, any of their old-fashioned recipes, pie or otherwise. At least my mom granted us kids full access to her kitchen, where we took turns making JELL-O 1-2-3 and no-bake cheesecake from a box. I also had my Suzy Homemaker oven, in which I baked minicakes by the heat of a lightbulb, but not pies.

Pie didn't feature prominently in my life again until I was seventeen. I was on a bicycle trip, heading down the West Coast from Vancouver, British Columbia, toward San Francisco. I was traveling with a fellow camp counselor from Iowa after our summer session at Camp Abe Lincoln ended. Pedaling down Washington State's dark and mossy Olympic Peninsula, we came upon a rare and welcome opening in the thick forest and feasted our eyes on an apple orchard. It was early September, so the trees were loaded with red, ripe fruit. The branches, so heavy-looking from the weight of all those juicy apples, seemed to be begging for relief. For two young and hungry cyclists, this was an open invitation to stop for a free snack. Besides, with all that bounty, who would miss a few? We got off our bikes, leaned our mighty steeds against the log fence and began to help ourselves. We had picked only three or four apples before an old man came storming out from the crumbling white farmhouse across the acreage.

"Hey! What are you doing on my property?" he shouted. His hair was white and uncombed, his face covered in gray stubble. His jeans were baggy and dirty, and he wore a grubby T-shirt yellowed from years of wear. He appeared unsteady on his legs, yet he charged at us with so much force we reeled back. For all our first impressions of him, he must have equally had his own ideas of us. He had every reason to be suspicious, dressed as we were in our black Lycra shorts, tight nylon shirts with rear pockets bulging with gear—and now apples—and funny little pointed shoes. Then again, given the thick lenses of his horn-rimmed glasses, he probably couldn't see us very well.

"We're riding our bikes down the coast," we said. "We're so sorry. We didn't mean to trespass."

He looked at us more closely, sizing up our tanned, athletic bodies and our cherubic faces. And then he softened. "Well, in that case . . . " The next thing we knew we were inside his home—making pie with our stolen apples. This grumpy old man, it turns out, was a retired pastry chef from the merchant marines.

The inside of his farmhouse was dusty, with stacks of old books and magazines piled up next to his threadbare sofa. The presence of kerosene lanterns and absence of lamps around the living room indicated that he didn't have electricity. We moved into his kitchen, where a large, round table crowded the room. Collecting his ingredients from the deep, dark cupboards, he dived right into what would be my first pie lesson.

To make the dough, he used two dinner knives, moving them against each other in opposite directions, to cut the butter into the flour. He added just enough water to hold the flour together. Then, he used his craggy, weathered seaman's hands to form two dough balls, and put the dough in his propane-powered refrigerator. While the dough was chilling, we helped peel and slice about ten small apples, saving the peelings for his compost and putting the slices into a bowl with the juice of a fresh lemon.

Dusk approached and he lit the kerosene lamps, so we had to finish baking by the dim lantern light. He rolled the chilled dough on his wooden slab of a kitchen table, first heavily flouring the surface, then flattening the dough into a circle with a heavy wooden rolling pin. We helped arrange the sliced apples in the pie dish. He added a cup of sugar, a few tablespoons of flour, a few shakes from his cinnamon jar, and placed a pat of butter on top. He covered the apple heap with the top crust. His hands crimped the crust's edge, moving around the circle with the deft and speed of a seaman coiling ropes. Whatever marines he'd sailed with were lucky to have him on their ship; spending months at sea were certainly made much nicer accompanied by his homemade pies.

As our pie baked in his propane-fueled oven, gradually the musty smell of his house was replaced with a heavenly apple-cinnamon-butter scent. We fell asleep that night in our sleeping bags on his living-room floor, content and nourished by pie. From that moment on, banana cream, be damned. Apple pie was my thing.

I'm not saying it pays to steal, but thanks to the apple-thievery incident, I continued to make pies throughout my college years and beyond. Whenever I encountered apples, I made pie. Because I went to college in Washington State—where forty-two percent of America's apples are grown—I made a lot of pies. Whenever I encountered a prospective husband, I applied my mother's strategy and made pie. And because I was a warm-blooded young woman— a fallen Catholic, no less—I made even more pies. I made an apple pie for every eligible bachelor I set my sights on. For Scott, the sexy chemistry teacher who lived in a tree house near campus. For Chris, the Hollywood screenwriter. For Rick, the environmental lawyer. For Mike, the surfer/entrepreneur. For Adam, the bike racer. For Kenny, the trust-funder. For Yoshiyuki, the macadamia-nut farmer. For Scott, the blind-date billionaire. For Matthew, the hockey player. For Dion, the banker. Jesus, I made a lot of apple pie—or, as I liked to call it, "lust in a crust."

"Delicious pie," they would all say. "No one has ever made me a pie before."

And yet, while two did propose (though, sadly, not the billionaire), none of these pies resulted in marriage—well, not until Marcus's pie, but that didn't come until much later. In spite of my pie prowess, my love life up to that point was like a greased pie plate—nothing stuck.

It wasn't until I quit the dot com job in 2001—when I said, "Goodbye, cubicle" (and "Goodbye, big paycheck")—that I shifted my pie intentions. Pie was no longer a wily attempt to impress guys. Pie became a way to restore balance. To soothe my tired, overworked soul. To get grounded after spending too much time in front of a computer and too little time interacting with people. Pie was a vehicle to transport me back to a time before computers and cell phones, when neighbors still stopped by unannounced for a back-door visit.

Instead of using my nimble fingers to type emails to the co-workers sitting in the cubicles right next to me, I put my hands to use, making something tangible and mouth-watering to be savored and appreciated by others. Just as my dad taught us kids to moan with pleasure over each bite of banana cream pie, I relished the joy with which my pie-loving customers, rich and famous or not, consumed my homemade pies.

My transition from my workaholic life in San Francisco to pie baking in Malibu was surprisingly seamless. Upon my return to L.A., I discovered a new gourmet-food shop had opened in Malibu. The place was called Mary's Kitchen and an article in the local *Surfside News* claimed it was known for its outstanding pie made by the café's namesake, Mary Spellman.

Mary was a transplant from the Hamptons in New York, where she had run the Sagaponak General Store. She had been persuaded by a customer-turned-investor to move West.

And now, in the Cross Creek Shopping Center (your basic L.A. strip mall), wedged between a Starbucks and a swimwear boutique, here she was. The front of her shop was decorated with picket fencing and picnic tables covered in vintage flowered cloths. Entering through the screen door, you were met by the hot deli section displaying a plethora of comfort food—meatloaf, mashed potatoes, macaroni and cheese with the emphasis on the cheese. In the cold deli section, there were countless wedges of white, yellow, blue, gooey and hard cheeses, and an endless row of salamis hanging from the ceiling. In the bakery section, brick-size brownies, cookies as big as dinner plates and zesty-looking lemon bars radiating with California citrusy sunshine all beckoned. There was a lot of good food. But there was no pie.

On my scouting trip, I inquired of the elegant blonde woman working behind the counter, "Where's the pie? I read that you have great pie."

She nodded and asked me to wait. "Let me go check with Mary."

A woman emerged from the kitchen in back, rounding the corner from behind the hot deli case. A six-foot-tall Amazon in a baseball hat, wire-rimmed glasses, black-and-white-checkered chef's pants and a white apron smeared with various representations of whatever she had been cooking—*this* was Mary. "Can I help you?" she asked.

"I came for pie," I said. "But you don't have any."

"We're too busy to make it," she replied in a brusque Long Island accent. Her voice was as powerful as her presence.

My response popped out like a premature champagne cork. "I'll make it for you," I said. When I had quit the dot com job and told my bosses I wanted to make pie, I originally intended the statement to be a symbolic one. I hadn't actually thought it through. But the opportunity magically presented itself, the genie was here to grant my wish. (Note to self: watch it on the subliminal wishes; they're always the most powerful ones.)

Mary stifled a chuckle. "What are your qualifications?" she wanted to know, sizing me up to see if I was serious. I hadn't seen the moment coming, but when it arrived, I realized just how serious I was.

"I'm from Iowa," I answered. I couldn't say I was a web producer or a freelance journalist to get *this* job. "I come from the land of pie." She just stood there, arms folded across her bosom. So I blathered on. "Actually, I learned how to bake from a pastry chef, a retired merchant marine. He taught me how to make apple pie when I was caught stealing apples from his tree." Yes, I am fully aware that sometimes I can be a complete bumbling idiot.

"Okay," she said with the hint of a smile. "Come back tomorrow and we'll see how you do. Be here at one. Oh, and the pay is $7.50 an hour. Are you okay with that?"

Seven-fifty an hour? To bake pie and not sit in front of a computer sixteen hours a day? To work in a bustling, cozy kitchen by the sea instead of a cavelike cubicle in a hermetically sealed high-rise? Yes, I was totally okay with that.

Looking back, however, I admit it was a miracle that I lasted beyond the first day in Malibu. In spite of all those pies I'd made for boyfriends, I was very much out of practice. Or, in reality, my pie-making skills weren't that polished in the first place. But Mary was an outstanding teacher.

When I showed up for my Malibu pie audition, Mary walked me over to what would be my work station, a small fluorescent-lit room off to the side of the kitchen packed with refrigerators, an industrial-size Hobart mixer, two convection ovens and a stainless steel table with flour and sugar bins stored underneath. A shelf above the table held a stack of dog-eared, stained cookbooks, and another shelf held a disarray of measuring cups and spice jars. The space was so tight you could almost stand in the middle and touch each appliance without moving.

"Let's see what you can do," Mary announced.

I froze. I hadn't actually made a pie in... Oh, shit, I had no idea when I had made my last pie.

"Let me show you how I do it," Mary said when it became clear by my catatonic state that I needed help. I stepped aside. She held a two-cup measuring cup in her bear-paw-size hands and scooped out flour into a gray tub, the kind normally used for bussing dishes. I counted along with her as she dumped twenty-two level cupfuls into the tub.

"I learned to bake pies from my mom," she said, as she pulled several pounds of butter out of the fridge. "She ran a boardinghouse in the Hamptons and cooked for all the guests. Pie was her specialty. She made pies of every kind—coconut cream, chocolate cream, lemon meringue, blackberry, blueberry, peach, apple, you name it."

She turned back to the refrigerator and pulled out a plastic bag full of something hard, white and greasy—like Crisco, only denser. "This is lard," she explained when she saw the puzzled look on my face. "My mom used lard. Some people don't like it, but that's how we do it here—half butter, half lard."

Using her bare hands, Mary worked the butter and lard into the flour. My eyes grew wide. "You use your hands?" I asked. "The merchant marine chef taught me to use knives."

"Hands work better," she said. "You work the fat into the flour with your fingers until you have the consistency of large peas." She talked as she mixed. "This is enough dough for ten pies. We'll just make one now, but you'll use the rest of the dough later." Next, she poured ice water into the flour mix. "The key here is to be light and gentle," she said. Though there was nothing light and gentle about Mary physically, from the way her hands moved through the dough, it was obvious she possessed a tender, loving side. She lifted the flour from underneath, letting it fall from her fingers to let the water blend in without forcing it.

"Don't overwork the dough. That's the biggest mistake people make. They knead it too much. Remember, we're not making bread. Pie dough only needs to be worked enough to hold it together. You work it too much and it gets tough." She formed her soft dough into balls, patted them into discs the diameter of cup saucers, then stacked them up next to the tub. She sprinkled flour on each to keep them from sticking together.

"Can you hand me the rolling pin?" she asked, pointing a flour-covered finger toward the corner of the table. Three rolling pins of varying sizes competed for space in a large ceramic crock jammed full with other baking utensils—wooden spoons, rubber spatulas, metal spatulas, lemon graters. "The big one," she said.

She moved the tub aside and sprinkled the table with flour. "Make sure you have a clean surface to start. The flour will keep the dough from sticking. The same goes for your rolling pin. You want to keep it clean. If the dough gets gunked up on it, scrape it off with a knife. You can also rub your rolling pin with flour." She sprinkled flour on the top of her dough and started rolling. "Only roll in one direction, starting from the middle and working outward. Don't roll back and forth. People like to do that and it makes the dough tough."

As her dough began to flatten, she paused. "Now you want to turn your dough. Lift it up like this." She demonstrated by picking up the now thinner and wider disc and flipped it over as if it were a pizza. While the dough was still airborne, she quickly ran her hand underneath, dusting the table with more flour. The dough landed on its opposite side, she sprinkled the new top side with flour, and went back to rolling. Her big hands worked quickly, expertly, and yet gently, until the dough was thin, flat and covering most of the table. "My mom had a striped vinyl tablecloth on her kitchen table. We rolled right on it and you would know your dough was thin enough when you could see the red lines through it."

I leaned over and tried to picture the red lines. As it was, the stainless steel table had no markings to indicate her dough had passed the test, but after many years of pie making she instinctively knew when to stop.

"Do you see these white-and-yellow dots in here?" Mary asked, pointing to an irregular marbled pattern in the flattened dough. "That's a good thing. You want that. That's the butter and lard and it will melt into the flour as it bakes. It's what gives your pie crust the flakiness."

"That's good to know," I said. "My crust has a tendency to be a little hard."

"That's because you overwork the dough," Mary responded.

"Yes. A friend of mine from Iowa, whose 104-year-old grandmother wrote a cookbook, accused me of that. Whenever we make pie together, she yells at me, 'Don't manhandle the dough!'"

"We're going to make apple today. I'll show you a shortcut that I learned from my mom. We're going to put this crust in the pie plate now and leave it there. We'll roll out the top later, when we're ready for it." Dough overflowed from the plate, draping over the edge of the dish and onto the table. Mary noticed me examining its droopy excess.

"I'll show you how to deal with that," she said, and came back with a large pair of scissors. "You can use a knife to trim it, or you can just use these." She snipped at the dough with the confidence of a Beverly Hills hairdresser until she had gone all the way around the pie plate. "Leave an extra inch from the rim because we're going to need it when we put on the top.

"Okay, Pie Girl. Are you ready to peel some apples?" Mary motioned to the boxes of Granny Smiths stacked up in front of the refrigerator. "Here, take a knife and have a seat." She handed me a paring knife and grabbed another one for herself. We sat on milk crates in the middle of the tiny baking room with a giant silver bowl between us. I picked up an apple and started to cut out the stem. "You don't have to do that. Leave the stems and I'll show you the shortcut I was talking about when we're done peeling."

I took a breath and moved my knife around the apple, the waxy green skin coming off easily with the sharp blade. "I guess my knives at home must be pretty dull," I said. "This one is working really well." I put my one skinned apple into the bowl, next to the four Mary had already peeled, and started in on another.

"One pie takes about seven or eight of these large apples," Mary explained as we filled the bowl. "Now here's what I want to show you—the shortcut." Taking an apple in her mama-bear hand, she sliced the apple directly into the pie shell.

"Don't you slice the apples into a bowl and mix them together with the sugar and cinnamon?" I asked. "That's what that old pastry chef taught me."

"No, that's the way most people do it, but this is what my mom taught me. It's easier and faster this way. Make sure you slice them all the same size so they cook evenly. You don't want them too small or they'll bake down too fast. And if they're too big, they won't bake through. We're going to put in half of the apples and half of everything else—sugar, cinnamon, pinch of salt and enough flour to thicken the juice—and then repeat it."

She sliced, sprinkled and pinched. Then, just as she promised, she sliced more apples and dumped the remaining half of the other ingredients on top. "Don't worry. It will all blend together as it bakes." Reaching for a stick of butter, she cut off an inch and placed it on top of the apple pile. "Don't forget a pat of butter before you lay the top crust over it."

"That's a lot of apples," I commented on the slices stacked up into a mountain peak.

"You don't want to be stingy, but you also don't want your apples too high because they will shrink as they bake. The crust will stay high, and you don't want to be left with a big gap underneath." She rolled out another ball of dough until it was flat, round and a few inches wider than the pie plate.

"To pick up the dough you can fold it in half like this." She lifted an edge and slowly brought it to meet its opposite side, ending up with a half-moon shape. "Or you can use the rolling pin by pulling the dough onto it and move it over to your pie." She lifted the half-moon by its edges and dragged it over to the waiting pie without breaking it. She lined it up with the center and unfolded it, until it laid flat across the fruit-filled heap.

My previous pies never had that kind of excess dough hanging off the sides, nor had I ever managed to roll my dough as smooth as hers. My pie dough was always cracked and crumbly with jagged edges that barely reached the edge of the pie plate. My dough required an all-star wrestling match to get the top and bottom crusts to join together. But this pie already looked like a masterpiece—the outline of apple wedges visible, snugly tucked under their supple blanket of dough. And she wasn't finished with it yet.

"I'm going to trim the edges." Again, she grabbed the scissors and cut with abandon, trimming the overflow. She measured her progress by poking her finger under the rim of the pie plate. "We'll leave about a fingertip's worth of dough. Now we pinch the top and bottom crusts together to seal in the juices." Her fingers raced around the perimeter, thumb and forefinger on one side, pushing the side of her index finger in between them from the other. The dough elevated with each pinch, creating a fortress from which no pie filling could ever escape. There would be no dripping of apple juice into *her* oven. The end result was a decorative fluted edge.

"Before it goes in the oven . . ." Mary stopped midsentence and said, "Will you make sure that top oven is set to 450?" I walked over and turned the knob. "Before it goes in the oven," she continued, "we need to brush it with a beaten egg." She painted the top crust with egg, using a small brush until it was shiny and yellow. "But don't overdo it. You don't want egg collecting in the little troughs. And now we poke holes in the top for the steam to vent." Picking up her paring knife again, she said, "My mom always made this pattern, sort of like chicken feet and, because she's a Christian, a little cross in the middle." She punctured the dough until it was covered in slits, a set of chicken footprints that lined up as if marking where to cut the pie into quarters.

"Open the oven for me, will you?" I opened the door and got hit with a blast of industrial-strength hot air convection. She slid the pie inside. "We'll set the timer for twenty minutes, enough time to set the crust. You want the crust to cook first, get it a little brown, then turn the temperature down to 375."

Not caring any longer if I sounded like a novice, I asked the classic "Pie Baking for Dummies" question: "How do you know when it's done?"

"You stick a knife in it. You want the apples to be soft, but still have a little resistance. If you overbake it, the apples will come out mushy, like applesauce. But you want to bake it until the juice bubbles, so you know the fruit is cooked."

After twenty minutes, sure enough, the edges and top had transformed from white and doughy to brown and crusty. "We'll turn down the temperature now and leave it in for another thirty or forty minutes."

Time passed much faster in the crammed and hot kitchen than in my dot com cubicle. "Here, stick the knife in and see what you think," Mary said when the timer went off. The knife gave way beneath my touch.

"I would say it's done." Even though the knife went in easily my confidence was tentative.

She took the knife from me to see for herself. "Yes, you're right. It's done." She pulled out the commercial-size baking sheet upon which the pie sat. The pie. The gorgeous, golden brown, sky-high apple pie. Steam rose from its vents, bubbling juices pooled in the crevices of the fluted edge, the familiar sweet apple-cinnamon-butter scent filled the kitchen.

"It's beautiful," I said. I didn't want to point out the one flaw I observed, but I couldn't help but ask: "Do you think we should cut off that one edge that got a little darker than the rest?"

"No," she snapped. "That's part of this pie's personality. Every pie is going to look different. Pie should look homemade."

Pie should look homemade. What a concept. A pie made by hand will never be perfect, but it will be real. You will know that someone crafted it with their hands, putting their own unique signature on it the way an artist signs their name on a canvas. I leaned over the steaming vents to breathe in the apple and spice, a soothing, heartwarming scent I never, ever tire of.

With Mary's mentoring, I found my way back into a healthy world again and, as a bonus, I perfected my pie-making skills.

I went on to bake some two thousand pies over the course of that year. I baked strawberry-rhubarb pies for Dick Van Dyke. I made coconut cream pies for Steven Spielberg. I watched Mel Gibson wolf down a slice of my apple crumble pie. I sold more than one peach pie to Robert Downey, Jr. And once, on a tight deadline, I whipped up a lemon meringue pie for Barbra Streisand, who had ordered it for a dinner party. (That pie, however, didn't survive the trip to her house. Her driver took the speed bumps in Malibu Colony too fast and the meringue stuck to the top of the bakery box.) The biggest challenge came at Thanksgiving, when I pulled an all-nighter, baking two hundred pecan, pumpkin and apple pies in a twenty-four-hour stretch to fulfill all the customer orders, leaving me with sore muscles, swollen hands and bakers' burns on my forearms. I still bear the scars proudly.

CHAPTER

5

It was because of this lifelong pie history—and the ease with which I had landed the pie-baking job in Malibu—that I assumed I could approach the bakeries and coffeehouses of Portland and have a job nailed down within a few days. And so, two months after Marcus's life ended and my grief began, I set forth on my job-seeking mission.

Portland may be renowned for its food scene—its socially conscious cafés supplied with locally grown produce and free-range, hormone-absent meat, its proliferating gourmet food carts and its frequent glowing reviews in the *New York Times*—but at the time, Portland did not have any pie shops. Still, it had decent pie. Not mind-blowing-delicious pie, but there was pie all the same. And pie is what I needed. Like a gardener savors digging their bare hands in the earth, drawing energy from holding a clump of root-bound soil between their palms, I needed pie dough. I needed to bury my hands in flour and butter to evoke that grounding, energizing sensation. I made a list of the places where I would apply: Crema, Random Order Coffee House, Bipartisan Café, Grand Central Bakery, Baker and Spice. Out of five places, I was sure to get a job. After all, I was highly qualified.

At least by my definition I was qualified. Granted, it had been eight years since I worked at Mary's Kitchen. But I had spent a full year there making pies, and my on-the-job training had to be as valuable as a culinary school certificate.

If my pies passed the test from Hollywood's A-list celebrities, I was certain my pies would hold up to Portland's precious culinary standards.

First, I applied at Crema, a hip little bakery in Portland's northeast quadrant. I was attracted to the contrast of wholesome, hearty baked goods—scones, muffins, cupcakes and pie—sold in an ultramodern glass-front building with concrete floors. It's what Marcus would call a "style-mix." In truth, I went to Crema first because it's a place Marcus and I liked. He had taken Alison there for a thank-you breakfast just days before he died. She told me about it later, about their conversation, about how sad he was over our divorce. I still had the receipt from their breakfast, which I found in his wallet, along with the other sales slips that tracked the movements of his final days. Even when I was not conscious of it, everything I did, everywhere I went now, was motivated by staying connected to Marcus.

I approached the twentysomething dude with the plug-pierced ears and scraggly beard behind the cash register. "Oh, man, sorry, we're not hiring," he said. "But you can leave your number."

I didn't scribble my number on the scrap of paper he offered. I left my card. I had come a long way since my baking days in Malibu. I took pie so seriously now I had a business card printed with "The World Needs More Pie" as my company name, complete with a red-and-white-checkered border and a steaming pie logo on it. Crema's manager was sure to call me back. Not only was I professional in my approach, I was perfect for this place. The kitchen behind the bakery counter was calling to me. I was already visualizing myself pulling my gorgeous pies out of their ovens, joking and laughing with the other bakers, making friends with the pie-consuming customers, maybe even getting this cashier dude to help me peel apples. This was a place where I could relive the good old days of Malibu. They *had* to call me back.

Next, I went to Random Order Coffee House about a mile farther northeast. In the heart of the Alberta Street district, Portland's grunge strip, the predominant feature of this tiny coffeehouse was its display case of handmade pies. Not cheap by any city's standards, their pies sold for twenty-eight bucks each. Pretending I was looking for the restroom, I poked my head into their baking kitchen in the back. It wasn't a kitchen exactly, it was more like a closet. A very, very small closet. They were baking all those pies in a bloody toaster oven. No, we weren't in Malibu anymore. I inquired anyway. No. Not hiring. Whatever. I left my card.

Bipartisan Café is a longer trek east, as far opposite of my Grieving Sanctuary as you could get and still be in Portland. But their pie was as good, plain and simple as a grandmother—er, in my case, great-grandmother—would make. Their specialty was Northwest berry pies—marionberry, blackberry and raspberry—all served with a giant dollop of whipped cream. From what I could tell, the pies were baked right behind the counter, a space already congested with coffee machines and their harried staff members preparing soup and sandwiches. I stayed to eat a bowl of chili—one that actually had meat in it (surprising for vegetarian-centric Portland)—and after some subtle questioning of the waitress, I learned that they might be hiring extra help for

Thanksgiving. Unfortunately, the baker was out of town for two weeks. I left my card.

After that, it was on to Grand Central Bakery. This was the biggest of the bunch. Grand Central Bakery was a chain started in Seattle, and had recently released an impressive new cookbook. Their wholegrain breads were sold in grocery stores, and they had started a new line of frozen pie crust and unbaked frozen pies. A burgeoning pie enterprise? They could use my help. Of their three Portland locations, the one closest to my house had a public viewing area to watch the bakers make bread in a warehouse-size kitchen. I watched. I liked. The bakers worked as a team, as one completed their task they passed the bread dough on to their coworker for another task, chatting and smiling all the while. I wanted to join in the camaraderie. I was even willing to change camps and make bread instead of pie. If they were hiring. My neighbor, Robin, worked there part-time as counter help. Even with her hand-delivering my application and putting in a good word for me, I never got a call back.

Baker and Spice, out in the suburbs, was my last resort. When I thought of getting a pie-baking job to help heal my grief, I had envisioned riding my bike to work, like I did in California. Those were heavenly days when I could pedal the forty-five minutes from Venice to Malibu along the warm and sunny coast, watching pelicans dive for fish and surfers catch waves.

Heaven did not exist in Portland, where rain clouds dumped their moisture 24/7. Riding my bike in the rain was one thing. Riding my bike in the rain to the suburbs was another. It didn't matter. They didn't want to hire me anyway. The girl in the ratty braids and T-shirt too small for her chubby figure made it clear I wasn't welcome.

"We. Are. Not. Hiring," she spelled out in her snotty-pants tone. She wanted me to know I wasn't one of them.

But what was "them?" I could not figure it out. What was I doing wrong? Maybe Portland bakeries thought my background as pie-baker-to-the-stars was too glitzy and glamorous for their granola-crunching taste. If I was twenty years younger and had Portland's prerequisite facial piercings and arm-length tattoos, would I have qualified? Or could they see straight through my forced, fake smile and into the sadness behind my tear-swollen eyes?

I started to get mad at Marcus. *Is this how you're punishing me? You've turned me into a hideous, repulsive hag. My eyes are so red and puffy, my grief so palpable and heavy, my depression so obvious, no one wants me near them.* I was in such bad shape I couldn't even get a part-time, minimum-wage-paying, pie-baking job. I used to make six figures a year and now I was an unemployable grieving widow. How far and fast we can fall. Fine. I deserved it.

I tried not to be mad at Marcus. To make peace with him, and with myself, I wrote him letters almost daily. I wrote in a notebook that had started off as my journal, but from August 20—the day after his death, during my flight from El Paso to Portland—I wrote him letters in it. I haven't stopped writing since. I'm on my fourth notebook, all letters to Marcus, explaining how I would do things differently—not complain as much, have more sex, cook without copping an attitude, stick it out instead of running away, be a better wife. I wrote and wrote and wrote—still write—and asked him for forgiveness.

I also wrote in my letters that I needed *him* to do things differently: come home earlier from work, watch less television, be more romantic, give me more compliments (easier said than done for a German!), take me out for dinner on my birthday. I don't need a birthday present, my love, but would a card be too much to ask? Talk about our issues instead of staying silent and stoic, don't be late, don't keep me waiting.

Everything was written in an apologetic and loving tone. Mostly. There were the days when all I wrote was *WHY DID YOU DIE? WHY DID YOU DIE? WHY DID YOU DIE?* And other days, when I wrote *I MISS YOU. I MISS YOU. I MISS YOU.*

I continue to fill entire pages of my notebook with these words. And yes, in all caps. I am repetitive in my requests, my pleas, my apologies, but since he can't reply, I can never get the resolution, the consolation, the closure I need. And so I keep writing, repeating myself, hoping I might come to my own resolution some distant day, no matter how many notebooks it might take.

The days dragged on. None of the bakeries called me back—even after leaving phone messages and revisiting all of them, dropping off extra cards, just in case.

I kept busy, reading my grief books, adding new titles every day, like, *Widow to Widow* and *The Tibetan Book of Living and Dying*. I settled into somewhat of a routine—I choke on the words to say I was adjusting to my "new normal." Normal or not, routine—or any kind of structure—is a useful thing to a grieving person. I had developed a triangular pattern of movement. I went from my house—and my daily long, meditative dog walks on the muddy hiking trails behind it—to Susan's counseling office across town, where I obediently and eagerly attended my private sessions. From there, I went to Alison and Thomas's house for movie nights with Alison, when Thomas was working late or out of town. Alison and I would eat popcorn and slice-'n'-bake chocolate chip cookies while watching romantic comedies (basically, movies Thomas would never watch) and tried to stay warm under piles of fleece blankets.

Because our storage unit was too full, Marcus had left his red leather Stressless chair at Alison and Thomas's. It was Marcus's European version of the Barcalounger—sleek, minimalist and modern. Its temporary home was the TV room and whenever I came over I was allowed priority seating in it. Even when I would just drop by to say hi, I would secretly take a few minutes to sit in the chair. While Alison was busy in the kitchen or bathroom, I would squeeze the arms, channeling Marcus, pretending I was sitting on his lap, pretending that the chair was him. I pressed my weight into it, hard, to absorb into my skin any hint of his lingering presence.

I had a love-hate relationship with this chair. Marcus bought it when we lived in Portland, and then moved it to Mexico. He spent his weekend days in Mexico lounging in that recliner, dragging it outside onto our sunny terrace where he read, drank lattes and ate toast smeared with Nutella for breakfast and toast piled with sliced avocado for lunch. He would still be in that damn chair in the afternoons, when he switched from coffee to pilsner, and swapped his business books for motor-cycle or mountain-biking magazines. I realized he was tired from his work week and needed his rest. The fertile beauty of the pecan farm, the vitamins from the sun on his naked body (Europeans don't like tan lines) and the quiet contrast from the truck factory construction site, all helped to revitalize him from his stressful job. Still, after being housebound all week—apart from my daily Spanish lessons—I blamed that chair for keeping us from taking weekend road trips to explore our new surroundings.

But, I had to admit, it was a good movie-watching chair. Moreover, it was in this chair, while drinking wine and talking with Alison that I was struck with some brilliant inspiration.

Since no one would hire me to bake pie for them, I would open my own pie shop. Ha! I had talked about the idea for years. Ever since I'd left Mary's Kitchen. Establishing my own shop would represent what Marcus always thought I was lacking: stability. He had left me a small inheritance. I would use the money to open a pie shop in Portland. I would name the shop after him, or at least offer a rotating pie-of-the-week and call it "The Marcus Special." I would write the names of his pies on a chalkboard. I would have red-and-white-checkered tablecloths. I would create a cozy place where people would sit with friends to share pie and conversation, and feel so welcome they would linger for hours. I would make Marcus proud.

I told Susan about my idea in our next session. She nodded and smiled and gave me a gold star for the concept.

"Making plans is a good sign," she said. Any sign that I wasn't going to slit my wrists or hang myself with Marcus's bathrobe belt was a good sign to her.

The excitement about the idea lasted approximately one day. All I had to do was sit down at my computer and start an Excel spread sheet listing the expenses it would require, and I was instantly reminded of why I had never opened a pie shop before. I scrapped the idea and went back to bed. But that one day of excitement, fleeting as it was, was better than nothing.

CHAPTER

6

If I thought it was expensive to open a pie shop, I learned that it's even more expensive to die. I know this because I had to deal with Marcus's affairs. I had to pay the ambulance bill. And the emergency-room bill. And the emergency-room doctor's bill. I paid the funeral home for the service and the casket and the courier service to get Marcus's paperwork from the German consulate. There was the Portland reception, the pizza, the wine and, because Marcus's friends were mostly Germans, the beer.

In Germany, there was another casket to buy (a fancy wooden one used only for the church service—what became of it afterward, I still wonder), the cremation, the urn for the ashes, the burial plot for the ash-filled urn.

One is not allowed to keep the ashes in Germany, let alone scatter them at will. This is another one of those examples which underscores our cultural differences—countless American fireplace mantels serve as the final resting place for dead relatives, and U.S.

mountaintops and oceans are freely, liberally, legally sprinkled with the remains of lost loved ones. I'd settle for a place less grand, with less fanfare, perhaps a small field filled with daisies, preferably in the country. I'd like to think Marcus would rather his ashes be scattered in the juniper heath behind his parents' house—his favorite hiking spot, located on the northern tip of Germany's famed Black Forest—but then he was in no position to state his preference. And I was in no position to argue with his German parents, traditions or laws.

I took solace in my belief that it doesn't matter what happens to our remains. Marcus is not in that urn buried in the ground. He is flying around on a magic carpet, bar hopping at British pubs, making appearances in my dreams, checking in on his coworkers every so often and riding his bike.

A burial serves as a ritual to provide closure; a grave merely serves as a memorial, a shrine. I had no attachment to his grave. The grave was in Germany, a mile and a half from his parents' house. It was their shrine, not mine. I had made my own shrine in my Portland apartment, covering the top of our Chinese medicine cabinet in framed photos of Marcus, twenty candles at least, and the Happy Buddha statue I had bought him as what turned out to be his last Christmas present. My refrigerator door was covered with pictures of him—Marcus riding a horse on a beach (taken during our honeymoon in Costa Rica), Marcus running on a dirt road through an Italian vineyard, Marcus holding a cup of coffee while sitting on the front porch of a cabin (outside Seattle, where I had lived during our courtship). Anyone who entered my Grieving Sanctuary might have thought my shrine was over the top—it was far more elaborate than the headstone and flowers covering his German grave. You couldn't stand anywhere in my studio without facing an image of Marcus, but since it was my space, my shrine, *my* grief, I didn't give a damn what anyone thought. Besides, almost no one ever came inside.

Burial sites and shrines aside, thanks to my husband's sense of responsibility, his staunch belief in the importance of insurance, including a very generous travelers' insurance policy, I was reimbursed for most of the exorbitant bills.

And so, after his body and his emergency medical expenses had been taken care of, after all the checks had been written and the framed photos and candles positioned on my bureau, I had finally arrived at number five on my to-do list: Figure out What to Do with Marcus's Stuff.

I started with the motorcycle trailer. For as much as I would have liked to have kept the trailer, I couldn't tow it behind my MINI Cooper. In fact, the trailer was so big my MINI could have fit inside. Marcus had bought the enclosed, wood panel-lined storage-unit-on-wheels for our move from Portland to Mexico, to haul his BMW motorbike. When he bought the immaculate Wells Cargo trailer, I teased him, saying, "This would be the perfect mobile pie shop. We could just cut out a window here," I said, pointing to the side. "And we could paint 'The World Needs More Pie' here," I added, indicating the blank white area above. "Or I could use it as an extra room, a writing studio. It's got skylights and air vents. I could really put this to good use."

He smiled in the deep way that showed his dimples and said, "*Hände Weg. Verboten*," the German words for "Keep your hands off. Forbidden." He had used this expression with me ever since our first Christmas together when he wanted to make certain I didn't go looking for my present in his suitcase and to tease me, he placed a note, in German, saying as much on top of his luggage. I still have the note, written in his bold, blocky handwriting.

The trailer had journeyed to Mexico and back, packed with Marcus's motorcycle, our sofa and boxes and boxes of household goods. The roads in Mexico were so bad, so full of potholes and the pavement ultra-slippery when wet, he never did ride the motorcycle there. And after learning of his transfer back to Germany, he had shipped the motorbike directly from Mexico to Stuttgart. The sofa and household goods, however, had all made the return trip to Portland and Marcus's August vacation was his first chance to unload the trailer. He had spent a full week emptying the trailer and reorganizing our Portland storage unit.

While in the midst of this reorg, he wrote in an email to me in Texas, "Good news. Our storage unit is now packed with the couch, chairs, Chinese medicine cabinet, amazing memory-foam mattress, bar stools, the boxes and all the large tubs. Six small tubs needed to stay in the trailer along with the teak tabletop. Obviously, dealing with this is very 'un-vacationish.'"

I liked his twist on the English language, and that he even put the made-up word in quotes. I also liked how he noted the detail of the mattress type and called it "amazing." I had argued for the queen-size version—so we could sleep closer together, as I wanted and needed more intimacy with him—but with our dogs snuggling in bed with us, the king ended up being a good call. In spite of what a pain the thing was to move.

He could have spared himself the physical effort and hassle had he agreed to let his company move us. Instead my stubborn, frugal and fiercely independent husband took the ten-thousand-dollar cash equivalent/moving allowance paid by his employer and opted to do the heavy lifting himself. This was yet another case of me not being happy about his choice. "I am not going to do this self-moving crap again," I had barked at him, as I taped yet another box while packing for Mexico. But the end result of his decision was much worse and farther reaching than either of us could have ever imagined.

"It's the anaerobic activity that could have contributed to his aorta rupturing," I was told by a heart specialist in Boston for whom Alison's mother-in-law worked. "Moving heavy furniture by himself would have put more pressure on the aortic wall than regular exercise, including his bike riding. And you must understand, there is absolutely no evidence that emotional stress causes a rupture."

Yeah? Well, it would still require a lot more convincing than that to accept that I did not kill him. But for the time being my guilt had been replaced by resentment toward the trailer, the storage unit, the furniture and the fact that the company even offered a moving allowance. *If only he had used the company's moving services...*

I asked one of Marcus's coworkers to post an ad for the trailer on the bulletin board at work. The thing sold in two days and the poor guy who bought had to console me as I handed him the registration and keys. This man was excited to use the trailer for his Harley-Davidson and instead of being happy that the rig was going to be appreciated and put to good use, I diminished his enthusiasm over his purchase by having a meltdown in front of him.

"It's like I'm selling off a part of my husband," I sobbed. He put his arm around me to keep me from collapsing on the pavement. "This represents everything about Marcus's dreams. He wanted to turn this into an adventure camper for his mountain bike. How can I let go of this? It's like letting go of him." Surely the guy wanted to get away from me as fast as possible, but he was kind enough to squeeze me closer against his burly body and let me cry a little longer before driving away in his truck—with a piece of Marcus in tow.

Setting foot inside the storage unit for the first time was another form of hell. There were the couches, chairs, Chinese medicine cabinet, mattress, bar stools and boxes that Marcus had arranged himself. I had brought a crew of friends with me, all men, all friends of Marcus, to help transport some of the big items over to my guesthouse. *If only Marcus had asked these friends for help when he was moving the furniture...* I turned my back to them so they didn't see my tears. And when I composed myself enough to tell them what needed to be moved, I got us out of there as quickly as possible.

Like with every single post-death task, activity or encounter, spending time in the storage unit and going through Marcus's belongings was something that required conditioning. The first time for everything was inevitably the hardest, but over time and with repetition, emotional fortitude builds up like a muscle, making unavoidable tasks at least bearable.

I went back to the storage unit a few weeks later, on November 19, the three-month mark of Marcus's—what does one call it?—*passing*. I had gone only to look for a tax document but ended up staying three hours. I bravely peered into the black garbage bags that held the clothes Marcus had packed for his vacation, clothes that friends had tossed inside in our rush to make funeral arrangements.

Marcus had always taken good care of his belongings. He folded every shirt, sock and pair of underwear with painstaking precision. He wouldn't have liked his things being treated this way. So I emptied the garbage bags, folded everything—his bike jerseys, his running tights, his surfer shorts, his cotton turtlenecks, his jeans—and placed each article neatly in the large plastic tubs. What took me so long is that I had to sniff every item before putting it away.

I talked to my California-based friend Melissa that evening, commenting on how the majority of the storage unit was taken up by his things. She said, "Why don't you just pick ten things to keep and give away the rest?"

I snapped back angrily, "It was enough for me just to organize. I'm not letting go of anything!"

But the question had been raised. When would it be time to let go of his stuff? Six months? A year? Ten years? Never? The solution for me was simply this: do it incrementally. In baby steps.

My youngest brother, Patrick, who lives in Seattle, wears exactly Marcus's size and I suggested that I could give him Marcus's cashmere sport coat as he was about to start a new job. Patrick said yes and added that he was in need of more business clothes. It made my decision easy: the rest of Marcus's work clothes would go to him, keeping them in the family was a win-win. Marcus really liked Patrick and therefore would approve. And, unlike the trailer, I wouldn't feel like I was truly letting go of them.

I went back to the storage unit a week later to collect Marcus's dress shirts and wool trousers. As I rummaged through the tubs, I noted the abundance of Marcus's hats, gloves, socks, fleece jackets and sweaters. I had experienced a recent manic desire to clear out all clutter from my life, to simplify, to downsize (if one can actually downsize from a studio apartment), to lighten my load. In case I dropped dead, too (I lived in a paranoid world imagining anyone could disappear at any moment), I wanted to make sure I wasn't leaving much behind. I had already, impetuously, donated to Goodwill my doll collection consisting of Mrs. Beasley, which might have been worth something, and a handmade Raggedy Ann. I also donated my Catholic high school uniform, a pleated, plaid skirt with the "It's Better in the Bahamas" patch I sewed over the hole made from holding the iron down too long. The skirt still fit me and held many memories of cheerleading tryouts and student-council meetings, truancy and subsequent detentions, of first loves and first broken heart. And I let go of my baby blanket, made from light yellow bunny-print cotton filled with wool batting, still usable for spare bedding. None of these were doing me any good in storage and I had no one to pass them down to, so off they went in an unceremonious departure. Kicking them out of the nest, my childhood treasures were given the boot. (I came to regret this later, but that's grief for you. It erases consciousness and common sense, like a kind of temporary insanity.)

In this purging state of mind and rummaging through Marcus's things in storage, I considered giving away his warm clothing. "Winter is coming. Think of all the homeless people out there who could benefit from this pair of fleece gloves or this great hat," I thought.

But then the other side of the brain began arguing. "Yes, but he always wore those gloves to the park when he threw the stick for Jack. You bought him that hat in New York City, in Little Italy. He looked so cute in it. You had so much fun together on that trip . . ." No, I couldn't do it. I couldn't give this stuff away, *his* stuff.

With tears—those pesky, ubiquitous droplets that leaked from my eyes—dripping onto his clothes, I put away the hat, gloves and everything else, except for the dress shirts and trousers for Patrick. I also kept a box of German books to give to Joerg, as I was realistic enough to know I would never read them. (No later regrets about those.) I wadded up the empty garbage bags, snapped the lids shut on the tubs, pulled the storage-unit door closed, hooked the padlock and left the rest of Marcus's belongings where they were—secure, unused and waiting for some distant day that I might be able to let go. Let go, or at least go back and smell them again.

7

There is nothing like facing your fears—and overcoming them—to boost your confidence. The fear that filled me with terror was driving the recreational vehicle, the RV that Marcus had left behind. What we had referred to as "The Beast," the RV was (and still is) a twenty-four-foot camper built around a commercial-size Ford truck chassis. In RV terms, this is called a C-class. It is also known to veterans of the RV world, the ones who drive those shiny hundred-thousand-dollar buses, as "the runt of the litter."

Marcus, being German, possessed a dream very common among Europeans: he wanted to drive an RV around the country, visit all the national parks and camp.

"You call that camping?" I had growled at him. "If you buy one of those, you are traveling on your own." My bitchiness toward him may seem unwarranted—and it was—but I was used to *real* camping, roughing it. I had graduated a semester early from high school (it was either that or get kicked out for being "too disruptive") and instead of going to senior prom, which was no big deal to me seeing as I had already lost my virginity, I spent three months in the Rocky Mountains completing a semester at the National Outdoor Leadership School. Instead of shopping for a taffeta gown that spring, I was building igloos, crawling through caves, hauling seventy pounds on my back, sleeping under the stars and going for weeks at a time without bathing. I loved it; I had found my comfort zone.

I knew from experience, from our trips to Crater Lake and Umpqua Hot Springs and our hiking trips in the Cascades and the Alps, that Marcus liked wilderness camping, too. All I had to do was glance at our wedding rings to be reminded of it: the gold and steel representation of contrasts, our love for camping and five-star hotels. But an RV? There was no metal band on our rings for that.

An RV represented a definition of camping I could not, would not, subscribe to. RVs were for suburbanites who didn't want to ruin their manicures, people who couldn't appreciate how important bugs are to the ecosystem and killed (by poisonous means) every insect they encountered, "campers" who were so trapped by their creature comforts they couldn't fathom a night in nature without television. RVs meant you were so insulated from the elements you might as well have stayed home parked on the cul de sac. Further, RVs were gas guzzlers, road hogs and just plain stupid. But I didn't have a strong opinion about them.

Several months before we were scheduled to move to Mexico, we had dodged our first divorce attempt by landing in a very useful marriage workshop based on the teachings of John Gottman and his Seattle-based Gottman Relationship Institute. During these sessions, I learned what a bad wife I had been, and how my stance against the RV represented just how awful, how rude, how reactionary I was. As we attended the workshop, sharing our feelings, our frustrations, our goals, it dawned on me that regardless of how I felt about camping, I had no right to stand in the way of Marcus's dream.

Marcus thought it would be "cool" (his word) to drive an RV to Mexico, as it would be a cross-continent—even better, *international*—road trip. To which I replied, in my newfound (albeit temporary) role as Good Wife, "Love of my life, if you want an RV, by all means, get an RV." But my goodness went only so far, because I snidely added, "On the condition that I never have to drive it."

I was true to my word. I cleaned it, I loaded and unloaded it, I cooked, I made coffee in it, I made the bed, I navigated, I rubbed his shoulders. But I did not drive it. Period. I barely drove *in* it as it was, because we traveled to Mexico separately. I drove my own car down, making a weeklong pit stop in Los Angeles to visit my family on my way. Our paths converged in Laredo, Texas, planned that way, so we could make the official border crossing together. I followed him, The Beast and the motorcycle trailer, across the Rio Grande and through the mountainous terrain of Northern Mexico for the last three hours of the forty-hour journey, until we reached our new home in Saltillo, on the edge of the pecan farm.

We took a few RV road trips during our stay in Mexico—to the colonial towns of Zacatecas and Real de Catorce and to the Amistad Reservoir in Del Rio, Texas. I spent enough nights in it to get irreversibly hooked on sleeping in a nest of down comforters and pillows, waking up to café lattes made in the espresso machine and lounging around the breakfast table while running the heater. (Generators are indeed a wonderful thing.) Damn it, I hated myself for being such a hypocrite.

That is how The Beast came into our lives—the RV I didn't want, that I refused to drive, the RV that was now mine. What the hell was I going to do with this thing?

As with most questions in life, the answer presented itself in time.

When I wrote on my to-do list "Figure out What to Do with Marcus's Stuff," I meant it as in *all* of our stuff, including the storage unit I had kept in Venice Beach after moving to Terlingua, Texas. I still had a studio apartment's worth of furniture, books and pie-baking supplies to consolidate. God forbid I die with my life spread out over two states a thousand miles apart.

After conducting exhaustive research, it finally occurred to me that I already owned the perfect moving truck: the RV.

It was a practical concept. With the RV, I would have my own place to stay in L.A., my very own mobile Grieving Sanctuary, I could stay as long as I wanted, and I could bring my dogs. The only problem was I would have to drive it. Never mind that I would go from never having been behind the wheel of The Beast to embarking on a thousand-mile road trip across several mountain ranges in December straight into the city with America's worst traffic. That said, I was—to use Marcus's term—"pregnant with the idea." Translation: a quirky German way of saying I couldn't get the thought out of my head. And when I make up my mind, look out.

After losing three nights' sleep from the anticipation and anxiety of my inaugural RV drive, Alison drove me to the RV dealer thirty miles south of Portland, where The Beast had ostensibly been for sale. Marcus had left it there the week before he died, hoping to sell the RV on consignment. Make no mistake. Marcus may have been transferred back to Germany, but he had not given up his RV dream of traveling around North America. He merely wanted to sell it in order to buy a brand-new one.

With this new brainstorm of mine, the dealership had ended up serving only as a temporary parking lot. If Marcus only knew. Did he know? Was this his idea? Probably.

When Alison and I arrived at the dealer's lot, we recognized The Beast at first sight. It wasn't just that Alison was very familiar with it (it had been parked in front of her house the first two weeks of Marcus's August vacation), it's that not all RVs look alike. The unique identifiers of ours included a red stripe acquired when its previous owner side-swiped a building that was, yes, red. And on the upper right corner there were the prominent markings of "de-lam," short for delamination, as buckling, water-damaged fiberglass is called when it separates from the RV's inner wooden layer. When this happens you might as well start shopping for a new RV.

"Oh, it's a lot bigger than I remember," Alison commented.

"Uh, yeah." I nodded, gaping at the site of it. A flimsy white shell extended out over the truck's cab to the front and reached far beyond the rear wheels to the back, making it appear longer than—and less safe than—a school bus. The dually wheels alone were as big as an oven. "It's about the same size as my apartment," I said grimly to Alison. Though in fact, the RV seemed even larger than my one-room studio, given its layout of four separate rooms for the bed, shower, toilet and kitchen.

Alison, proving she was a brave and true friend, rode along with me and the old geezer from the RV dealership for a practice drive around the neighborhood. I learned how to turn right—"Pull further out into the intersection than you would with a car, then make your turn. You need to clear the length," instructed the man in the well-worn U.S. Army Veteran's baseball hat. And I practiced braking—"You need to allow yourself more stopping distance than you're used to," he warned.

Alison followed me home on the I-5 freeway, driving my MINI Cooper as I rolled along on my first highway outing at fifty miles per hour, which felt double that speed, given the tension in my body. One hundred percent of my concentration was focused on keeping the wide-bodied rig centered in my lane, getting used to the squishy power steering (this was not the "go-kart handling" I was used to), and avoiding bumping side mirrors with the FedEx trucks and other transport vehicles. From where I sat, as high as the semis and school buses, my MINI looked like an ant I could squash.

"Keep an eye on my MINI while I'm gone," I told Alison, hugging her as we said our goodbyes. "If all goes well . . ." *if I don't die in a fiery crash in this monster truck "* . . . I'll meet you in Arizona for Christmas."

I packed The Beast with some food, clothes, my two dogs and a new set of tire chains, which I prayed to Almighty God I would never have to use, and headed to California.

Once again on I-5, but this time traveling a thousand miles instead of thirty, my main mission—besides getting to L.A. without wrecking or rolling The Beast—was to avoid a breakdown of the nervous kind. My relaxation techniques for driving were many. I chanted a mantra: "Strength, grace, confidence, calm. Strength, grace, confidence, calm. Strength, grace, confidence, calm." I said the words over and over and over in a rhythmic cadence, saying them louder whenever a semi passed me, their drafts causing the RV to veer precariously to the right. I chanted the mantra words so many times my dogs could probably have recited them, too.

I played a CD Marcus had bought me that was called "Relax and De-Stress," a compilation of soothing classical music from Dr. Andrew Weil's "Music for Self-Healing" series—Marcus's not-so-subtle way of telling me to "take it easy," an expression he had used often with me. I almost melted the disc by playing it continuously for the first eight hours of driving, not even turning it off when I stopped for gas.

I reminded myself at least once every fifteen minutes to release my white-knuckle grip on the steering wheel, to stop holding my breath and breathe normally. As often as possible, I glanced over at the picture of Marcus I had taped to the center console, a visa photo of him in a serious, stern-looking pose that became my symbol of him overseeing my safety. A mug shot of my guardian angel.

And last but not least, I raised my left hand every so often, shaking it until I heard the familiar rattle of our wedding rings. I wore both of them now, my smaller one on top of Marcus's larger one to keep his from sliding off. Considering these were heavy, bulky rings individually, wearing them together was the equivalent of strapping a barbell to my finger. That Marcus had gone to Portland knowing we were filing for divorce and still had his wedding ring with him was a painful reminder that he wanted the divorce as much as I did. As in, not that much. Finding the ring right next to his passport had produced another one of those searing stabs of heartache, but that feeling gradually turned to relief knowing I could keep the ring safe. Even if *we* couldn't be together, at least our rings were. I took solace in the small things.

I made it from Portland to Lake Shasta in Northern California the first night and pulled off the highway into an RV park an hour after dusk had turned to complete darkness. It was only my first day and, in my determination to just get this stressful and scary trip over with, I had already broken my first rule: no driving at night.

I rolled down my window as the campground manager stepped out to greet me at the gate. "We have electrical outlets. You can plug in," he said, zipping his down jacket all the way up to his neck.

"That's nice, but I don't have a power cord," I replied.

He raised his eyebrow as if to say, I can see you are ignorant about RVs, and then said with a touch of compassion, "Let me show you where to find it."

Sure enough, there was a built-in cord. I plugged in to the power box and enjoyed the luxury of having both lights and heat. I don't know why I ever insisted on tent camping. Nor did I know why I was so afraid to drive the RV. Driving The Beast was a cinch, really, once you got used to it. And after my first 400 miles, I was not only used to it, I . . . *Oh, I'm so very, very sorry, Marcus*—I actually liked it.

♥♥♥

Santa Monica Canyon is an exclusive pocket on Los Angeles' far west side. Tucked between the Pacific Ocean, Malibu, the wild coyote- and sagebrush-filled coastal mountain range, and the mansions of Brentwood and Beverly Hills, this little canyon is an idyllic secret haven. Its prime location and elegant beach cottages could make even the most L.A.-despising person run to the nearest real-estate office.

As I maneuvered the RV from Seventh Street above down into the canyon onto Entrada Street below, it was not the elegant houses that were so striking but the colors and smells. Magenta, red and orange bougainvillea bloomed on bushes even bigger than houses. The cloudless sky was colored iridescent blue, its beckoning infinity interrupted only by the ridgeline of the Santa Monica Mountains, a pristine preserve free of development. I rolled down the window to sniff the air that carried a scent of the sea, slightly fishy, mixed with the distinct and pungent spices of sage and bay leaf. There was no smog here. (Nor was there the depressing solid gray cloud cover and steady rain I had left in Portland.) There was only sea breeze and sun. And one of my best friends, Melissa.

Melissa was my West Coast equivalent of my childhood friend Nan. One of Melissa's magical qualities is how she turns up at precisely the moment you need her. She came to Marcus's and my American wedding, on the farm outside Seattle, and found me alone inside the farmhouse, just as I was about to have a pre-ceremony freak-out. She calmly zipped me into my wedding dress, clasped my pearl necklace around my neck and recited the words from a fortune cookie that we had adopted as our self-help code. "I am not worried about your future," she whispered, giving me her blessing before I walked down the pine-tree-lined aisle. When Marcus died, she was on a family vacation, but immediately upon her return she took the first flight to Oregon. She and Nan over-lapped in Portland by one night, so Nan, needing to get back to New York, passed the baton of caretaker (and Suicide Prevention Watch) over to Melissa. Who needs tranquilizers when you have best friends?

I parked at Melissa's because I knew I could run my exten-sion cord from the RV to her garage to get power. That was my excuse anyway. The truth is, I was avoiding staying with my par-ents. I didn't want my grief to be scrutinized. I wasn't ready for their Midwest "just get on with it" practicality. I knew what to expect. My dad, when he accompanied me to Marcus's funeral in Germany, had said "Everyone has to die sometime" in response to my "I can't believe Marcus is gone" statement, and that was still grating on me. I was doing my best to move forward, but I didn't want to be pushed. I didn't want my grief to be ignored either. I wanted to talk about Marcus. But they didn't want to talk. At least not about death. "Let me show you my new outfit," my mom would say. "Let's have a martini," my dad would say. But they didn't say,

"We know this must be so hard for you. We're here to listen. Take as much time as you need."

Susan had given me her blessing before I left Portland to ditch my parents. The words she used were different than my driving mantra but equally useful: self-compassion, self-kindness, self-tenderness. I practiced saying them like the good grief student I had become. If anyone heard me talking to myself, as I was prone to do, they would have thought I belonged in a mental institution. And I probably did. Instead, I was in Melissa's newly renovated bungalow with the heated swimming pool and grassy, palm-tree-filled backyard, perfect for Team Terrier.

I was not the only one staying at Melissa's. She had another houseguest, Janice, her fellow television-producer friend from the East Coast. Janice and I had met several times over the years. She and Melissa started their careers at MTV together, where Melissa started *MTV Sports* and Janice worked on a show similar to *Road Rules,* the reality show that followed a group of kids traveling cross-country in an RV.

Janice, cheerful and tomboyish, lit up when she saw my RV. "That's awesome you're driving that," she said in her thick New Jersey accent.

"Yeah, it is," I replied flatly, not bothering to describe the gamut of emotions I had wrangled to get The Beast there, and knowing I still had a return trip to make.

The second evening I was there, Janice came back to Melissa's after work. She was beaming and bouncy, so much so I thought she was going to start doing cartwheels in the living room with Melissa's little girls. "I had an idea," she panted. "You write a pie blog, and you have the RV. I miss my days working on the travel show. I need a road trip. Let's take the RV, drive around the country and make a pie documentary. Better yet, a whole television series and we'll start by shooting the pilot." I must have looked slightly skeptical as she added, "I'm serious." She didn't have to emphasize the point because her eyes, glistening from under the brim of her "Life is Good" baseball cap, relayed just how interested she was. "I can take two weeks off in January. I'll fly back out here and bring my cameras."

Whether pie documentary or TV series or a handful of videos posted on YouTube, it was a no-brainer. It combined my favorite subjects and skills—travel, journalism, curiosity about other people's lives, and of course, pie. It would mean I wouldn't return to Portland for another month. But what the hell, I didn't have anything to go back for. I had my dogs with me. I had also brought Marcus's shrine (albeit a scaled-down version). And I had the RV with my down pillows and espresso maker. But best of all, I had something I hadn't found since Marcus died: a purpose.

Janice, like the Fairy Godmother of Grief, had waved her wand and presented me with a new direction, a project I could channel my energy into, a goal to strive for. Or, if nothing else, a constructive diversion from my constant sadness. And so it was, through a chance convergence with an old acquaintance, my Pie Quest was launched.

Or was it chance?

"Marcus? What are you up to?" I asked when I was alone in the RV, holding his mug shot and staring him in the eye. "You're trying to help me, aren't you?" I had been watching too many episodes of *Ghost Whisperer,* making myself believe he was actually hanging around all the time. Unlike in the TV show, he didn't materialize, and he didn't answer. Well, it didn't matter how—or who—or why it happened. The important thing was that I was about to hit the road in the RV again—the road to recovery, a long, slow, winding road that would take many more months and many miles to travel.

A wide open road paved with tears, but also bursting like ripe berries with goodness, kindness, generosity. A path filled with pie.
A whole lot of pie. Delicious, fruity, creamy, flaky, homemade,
hearty pie. If, like the Chinese proverb states, "The journey of a
thousand miles begins with the first step," then the journey of a
grieving widow begins with the first slice. I couldn't wait to get
behind the wheel again, to drive The Beast, the beloved Beast.

CHAPTER

8

Our game plan for the pie TV shoot was pretty loose. Because I knew the world of pie, I would come up with all the content ideas and conduct the interviews. And I would drive the RV. Janice, who knew the technical world of cameras, would do the directing and filming. And provide an extra set of eyes when I had to parallel park. We wouldn't follow a script, we would just make a list of the places, people and events we wanted to cover and then be like the renegades of *Road Rules* and wing it. The thread that would weave the stories together, Janice suggested, would be how pie had helped heal my grief.

The problem was, it hadn't. My grief was still raw, my eyes still extremely red from constantly crying, my vulnerability still visible. But I kept the faith in the healing powers of pie; I had had experience with its comforting capabilities, like when I had worked in Malibu and baked my way back to a balanced life. And as far as the TV show was concerned, I knew there were a lot of other bakers around the country using pie as a way to give back to society. Ways that helped others, that might also help me. Therefore, I went along with her suggestion.

I was in Los Angeles and still had nearly a month before Janice returned from New Jersey, so I began my pie show research. I started with The Apple Pan, a legendary diner known for its pie, in West Los Angeles, conveniently near Melissa's.

The Apple Pan is the twin sister, or perhaps more accurately, the glamorous cousin, of the Canteen, the diner of my childhood. On the surface, the similarities are many: the horseshoe-shaped Formica counter surrounded by red vinyl-covered barstools, the checkered curtains, the wood-paneled walls lined with a smattering of coat hooks and faded photos and a menu that unabashedly offers only three things—burgers, tuna sandwiches and pie—a limited selection with an air of time-earned confidence that stops short of saying directly, "Take it or leave it."

Like the Canteen, The Apple Pan—established in 1947, making it eleven years younger than the Iowa version—remains unchanged since it opened. The only differences are that The Apple Pan's burgers are formed patties (not loose meat), its counter is three times as big, and given its close proximity to Twentieth Century Fox's film studios, the lunch crowd is often star-studded.

Not that the Canteen hasn't had its brush with fame. Tom Arnold, a native of Ottumwa, Iowa, is a regular Canteen customer whenever he comes home to visit. And in his ex-wife Rosanne Barr's show, *Roseanne,* the Lanford Lunch Box restaurant was modeled after the Canteen. However, The Apple Pan, always one to upstage its rural cousin, laid its own claim to a television series: it was the model for the Peach Pit in the original *Beverly Hills, 90210* series. I know this because I worked on the hit show as a publicist.

♥♥♥

I may never have owned a TV, but I had some background working in the television industry. My first public-relations job was at a hotel resort on the Big Island of Hawaii and *Bob Hope's Christmas Special* was taped during my tenure there (I lasted eight months at the job, a personal best at the time). Because I was willing to help with whatever the production's public-relations firm needed—from getting coffee to rounding up soldiers from the local army base to fill the studio audience—they thought I'd make a good employee at their Los Angeles headquarters. (They weren't aware of my "entrepreneurial tendencies"...yet.) Several months later, claustrophobia from island living had set in—an affliction known as "Rock Fever"—and even though I had no desire to live in Southern California, let alone work in television, it was my ticket out of Hawaii, so I accepted the job.

My first day of work at the PR agency, I found myself in Aaron Spelling's private office, sitting on the couch next to a young hotshot producer wearing black velvet jewel-encrusted slippers. Cute guy, but those shoes? I may have been the first person in Hollywood to suspect he was gay. The guy was Darren Star, who later produced *Melrose Place* and the entire *Sex and the City* franchise; *Beverly Hills, 90210* was his first show. It was clear why he was here, but me? Didn't my bosses know I was a fraud? Not only did I not own a television, I never watched it. Who was Aaron Spelling anyway? Actually, I did know who he was. I would have had to be living under a bigger volcanic rock than the Big Island to not be familiar with his shows, *Charlie's Angels* and *Dynasty*. But what I also knew was that I had no business sitting across from him. I was a junior publicist, a guppy thrown into the pond with

Hollywood's top whale sharks. It was like my first day baking pies at Mary's Kitchen; I had no idea what I was doing.

But I got the job done. I got on the phone, used my most polite Midwest manners and lined up interviews for Jason Priestly, Shannon Doherty, Tori Spelling and company. Tori was so young then she didn't have a driver's license and I had to pick her up—at her family's mega-mansion—for appointments.

I left that job (surprise!), and public relations altogether—it was a thankless career, literally, as no one ever said thank you—to fulfill my childhood dream of becoming an outdoor-adventure journalist. I wrote for sports and fitness magazines, jumping out of airplanes, scuba diving with sharks and dogsledding in Alaska for assignments—basically, the assignments no one else would take. And then, ironically, the magazine work led me back to television—even though I still didn't own one. This time I was in front of the camera, appearing in two seasons of an inline skating show on the Outdoor Life Network. I was a perky and athletic host on Rollerblades, who said things like, "Why walk, when you can skate?" and "We'll be right back, so stick around." I wasn't bad at it. I had enough talent to smile, talk and skate all at the same time. Mainly, I surprised myself with my ability to memorize my lines, surprising because my memory is terrible. Marcus, whose photographic memory was off-the-charts impressive, used to get annoyed with me for not remembering things, like the date we met (I was off by a day) or the name of a movie we had seen the week before.

I already liked my new identity as TV producer, at least I liked the idea of it. It sounded much nicer than Grieving Widow. Still, I was both things. I was one of those multifaceted people known as slashers: Writer slash Pie Baker slash TV Producer slash Grieving Widow. I could have had many more slashes with all the other kinds of jobs I had had and quit. But that last one in the slasher lineup was a title I didn't want, a job I couldn't quit, couldn't even get fired from.

Marcus and I had talked about how awful it was going to be in the future to have to check the "divorced" box on tax and other official forms. Neither of us dreamed a different box would be checked. And that it would mean only one of us was alive to check it. "Widow." I hated the term, hated being put into this category, hated being part of this club. And yet, this had become my main identity. Before I could remember that I was anything else, I now thought of myself first and foremost as Grieving Widow.

I was also Husband Killer. I was still holding on tightly to that one.

"You know that 99.9 percent of divorces don't end in death," Melissa tried to assure me. "You asking for a divorce did not kill him."

I considered this. "Yes, but ... "

"Think how many people would be dead if every divorce ended in death. You didn't kill him," she repeated.

"I suppose you're right." Her hammer of wisdom had finally chiseled a little crack in my fortress of guilt over Marcus. But any progress was countered by a terrible, shameful thought: Melissa was filing for divorce, too. *Why couldn't her husband have died instead of mine?* Oh my God, I was bad, bad, bad for thinking that. Especially because they have two young kids. It's just that Melissa didn't love her husband the way I loved Marcus, and their divorce was most definitely not amicable. How would she have reacted had her soon-to-be-ex spouse died? Would she have been devastated, debilitated like I was?

Friends wrote me emails, complimenting me on my courage, strength and resilience. "I would never have the strength to handle it," they would say. I dismissed the notion that I was doing anything differently than any other widow, or anyone suffering any loss, would do. I was still living in spite of not wanting to, still getting up every morning, running through the basic daily functions. And crying.

I would never wish what I was going through on anyone, best friend or worst enemy. I take back what I said about Melissa's husband, even though the guy is kind of an asshole. But I couldn't stop asking the question: Why Marcus? Why a good and honest man who respected life so much he couldn't even throw out an avocado pit? *WHY HIM?*

What I never asked was "Why me?" I wasn't a victim. Marcus was the one who I felt bad for. My grief wasn't self-pity. It was loneliness, a void, an emptiness that couldn't be filled. Some devil had gouged my heart out of my chest and left me caving in, like a pie that's lost its filling.

Married or divorced, Marcus was still the person I was closest to, the one who knew the most intimate details about me, from my hot-and-cold sex drive to my infertility (due to the hyperthyroid) to the location of every birthmark and blackhead on my body. Likewise, I knew everything about him. Except for the fact that he was going to die at forty-three.

"Regardless of whether the relationship was good or bad, don't assume there is no attachment," Susan had told me in my first grief counseling session. "The dream that it could be different, that you could get it right, is gone."

Marcus had written to me almost identical sentiments just one week before he died: "Giving up this dream is what's hardest for me. We fought hard for this and that probably makes it harder to let go."

Self-pity? No. Losing a limb and having to learn to live without it? Yes. If only there was a prosthetic for grief.

Pushing the questions—and shameful thoughts—aside, I dug beneath the lard-heavy layers of grief to tap into whatever reserves I had left in order to get to work. In the same way I tackled magazine articles, I would identify who to interview, call them to schedule a visit and then show up to ask the questions. The biggest difference was cameras. And makeup. I was going to need a lot of foundation and concealer—definitely concealer—to hide my puffy, tear-damaged eyes and the stress-induced case of dermatitis, a growing rash that surrounded my eyes and nose with inflamed and ugly red spots.

The first phone call I made for the pie show was to L.A.'s top pie expert: my dad. My parents had moved from Iowa to California when the kids came back for fewer and fewer visits. Three of us had moved to Los Angeles and my parents spent so much time visiting us they finally got their own vacation apartment, which led to selling their house in Iowa, which led to early retirement by the sea. Smart people. They had spent the first two years of their marriage in San Diego, where they gave birth to the first two of five kids and conceived me. As far as I was concerned, my conception in their Ocean Avenue apartment meant I could lay claim to dual origins—part California girl (sunny and free-spirited—I used to be anyway, before Marcus died) and part Native Iowan (hearty and grounded), a fact that I like to publicize because it sums up the definition of me so well.

"You don't need to tell people that," my mom scolds.

"Why? Because people will think you actually had sex?" I tease her the way I learned from my dad.

They settled in Iowa, but always longed to move back to the West Coast. And they finally did pull up their Iowa stakes, in 2001, and have lived blissfully at the beach ever since. No sooner had my parents unpacked their moving van in L.A., however, I left my pie-baking job at Mary's Kitchen and moved to Seattle for a project (one that actually paid), then I married Marcus and moved to Germany, then . . . well, they couldn't keep track of me after that. My dad complained about me taking up so many pages in his address book. "You should see all the scratched-out entries I have in there," he said every time I added a new residence.

But I was in L.A. for the time being. Four months after Marcus dying. Staying at Melissa's a mere ten miles away. Avoiding them. I needed to do something to prove I wasn't the World's Worst Daughter. I didn't need to add another slasher title to my list, though its rank would have been obvious—it would come right after Bad Wife.

"Dad? It's Beth," I had to speak loudly since years of a dental drill whining in his ears had taken a toll. "Can I take you to lunch?"

"Hi, Anne," he said. "What are you up to?"

"No, it's *BETH*. Are you free for lunch? There's a diner in West L.A. I think you'll like." I didn't tell him I was using him as a cover for my location-scouting trip, as they call it in "the Biz." He wouldn't have cared about my ulterior motive, though, because I had a selling point he couldn't refuse: "They have banana cream pie."

The Apple Pan is best known for its outstanding apple pie, but their second-most popular pie, banana cream, is even better. Moreover—okay, I'm just going to say it—it's far better than my mom's. Especially since my mom had adopted a few shortcuts over the years. First it was just one or two easier steps, but she took it an ingredient too far, entering that dangerous territory my grandmothers had landed in, and eventually arrived at the point-of-no-return. Her made-from-scratch banana cream pie had morphed into one of store-bought graham cracker crust, packaged pudding mix (worse, instant pudding), and—oh, the horror—Cool Whip topping. The only thing that hadn't changed was the bananas. But even that part had been altered as my mom put bananas in only half the pie because she couldn't eat them. Didn't matter. My dad still loved her pie. And he still loved her.

The Hispanic man behind the counter placed two burgers on the counter in front of my dad and me. Just like the old days at the Canteen, they were wrapped in wax paper. The Apple Pan's staff was made up of dark-haired men in white paper hats and not, like at the Canteen, grey-haired ladies in hairnets. We weren't in Iowa anymore. Gender and race aside, what was remarkable about both places was the longevity of employment. Ask anyone on The Apple Pan's staff how long they've worked there and you will not get an answer less than, "Thirteen years." The longest stint was held by a man who retired a year earlier; he worked there fifty-three years. God forbid they hire me. I would ruin their track record. Ditto for the Canteen, where fifteen to twenty years was the average employment duration. Wow. What were these diners doing right? They couldn't have been paying huge salaries. My deduction—verified by the empty plates on the counter—was the pie. It had to be the pie. And we were about to be served ours. Two heaping slices of banana cream bliss.

Pie was a connection for my dad and me, but pie didn't inspire the deep and meaningful, philosophical conversations that were possible with him. Our most revealing talks were usually assisted by a three-olive martini or two—and hearing aids.

Our eyes lit up as the waiter set the pie down in front of us. We lifted our forks in unison, diving into our individual slices, cutting through our layers of whipped cream, thin blankets of vanilla pudding and down into the most generous stack of sliced bananas

I had ever seen in a pie. Our forks cut through the delicate flour and butter crust until there was nothing left to stop them but the plate.

We ate in silence—with the exception of the familiar, telltale moans expressing our utter satisfaction with the dessert. We didn't need to talk. There wasn't anything to say. It was enough that I was there with my dad. Eating his favorite pie. He was still alive and I was grateful for that.

He may not have been able to talk about Marcus, but forgiveness came more easily when I reminded myself that he was grieving Marcus, too. My dad had visited Marcus and me in Germany twice in the two and a half years I lived there, and both times we took week-long motorcycle trips, one time crossing the Alps to Italy and the other to the Alsatian wine country of France. Marcus and my dad bonded over their love for these two-wheeled adventures, but I'm convinced they would have had the same friendship and respect for one another even if they hadn't had me or even the motorcycles as the common link. What stood out most is how, during my heart-to-heart talks with my dad over martinis, when I confided in him how much I was struggling in the marriage, he would always say, "I like Marcus; he's a good man." And then he always added, "You two have something special. I know you will be okay." But we weren't okay. And now Marcus was gone. And now, with or without the assistance of a lip-loosening martini, my dad and I didn't know what to say to each other anymore.

Regardless of our inability to talk, I didn't take my dad for granted. I couldn't. He could be gone any second. Anyone could.

When we finished, I paid the bill. That was a change from our childhood Canteen outings, but one thing had stayed the same. When we stepped outside into the warm sunshine, I didn't have to remind myself. It came out, like a reflex, and I genuinely meant it. I said, "Thank you, Dad."

9

With The Apple Pan securing the Number One position on my Must See TV pie production schedule, I continued making phone calls and doing Internet searches until I had filled the rest of the two-week shoot with other pie-related appointments. It was a week before Christmas and all I could do now was wait for Janice's return to L.A. in mid-January. That, and get through the holidays.

I needed to answer the question that had been looming for weeks: "How would I survive my first Christmas and New Year's Eve without Marcus?" Many friends worried about me, calling and emailing to offer their good wishes and support. My grief counselor worried about me. I worried about me, too. But I had discovered something important during my drive from Portland to Los Angeles in The Beast: I felt best when I was in motion.

"Perpetual Motion" is the name of the second song I learned to play on the cello using the Suzuki Method. Perpetual motion is the physics theory stating that motion would go on indefinitely if not for the presence of friction. Perpetual motion, and my need for it, is why I left Melissa's after several weeks there and kept on driving—four hundred miles east to Phoenix, Arizona. I hadn't planned on traveling to America's fifth largest city for Christmas, but Alison had invited me to join her and Thomas at her mother's condo in the suburb of Scottsdale.

After barely surviving my first Thanksgiving without Marcus, I had a valid reason to be worried about Christmas and New Year's. And even more reason to seek refuge in Alison's soothing company.

As a pie baker, Thanksgiving was my most revered holiday. Forget the turkey, stuffing and cranberry sauce, the feast's sacrosanct dish was pie—pumpkin and pecan. Thanksgiving was also sacred, as it was the one holiday Marcus and I had never spent apart. Through all the job transfers, moves and other upheavals in our relationship there was one, and only one, consistent thing: Thanksgiving. We had celebrated the past seven Thanksgivings together—two in America with my parents, two in Germany with his parents, one in Switzerland with my friends in Bern, one in Mexico with his boss and other American coworkers and one on board a Lufthansa flight somewhere over the Atlantic the year Marcus's grandma died.

Three months after my return trip from Marcus's funeral on that same German airline, I didn't feel much like celebrating Thanksgiving, let alone making pie or even eating it. But Alison, ever-present, ever ready to cheer me up with her laugh, insisted I join her at the gathering of twelve in her home.

"And would you be able to bring the pies?"

"Yes, yes, of course, you can count on me." I was glad for the assignment.

The Spurs Award. You fall off your horse, you run after it, chase it down, get back on and ride again. If pie baking was my new proverbial horse, my mixing bowls were my saddle; my rolling pin, my reins; my apron, my cowboy boots.

With the late November rain lightly tapping on the skylights in my tiny studio apartment kitchen, I turned up the volume on my iPod to fill my ears with the Bach cello music from our wedding and drown out my thoughts. With my hands moving to the rhythm of the string instruments, I rubbed the butter and shortening into the flour. The soft white powder and tender yellow and white fats melded together between my thumbs and forefingers. I never tired of the process; I loved watching textures combine to create a new, even softer one.

Alison refused to make pie dough with her hands. She made ongoing jokes about her love affair with her food processor. But to me, it wasn't funny. Making pie dough was all about the senses, the tactile experience, the sensory messages sent from the fingertips to the brain signaling the right consistency had been achieved. Only with your bare hands could you be sure the dough had enough moisture, and have the confidence, the intuitive knowing, the connection with your food. Only by touching the dough, having direct contact with it, could you imagine yourself as a sculptor, or awaken your inner child, the one who loved making creations with Play-Doh. You just couldn't reach that sensual depth with a Cuisinart.

I filled four crimped crusts, two with the liquid pumpkin-spice mixture and two with the viscous pecan concoction and placed them in my oven that was so small the pie rims touched. My precious babies baked and browned; their sweet scents permeated my tree house and evoked a sense of pride. Hooray for me. I had done something productive, gratifying—making pie for friends, people I loved, people who loved me. I was relieved to discover I still possessed a bit of my "old normal."

A friend who had witnessed my transition from dot com producer to pie baker at Mary's Kitchen had commented back then, "Beth, you're happiest when you're making pie."

He was right. Though I couldn't yet say I was "happy," making these pies, my first since those hot August days in the Texas miner's cabin, had reminded me I could still get that peaceful, easy feeling. Hell, I hadn't even cried all day. For a fresh widow going through her first major holiday alone? Damn, I was doing great. Bring on the gold star for the grief student.

I dropped off the pies at Alison's that night, on Thanksgiving Eve. I must have had a premonition that I might not make it to her dinner party.

By five o'clock on Thanksgiving Day, I was dressed and ready to face the holiday, flying solo. I had put on nice jeans, a paisley blouse and, as a nod to Marcus, my Bavarian *Trachten* wool blazer. He would have liked that. I had spritzed myself with perfume and applied the final strokes of mascara. I grabbed my car key off the hook by the door and then... Oh, I should have seen it coming, should have known it was going to happen, should have been prepared. I felt a sudden stabbing in my heart. Tears shot out from my eye ducts without warning. My mouth dropped open to release a silent scream. My knees buckled and I slumped down on the floor, my forehead pressing into the wood, rolling back and forth the way it had done on the concrete in Texas the night Marcus died. The tears raced out so fast and forcefully I thought I might vomit. Forget the turkey, some kind of electric carving knife had found its way into my chest.

"A grief burst," Susan explained later. "That's what you had. It's the sudden and overwhelming onset of grief. They can happen anytime and they come without warning."

My grief burst and its crippling onslaught of despair caused me to miss the appetizer and cocktail portion of the festivities. When Alison and family were ready to sit down for the main meal, wondering why I hadn't yet arrived, I got a phone call.

"It's unlike you to be late. Are you okay?" Alison asked.

"I'm sorry. I can't come," I told her. "Every time I try to leave the house, I start bawling again." As it was, I couldn't talk on the phone without gasping in between sobs.

"I'm coming to pick you up. Don't worry about packing for the dogs; we have food for them. Just bring your pajamas." She put the roasted bird back in the oven to keep it warm, drove the twenty minutes across town to my house, and sat with me for another fifteen minutes at my kitchen table to talk me down from the ledge.

"Don't jump," she might as well have been saying. "But if you do, I will use my net to catch you." Patient, loving, kind, even with ten people and a turkey waiting at home—this is why Alison was voted Homecoming Queen, why her number was right next to Nan's and Melissa's in my speed dial. And why I would spend the next holiday with her. Christmas. In Arizona.

♥♥♥

In spite of parking the RV upon arrival in Scottsdale, I stayed constantly in motion—hiking every morning in the local mountains, swimming every afternoon in the condo's pool, cooking big meals and making pie, a blueberry crumble, since we bought a bulk-size carton of blueberries from Costco.

Also during my week with her, Alison got me to do something I've never done: color my hair. Alison's sister Emily helped pick out a boxed blond shade from the grocery store and the two sisters played the roles of both beautician and therapist and lightened me up. Really, I did feel lighter. Not just because of my new hair color, but because I had made it through Christmas without having a complete Oh-My-God-I-Can't-Believe-Marcus-Is-Dead Meltdown. Too bad they couldn't do anything to fix my puffy eyes. When Alison and Thomas's vacation time ended, I couldn't bring myself to leave the desert and its brilliant, blazing sun. If staying in motion was helpful, being in the sun was doubly so. Seeing as I was unemployed, lost, confused and still mired in grief—and didn't have to be back in L.A. to meet Janice for another few weeks—I simply drove The Beast twenty-some miles down the road to my aunt and uncle's home in Mesa.

Uncle Mike and Aunt Sue were snowbirds from the Midwest, meaning they retired early and spent their winters golfing in Arizona rather than shoveling snow in Iowa. They lived in a trailer park for people age fifty-five and over, and though I didn't qualify in the age category I was nonetheless welcomed as a guest. The RV fit right in to the scene, parked among the double-wides, and we settled into a busy schedule that included more hiking, swimming, hot-tubbing and watching movies from the horizontal comfort of La-Z-Boy recliners. Escaping into films like *The Secret Life of Bees* engaged my heart and mind enough to help me forget.

Lest I get too comfortable in retirement mode—and I could have easily seen myself getting accustomed to the recreation-packed lifestyle—I packed up the dogs and drove out of the trailer park. Unsure of where I was going next—maybe back to L.A., maybe find a campground outside Phoenix, maybe head north to Sedona—I was stocking up on supplies at a local Trader Joe's when my cell phone rang. It was Maggie. Maggie was a friend from Chicago (who I met in passing at a hotel in Nairobi, Kenya—but that's another story), whose husband, Paul, had died of a ruptured aorta six months before Marcus.

"I'm in Phoenix, staying with my friend Christina," she said. "Come join us for lunch." So I drove the RV only ten miles west, to downtown Phoenix, parked the RV under the trees of Christina's old town hacienda-style home and went out for lunch.

Lunch lasted two and a half days. Christina was also a widow. Her husband and Maggie's husband were best friends. We recognized the irony of being "Three Merry Widows" and thus glommed together like undercooked pie dough. "If you don't have to be anywhere for New Year's Eve," Christina said, "then stay here with us."

How else would I have gotten through the hype of this dreaded holiday? Instead of being forced to fake that we were happy about welcoming a new year—a year that would be void of the men we loved—we got busy in the kitchen. Christina grilled steaks (Marcus would have loved that), Maggie made the salad and, naturally, I baked a pie—apple.

As the minutes ticked past 11:59 p.m. to 12:00 a.m. to 12:01 a.m., I breathed a sigh of relief that, officially, the holidays were almost over.

Just as I was gearing up to finally leave Phoenix, my cell phone rang again. This time the call was from Nan, who was en route from New York to L.A., where she would be spending the next five months directing and starring in a new play she wrote. Phoenix was not a planned stop on her trip, but she and her husband, Steve, had a last-minute change in plans.

"Come stay with us at my sister's house," Nan insisted. That took no convincing as Nan, the designated leader of Team Marcus (my support group that included Alison and Melissa), was my biggest salve. I had stayed at her sister's house once. It was a stunning palatial estate in the shadow of Phoenix's Camelback Mountain. How could I not look forward to a night soaking in the infinity pool and sleeping in the guest room on the five-thousand-count sheets?

I drove the RV all of five miles from Christina's house to Nan's sister's—I may have been back in motion but I wasn't getting too far—and parked in the circular driveway, just in time for a multimillion-dollar view of the sunset against the Camel's red rocks. The next thing we knew, one overnight turned into "Let's stay another night."

Phoenix seemed to have an odd grip on me. Two weeks after I arrived, I was still there. Two weeks is how long it took me to recognize that the Phoenix is the bird who rose from the ashes. A Phoenix symbolizes rebirth. Duh.

This realization hit only on my last night when Nan, Steve and I raided the wine cellar and opened an expensive bottle of pinot noir. We wrapped ourselves in blankets and sat on the grass, propped up on cushions around an outdoor fire pit. In a New Year's ritual, Nan made us all write down on paper what things, what qualities, behaviors, whatever, we wanted to get rid of from the past. We were to then throw the paper in the fire and start the New Year by leaving these (presumably negative) things behind. I looked at my blank piece of paper for a while and turned to Nan.

"I don't know what to write," I said.

Nan—who is the only person who knew me as well as Marcus (minus the sex and birthmark on the inside of my thigh)—replied, "I do." She took my paper and wrote "Sorrow."

I threw the slip of white paper into the fire and watched, with tears streaming down my face, as it burned in the flames. Did letting go of my sorrow also mean letting go of Marcus? I didn't want to let him go. But I understood Nan's message: letting go of the sorrow was the only way to keep living. And if I had learned anything at all in the four and a half months since Marcus's death, it was simply that our job as humans is to keep living as long as we're graced with the opportunity to be here.

The paper continued to burn into white ashes, floating up to the heavens, carrying a little bit of my sorrow with it, making room for rebirth, for new life.

I wasn't reborn, but it was a symbolic start and the perfect culmination to the holidays. With the help of some very special old friends and some new ones—Alison, Thomas, Alison's sister and mom, Uncle Mike, Aunt Sue, Maggie, Christina, Nan and Steve—I made it through my first holidays without Marcus. I had only begun my journey through grief, but in Arizona I had discovered some additional elements I would need to bring along for the healing ride: sun, movement, openness—the ingredients for resurrection.

And now, I had to return to L.A. I had a TV show to make.

10

The best, most priceless television footage cannot be planned; it just happens in the same way real life unfolds. Like when three little boys crash their sister's pie party. Eight-year-old boys with unruly hair and shirts that hang out from their knee-stained jeans. Boys who make exaggerated faces, wrinkle their noses and say, "We're not going to make any pie. Pie is stupid. Pie is for girls."

I nodded at the little boys and their reluctance to participate. I had expected it. But I just smiled to myself inwardly, because I knew what would happen next.

I had just picked up Janice from the Los Angeles Airport in the RV and we were at the home of my former landlord in Venice, where I had lived in the guesthouse above the garage (similar to my place in Portland but with an ocean outside the door instead of a five-thousand-acre forest). I had promised my landlord's daughter, Margaret, months earlier—before my life fell apart—that I would give her a pie party as her birthday present. She had turned nine and I told her she could invite up to five friends. Determined to make good on my promise, though she was already closer to turning ten, I asked her mom if I could still have a party for her and, "Um, would it be okay if we film it?"

My former landlord had called the day before in a panic. "I don't have a babysitter for the boys. And if they're around I'm afraid they are going to be very disruptive. Maybe we should cancel the whole thing."

"Nonsense," I told her. "The boys can make pies, too. Trust me. Once they get going, they'll be very into it."

So when the macho little rug rats scoffed at making girlie pie, I simply suggested, "Well, maybe you can just make some little ones."

And they said, "Well, okay."

And then, once they started forming balls of dough in their baby-size man hands, they said—they *insisted*—"We want to make big pies."

Of course they did. They always did. Once people got past the initial reluctance to get their hands dirty, finding the sticky, doughy mess to be less distasteful than they had imagined, once they initiated the creative process, they wanted to keep going. No matter what their age. I had been teaching groups to make pie for a few years; I had seen it many times.

With the camera rolling, I began my pie class. I covered the family's kitchen table in my picnic-table-print vinyl cloth. I handed each of the seven kids one of my colored plastic mixing bowls, along with an apron and an adult-size rolling pin. "Everyone measure out two and a half cups of flour," I announced, holding the huge sack of flour open for them. They were an obedient and excited bunch, and just nervous enough to line up behind one another without fighting. "Okay, now unwrap the stick of butter that's in front of you and put it in your bowls. I'm going to come around and add a half cup of shortening to it."

Janice, with her big video camera balanced on her shoulder, moved around the table, capturing the serious looks on the kids' faces.

"We're going to work all these ingredients together until you have lots of lumps in your bowl," I continued. "Let me show you what I mean." I demonstrated with my own bowl of flour, butter and shortening, then walked around, helping each one with their technique. My landlord watched in amazement as her young kids and their friends kept their focus.

The inevitable "Ooh, yuck" was heard from several of the boys when it came time to add water to the dough, but the disgust was short-lived once they were ready for the rolling pins. This was always a tricky stage, trying to keep everyone at the same pace, keeping dough from sticking or cracking, and getting the desired thinness for the crust. "It doesn't matter if your crust breaks or doesn't look perfect," I assured them. "No one will see the bottom of your pie once you put the fruit in it."

Having planned ahead for the age group by eliminating the knives we would have needed for apple or peach pie, we added mixed berries into the pie plates. The kids grabbed handfuls of the not-quite-thawed berries from the huge bowl I had dumped them in, their fingers—and aprons—quickly staining with shades of red and purple. And at last we were ready to put our top crust on the pies-in-progress.

Cookie cutters are a wonderful thing for first-time pie makers. Adults and kids alike expect their pies to look perfect. And when they don't, they get discouraged and give up on pie altogether. But with cookie cutters, or scissors or a paring knife, you can turn an unruly top crust into a one-of-a-kind art piece with cut-out pieces of crust decoratively laid over the filling. The only downside to this technique is that it's so much more fun than slapping on a plain old top crust. Therefore, everyone gets caught up in the creativity and it takes a lot longer to get the pies in the oven. The kids forgot they were making pie; they were making artistic masterpieces.

"I'm going to do butterflies," announced one of the girls.

"I'm going to do hearts," replied Margaret.

"I'm going to do snakes," said her youngest brother.

I didn't care what they did as long as they weren't running all over the house getting dough on the furniture. There was a giant dusting of flour all around the kitchen table as it was.

Once all the pies went into the oven, Janice lined the kids up at the table and interviewed them while I cleaned up our mess. "Why do you love pie? What's your favorite kind of pie? How do you think pie can make the world a better place?" she asked.

The kids smiled, fiddled with their hair, looked down at their feet, pulled on their aprons. Some mumbled and some shouted their answers. "Pie tastes good. I like apple pie. I like chocolate pie. I like it when my mom makes pie."

While Janice had the kids' attention, mine wandered out the back windows to my old guesthouse above the carport. Marcus had stayed here with me many times, providing a welcome respite for him from his stressful work in Mexico. The place in Venice Beach was immaculate and modern, similar to my tree house in Portland. Though it was smaller, it was much nicer. Sliding-glass doors looked out into the palm trees and blue sky. A Jacuzzi bathtub worthy of a five-star hotel occupied the bathroom. And the kitchen was so efficiently designed there was more than enough storage in the glass-front cabinets and full-size stainless steel appliances, and—always a criterion—plenty of counter space for rolling pie dough. When Marcus visited, we went on early morning hikes in the Santa Monica Mountains, rode bikes to our favorite cafés and took walks on the beach. He went to yoga classes and walked the dogs while I worked at my speakers' bureau job. He shopped at Whole Foods and came back to fix meals for us. And at night we would spoon in my Murphy bed, watching DVDs on my laptop, falling asleep wrapped around each other. Marcus, a guy who didn't readily give compliments, couldn't stop saying, "Good job on finding this place. Well done, my love. This is a beautiful apartment." These were some of our calmest, most intimate times together. We always had a hard time saying goodbye after those days spent together. Fortunately, I was too busy with the kids and our shoot to reminisce for too long.

When the pies finished baking and browning, when the berries were bubbling and threatening to cover the bottom of the oven with their sticky overflow (and ensure I would never be invited back), we lined up the kids' showpieces on the table and took a victory shot. The pride in the room was palpable, visible in their beaming faces and bouncing bodies (much in the same way Janice had expressed her excitement at the idea of making the show). They wanted to touch their pies.

"That one is mine!" the older of the boys said, pointing to his freeform top crust adorned with extra dough that might have been a turtle or an army tank, I couldn't quite tell which.

"Be careful, guys. The pies are really hot," I cautioned. "You all did an excellent job. Your pies are gorgeous." The pies were beautiful, each one an art project made by kids under ten. Their edges were rounded and uneven as their little fingers couldn't quite form the sharp-edged fluted crust. Berry stains had leaked through the tops, leaving ink-blotter patterns. *Asymmetrical* could best describe at least two of them. They all looked perfectly delicious and their summerlike juicy scent that filled the room was making everyone impatient for a slice. Janice, who had made it known that berry was her favorite pie, was practically salivating on her camera lens.

"I'm really impressed at what good pie bakers you are," I told them. "Thank you for letting us come here today. And now, there's one last thing we need to do: sing 'Happy Birthday' to Margaret."

Janice got the singing on tape and at the end asked the kids to say, "The world needs more pie" to the camera. Janice, my Fairy Godmother of Grief, in action. Was she doing this just for me? Did she know how it would make me feel? To hear seven childlike voices chant my pie slogan at the top of their lungs, seven kids who had just made seven delectable-looking pies, was so moving I almost started crying. (To not break down and sob in public at this point was an accomplishment in and of itself.) Children represented the future, the circle of life. These adorable, curious, well-behaved kids with the messy hair and scuffed-knee jeans had no idea what their presence and enthusiasm meant to me. But I knew. This pie party was not a gift to Margaret; it was a gift to me.

♥♥♥

We couldn't make a pie documentary without including the place that had shaped me, mentored me, nurtured me. We were headed next to Mary's Kitchen in Malibu. Except that it wasn't called that anymore, since Mary had returned to her former New York home in the Hamptons. She and her business partner, Bill, parted ways after too many clashes over their different business styles. Mary always said, "Yes." For Mary, customers came

first. "It's four o'clock and you need the pie by five? No problem."
Whereas ask Bill, "May I have that turkey sandwich with mayo *and*
mustard?" and you would get a harsh and resounding, "No!" Bill
was Malibu's equivalent of *Seinfeld's* Soup Nazi. Poor overworked
Bill, the former music producer who had no idea how hard it would
be to run a gourmet take-out café in demanding little Malibu. He
didn't just take his frustrations out on the customers, he dished
out the bulk of them on Mary. So she finally packed up her cookbooks and headed back East.

I had an unrelenting loyalty to Mary, but still, I couldn't dismiss
my entire pie education because the teacher had left. So Janice
and I drove the RV up Pacific Coast Highway in the middle of a
torrential downpour, braving the potential mudslides the fragile
cliffs were notorious for. It was like playing vehicular Russian
roulette. But we were granted safe passage and finally entered
through the familiar screen door into what had been renamed
Malibu Kitchen.

Bill greeted us, smiling behind his beard that had become
much grayer since I had last seen him. Even after Mary left,
I made a point to pop in once in a while, to say hi when I was in
town, order a meatloaf sandwich and check on the pies. Sadly,
the pies had given way to precious, too-perfect-to-look-home-
made berry and lemon tarts in the display case. The tarts were
dwarfed by the supersize cupcakes, red velvet and white-frosted
chocolate monstrosities the size of whole cakes but wrapped in
the prerequisite accordion paper to make them appear like cupcakes. Sheesh. Even the bakeries could not escape Hollywood
special effects.

"Good to see you, Pie Girl," Bill said. He seemed genuinely
happy to see me, and there's no reason he shouldn't have been
as I had bolstered his income and his reputation during my year

of pie sales. "Are you going to bake today? The kitchen is yours. I've got everything you need to make a few coconut cream pies."

We hadn't confirmed our shooting strategy. I thought we would just film the place for atmosphere, then interview Bill about the business. To bake again in my tiny kitchen by the sea? "Really? I'd love to."

Apart from the white aprons, nothing was the same. For starters, Mary wasn't there. I didn't know anyone working there anymore. The stacks of ratty cookbooks and the overstuffed crocks of rolling pins and knives were gone. The spice rack above my work table was empty. And there was no food-stained sheet of notebook paper taped to the wall listing the day's pie orders. When Mary and Jane and the rest of the girl gang left, the soul of the place had gone with them.

"I'll leave you to do your thing. Just come and find me when you're done," Bill said. He scurried away and I stood there, dazed, under the glare of the florescent light which was much harsher than I remembered.

"Right," I said to Janice as I tried to get my bearings and ignore the fact that her camera was pointed at me, its red light beaming like Rudolph's nose to indicate it was on. "I feel like I'm on a reality show. It's like *Survivor* and I was dropped on an uncharted island. I don't even know where to start, let alone find anything. I hate to waste your tape." She was silent and kept her camera rolling. "Yeah, great," I mumbled.

I scrambled around, trying to find mixing bowls, utensils and ingredients, while making ad lib commentary about my former baking days there. I also tried not to appear panicked as I searched the bare kitchen for a recipe. I could make apple pie blindfolded, but I hadn't made coconut cream pie often enough to know it by rote. Cream pies can be one of those persnickety types where if you don't get the amounts just right, or add them in the right order, at the right speed—like whisking the beaten eggs into the hot pudding fast enough—you could end up with a disaster. Vanilla pudding with chunks of scrambled eggs does not make for a saleable cream pie.

I finally located all the supplies—and a recipe—and settled into what was familiar and fun: making pie. From the moment I began mixing the dough with my hands, I entered my comfort zone, which made it much easier to ignore the camera and forget just how much Mary's Kitchen had changed.

Once the dough had the degree of tackiness I liked (just slightly gummy), I rolled it out on my old table, prodding and cutting it into shape, and lined six pie plates with it. I pricked the bottoms and sides of the dough with a fork, placed a sheet of foil over each pie, and filled them until they were heaping with dried beans, which served as weights. I didn't skimp on the beans as I too often had experienced that common blind baker's error of using too little weight, resulting in the crust shrinking and thus rattling around in the pie plate.

While the crusts baked in the convection oven, I moved over to the stove in the main part of the kitchen. The place was deserted except for one lone guy washing dishes in the far corner of another side room. Where was everybody? Why wasn't there the usual bustle of soups cooking and salads being prepped for the next day? As I stirred—and stirred and stirred and stirred—waiting for the liquid mixture of milk, sugar, vanilla and cornstarch to thicken, I wondered if I could ever be happy working here again. It was so lonely. And colorless. When I was employed here, the worktable opposite the stove always had a huge cutting board covered in vibrant red tomatoes being sliced for sauce, or bright orange carrots being grated or chopped for one of the many deli salads, or glowing yellow ears of corn whose kernels would be shaved off for one of my favorite dishes: Mary's corn salad. And there were always at least two or three people there, whose productivity could be gauged by the steady hammering of their knives.

It was hard to wax nostalgic with a Sony high-definition digital video recorder in my face, so I just pretended to look cheerful, as if it were nine years earlier and I was surrounded by the Ghosts of Baking Past. I could almost hear Jane's British accent, slinging one of her wicked jokes while pulling a tray of scones out of the oven. I could see Mary hovering around, her signature baseball cap tilting back as if to say "Get back to work, girls," but secretly approving of our constant chatter.

My reverie was interrupted when Bill popped his head into the small side kitchen, where I had returned with my steel pot of cooked pudding. "How's it going?" he asked, checking on our progress. By this time I had poured the vanilla custard into the pie plates and was putting the egg whites I had separated earlier into a mixing bowl. (The yolks had been used for the pie filling.)

"Just getting ready to make the meringue," I answered as I fiddled with the beaters, trying to attach them.

"You know, Robert Downey, Jr. is still a good customer. We should make sure he gets one of these pies."

Bill's reference to the actor was due to the crush I had on him back in 2001, and everyone at Mary's Kitchen was aware of it then, including Bill. Robert came into the café every day for lunch—and pie. Someone from the deli would send word back to the kitchen to let me know when he had arrived, so I could bring out fresh pies, making the timing appear coincidental. I did talk to him a few times, and tried to flirt with him by asking him how he liked the peach pie I had made. Once, when I was standing next to him at the cash register, our forearms touched. I felt the electricity surge through my body.

"It was so strong, he had to have felt it, too," I told Jane afterward.

"He's in rehab," she chirped back. "He can't feel anything right now." It was true. The reason he came into Mary's Kitchen every day is because the rehab center he had checked into was nearby. The better-adjusted clients were allowed to go out for lunch—supervised—and transported in the clinic's unmarked van, proof that Robert was on the mend.

"You don't understand, Jane. There's definitely chemistry. And anyway, he's a good person. I can see past his problems and into his soul. I'm in love."

Janice stopped video taping to chime in. "I know! We should take a pie with us and deliver it to his house," she said, almost shouting to make herself heard over the noise of the electric mixer and the convection ovens. "We could get one of those Star Maps to find out where he lives."

I laughed and mustered the enthusiasm to reply, "That's a great idea," before returning my attention to my task. I let the mixer run until the egg whites were whipped into a bubbly froth, then added a few tablespoons of white sugar.

As the beaters raced at full speed, so did my mind. In the bowl, the eggs expanded and grew into a mountain of fluff. In my head, my thoughts wandered back to handsome brown-haired men. A little like how Robert Downey, Jr. had conquered his demons, moved back to Beverly Hills and gotten married, I had restored my spirit baking pies and then gotten married, too. To Marcus, who was every bit as gorgeous as Robert—and actually looked a little like him, but had a much sexier accent. Yet here I was again, standing in the place where I had started nine years earlier, with my heart cracked and broken like the two dozen egg shells I had just tossed in the garbage.

I was glad Janice had put her camera down so she didn't capture on tape how my smile had turned into a grimace. Still, amazingly, I had shed no tears. This TV show stuff was working miracles in that department. I hadn't cried for two days in a row. This was a record for me. I had gone from measuring my personal bests based on how long I could hold a job; now I was calculating how long I could go without crying.

When peaks finally formed in the meringue, I shut off the mixer and with a rubber spatula scooped the airy white sweetness onto the tops of the pies, dividing it evenly into heaping mounds.

Janice quickly picked up her camera again to record the rest of the process.

Taking a large serving spoon, I went through the quick-handed motions that Mary had taught me, dipping the back of the spoon into the meringue, gouging into it and then lifting the spoon high as I pulled it out. I immediately dipped down again into a new place on top of the pie, until I had created a haphazard pattern of curlicue spikes. When I was done with my spoon attack, I sprinkled a few handfuls of shredded coconut on top and put all six pies in the oven for seven to eight minutes for the final touch—toasting the meringue to a golden brown.

"Those pies are stunning," Bill commented as I placed them one by one on the worktable. "You certainly haven't lost your touch."

Bill had no idea how loaded his statement was. No, I hadn't lost my touch for pie, but I had lost what seemed like everything else.

Janice and I didn't drop off a pie at Robert Downey, Jr.'s house, even though the idea did make me slightly giddy.

We did, however, deliver a pie to my parents in Playa del Rey. It was my mother's seventy-third birthday—January 19 (also the five-month anniversary of The Phone Call)—and I had missed a family lunch in order to make pie in Malibu. Considering coconut cream was her number one pie choice, at least I could make up for not joining in the family gathering by bringing her the ideal birthday present. With the camera ready, pointed on the door, I rang the bell. This was turning into a reality show after all—*Candid Camera*. My mom answered, I handed her the pink bakery box, sang "Happy Birthday" (for the second time in two days), and left.

The short duration of our drive-by visit was nothing personal. While it's true, I was still punishing her for not understanding my grief and had seen her only once—for breakfast—in the month since I had come down from Portland, the birthday pie delivery was the only time I could manage. We couldn't stay because we had another pie party scheduled and we were running late.

The TV shoot included two pie parties, the second of which was decidedly different than the first. Instead of kids, I was teaching a group of thirtysomething single women. The premise was that baking a pie for a man is a guaranteed way to land a husband. "I am living proof of this," I assured the women as we assembled at my friend Susanne's house in Venice.

By "proof" I was referring to the first apple pie I had made for Marcus, the one I made at my friend Uschi's apartment in Bern, Switzerland, borrowing her ten-inch shallow metal tart pan with the pleated sides because that was the closest thing to an American-style pie plate she had in her cupboards. I had woven a lattice-top crust—an extra effort I reserved for special occasions—and the pie had finished baking just in time to catch my train to Stuttgart, where Marcus lived.

Our romance had begun only ten days earlier when he accepted my invitation to meet in Italy for my American friends' wedding, John and Laura, whom I knew from my dot com job in San Francisco. I had met Marcus six months earlier, at Crater Lake National Park, where we had talked for twenty minutes in the Crater Lake Lodge. Because our meeting in Italy was going to be our first date, we planned to keep it short; he was going to stay two days. But things went so well—as in, our greeting at the Milan airport was so charged we almost had sex in baggage claim—he stayed with me in Tuscany for the whole week.

I knew "romance" had turned "relationship" when, at the end of the wedding week, I left Florence to visit friends in Bern and he invited me to come visit him afterward in Germany. Leaving Uschi's in Bern with my hot, steaming apple pie in hand, I boarded the InterCityExpress for Stuttgart. Seven hours later, four on the train and the three I waited for Marcus to pick me up (establishing his lack of punctuality early on), I delivered the goods. He may have been more excited about that pie than he was about me, because he set it on his glass dining-room table, arranged the pie and the lights until they were just right and shot photos as if he was a paparazzo and the pie was a celebrity on the red carpet. The apple pie impressed him so much he broke his dating rule and introduced me to his parents. We took the pie with us the next day to their magnificent home in the country and, seated in their Queen Anne chairs under the twinkling crystals of the chandelier, ate more of the pie, served by their housekeeper on china plates with silver forks.

That pie led to a marriage proposal, all right, but for the purpose of this party, for these single husband-seeking women, I didn't tell that story. But it wouldn't have mattered if I had, since the group already knew I was a new widow. One of the women, Elissa, who was ten years younger than me, had already been widowed twice, having lost both of her husbands to cancer.

Gathered around Susanne's butcher-block kitchen island, glasses of sauvignon blanc were poured for everyone while I explained the fundamentals of pie. "Pie is about comfort and sharing. Pie is not about perfection. And contrary to what you might think, pie is actually very easy to make. You don't even need a recipe, if you just follow these basic guidelines." I paused my lecture to take a sip of wine and continued. "There's a simple formula, I call it 'the three to one rule.' For the dough, it's three cups of flour to one cup fat. For the filling, it's three pounds of fruit to one cup sugar. Easy. Three to one. That's all you have to remember." I didn't bog them down with the minor details—that you start with two and a half cups of flour for the dough with the rest getting worked in during the rolling stage, and how I almost never use more than three-fourths of a cup sugar as most fruit is already sweet enough. I would explain it later, as the ladies didn't want to wait. "Now, let's get started."

I took another swig from my glass. I was tired. Tired from the phone calls and shopping I had done to prep for the shoot. Tired from the two days of taping we had already done. Tired from having to fake-smile for the camera. Tired from grieving. Marcus had been gone only five months and adjusting to life without him was exhausting. The feeling that I was grasping at air was constant, as was the sensation that my heart was a pail shot full of holes; its contents could not be contained and simply leaked right out. To perk myself up—and because it seemed fitting for the party theme—I had worn my new T-shirt from Target, gray with a huge pink sequin heart and black letters spelling *Love* on it. It was my feeble attempt at bling, my subconscious suggesting that life still held some sparkle.

Janice moved around the island, getting close-up shots of the women's flour-covered hands and the smiles on their faces. Every so often I heard Janice say, "That's great" or "Can you do that again so I can shoot it from another angle?" Mostly I heard Janice laugh, an easy giggle that told me she was having fun. Janice was no stranger to grief herself, as her mother died when she was seventeen. All I had to do was look around the room to see that you can lose your loved ones and still have fun, and not live like your heart is caged behind iron bars.

I kept the class moving, keeping an eye out for the type-A personalities. The corporate women were always the biggest baking offenders. They approached their pie dough the same way they did their jobs—aggressively, competitively, with perfectionism, putting in long hours. They couldn't help but overwork their dough. It was in their nature. The group included an investment banker, the president of a mattress company and a public-relations vice president, so I hovered over them accordingly—and left the yoga teacher alone.

When I wasn't instructing, I was observing Elissa. How on earth was this woman still functioning, still sane, *still alive* after losing not one but two husbands? How could she ever trust life again? And yet there was not a trace of bitterness about her. She had not turned into a gooseberry pie with no sugar; she was all sweetness and tenderness, like peaches and cream in an all-butter crust. Not only that, she was using her experience to help others and worked as a life and health coach, aptly calling herself "The Healthy Life Guru." And here she was, calmly peeling apples, joking and smiling, as if her heart had never been broken. Twice.

The apples were skinned, the pies brushed with beaten eggs and placed in the oven, and after an hour—which we spent doing yoga in the living room—we arranged the bubbling pies on the island for the victory shot. There always has to be a victory shot. This final pose is what sustains me, restores my energy, reminds me that in my own small way, like Elissa, I too am trying to help others in spite of my own hardship—or because of my hardship. (It was too soon to know.) Seeing the joyous pride in everyone's faces as they stood by their finished pies would have been enough in itself. But to hear the excitement in their voices—their confident claims like, "I'm taking mine to work tomorrow to share with my coworkers," "I'm taking mine home to share with my boyfriend," "I can't believe how well mine turned out," "I can't wait to make another one"—added to my own sense of accomplishment. Maybe someday I would be as well-adjusted as Elissa and call myself "The Pie Guru." One could dream.

11

Malibu Kitchen may have had its pie-loving celebrity customers, but so did Mommie Helen's in Colton, California, an hour and a half away. Driving The Beast the following day to the easternmost reaches of Los Angeles, Janice and I set off to interview Dorothy Rose Pryor. Dorothy was owner of Mommie Helen's and supplier of sweet potato pie and pecan pie to NBA stars Shaquille O'Neal and Magic Johnson and America's biggest idol herself: Oprah.

Pulling into a typical L.A. strip-mall parking lot, nothing seemed special about this place at first glance. You wouldn't even notice the generic shop if you weren't actively looking for it. Mommie Helen's was deceiving, like a pie that looks machine-made and manicured, but after one bite you're surprised to find it was homemade. That's what it was like walking in the door, straight into the bear hug of Dorothy.

"Welcome, welcome," she said. "It's so nice to meet you. Thank you so much for coming out to see me." She exuded such warmth

I thought I might melt like Baker's Chocolate in her arms. I missed being touched, being held. Besides snuggling with Team Terrier, I wasn't getting much physical contact. I wanted to stay there in her embrace all day.

"Thank you. It's nice to be here. But don't squeeze too hard," I warned her, "or you'll squeeze my tears out." I had let her know when I spoke with her by phone that a premise of our show was to explore how pie can help heal grief. My grief.

"I know what you're going through, honey," she said. "I lost my sister and my mom and I miss them every day. But the Lord knows what he's doing. We have to trust in God's will and have faith." She let go of me and patted me on the shoulder while I wiped the wetness around my eyes.

I appreciated her sentiments, but I wasn't able to buy into the Lord's work thing. I had tried. I was raised Catholic but had rejected the notion of organized religion early on. I was too much of a feminist, too rebellious, too skeptical. But when Marcus died and I was desperate for ways to connect with him, I was open to anything that might help, anything that might bring me peace, calm, keep me from wanting to end my own life. So I went to church.

After I settled in Portland, I attended a Lutheran service at St. James' Church, where Marcus had gone at least once. At least I assumed he had gone there, because I found the church's newsletter in his files. The inner sanctum of the church was cold and stark, there were only two candles on the altar and about as many people in the congregation—on a Sunday. I attended a service at the Unitarian Church where our marriage workshop had been held, and while it was a more colorful and more musical affair, I couldn't connect with its religious pep-rally atmosphere and crying babies, so I left early. I even set foot inside a Catholic church again, to see if that might inspire the conversation with God—and with

Marcus—I was longing to have. But all that ritualistic, ceremonial, male-dominated pomp and circumstance sent me running for the door and back to the woods, literally. I had access to five-thousand acres of spirituality right outside my house. The forest was my church, it's where I felt the greatest connection to a higher power. I didn't need bible verses; I only needed an open heart, receptive ears—and rubber boots.

Starting from the front of the store, where the bakery display had only a few sweet potato pies in it, we worked our way to the back, to the enormous kitchen where all the action was taking place. A large vat of orange liquid was being stirred by a Hobart mixer as big as the young man in the white apron attending it. Right next to him was an oven of even greater proportions. It was the size of an entire wall and, inside, each of its rotating racks was filled with sweet potato pies, riding a Ferris wheel as they baked. The shelves of a nearby bakery rack were already packed with at least thirty pies left there to cool. The room was bathed in bright white light, lined with shiny silver appliances and accented by a sea of orange pies. It was a vision of heaven—if heaven were a sweet potato pie factory.

"We ship pies all over the country," she answered, as if she had heard the question in my mind: How could you sell that many pies here in this odd location? "But you should see this place at Thanksgiving. We get six hundred people lined up out the door. People get so desperate for our pie they fight over it. One year, a woman tried to buy a pie off someone else. I had to go out there and tell everyone that no one was going to get their pie unless they behaved."

"Here is our crust room," said Dorothy, pointing to the steel door with the padlock on the outside. "It is off limits to everyone except the two people who make the dough. People look through our Dumpsters to find out what is in our crust, but they won't find anything."

I turned and made a face at Janice—at her camera lens—but I don't know if she could see me rolling my eyes. What could possibly be in Mommie Helen's dough that was so top secret it required a padlock on the door? I had seen recipes that called for vinegar, almond extract, heavy cream, eggs or even vodka. (Vodka supposedly keeps your crust from getting too glutinous. I would argue just don't overwork your dough and save the vodka for martinis.) I was of the puritanical pie mind that kept my crust recipe to the basics: flour, butter, shortening, water and salt—but just a pinch.

The mystique Dorothy created around her crust may have been a gimmick—as opposed to anything illegal—but we would never know. If it was merely a marketing ploy, it was working so well that even inmates on death row were requesting a slice of Mommie Helen's pie for their last meal.

Dorothy packed up a couple of wedges of sweet potato and pecan pie for Janice and me to take with us. The second we dropped the camera gear in the RV, we dug in with our plastic forks. Indeed the Southern-style dessert was outstanding. Worthy of waiting in a line with six hundred people or ordering as a last meal? That I couldn't say. But it didn't stop me from devouring a slice of the sweet potato's nutmeg-laced custard without stopping to swallow in between bites.

♥♥♥

Our road trip may have been loosely structured, but it was tightly scheduled. We debated postponing our next stop due to bad weather. We were heading to Oak Glen (elevation 2,800), Southern California's apple-growing region eighty miles east of

Los Angeles, and only an hour's drive farther east from Mommie Helen's sweet potato pie palace, but if we postponed, we would have had no chance of coming back.

It had snowed in Oak Glen the previous day. If you were a skier, you would be happy about that; if you were driving a twenty-four-foot RV, you would not. I had become more and more comfortable driving The Beast, but I wasn't going to knowingly put myself in harm's way—even though I bought snow chains before leaving Portland. Alas, after much discussion and constant checking with the weather service, we motored up the mountain, climbing higher and higher in the rain. There were no signs of snow—only safety billboards flashing warnings of mud slides—and we arrived safely in the orchard-filled mountain town.

There may be no better way to spend a cold, miserable, wet day than to sit inside a wood-heated mountain diner in a cozy booth talking about—and eating—pie. Cinnamon-sauce apple pie à la mode. With endless cups of coffee. No offense to Susan in Portland, but this might have been more effective than grief counseling.

We were at Law's Oak Glen Coffee Shop, meeting with three generations of pie bakers and apple growers. Sitting across from me in the booth was Theresa Law, the matriarch of the family. At age ninety-two, impeccably dressed in her pale blue sweater and tweed scarf, her hair dyed blond and expertly curled, she was still clearly in charge. Her daughter Alison, who looked to be about sixty, sat next to her, trying to finish Theresa's sentences, but her mother ignored her and kept on talking. She was telling us about the history of Oak Glen.

"The Mormons settled the area in the 1800s and planted the first apple orchards here," the matriarch said. "I lost my first husband in World War II. I got remarried and drove cross-country in the 1940s, from Maine all the way to Oak Glen, with my second husband. I first baked pies in my wood-burning stove in my home. When we opened the diner, we sold out of pies the very first day."

"Her baking record is 657 pies in one day," Alison touted.

"How is that possible?" I asked. "My record is two hundred in one day, but that included an all-nighter on top of one week of prep. And I was left with swollen hands, sore muscles and burned arms."

"We had help," Theresa admitted. "But you should have seen the customers. They just kept showing up at the take-out window."

The waitress poured more coffee and said, "Kent is ready for you to come into the kitchen to film him making pie." Kent was Theresa's son, who ran the restaurant.

I followed the waitress and Janice and the camera to the kitchen, just behind the diner's counter. Kent, Alison's gray-bearded brother who looked more like a construction foreman than a baker, showed us his pie-making equipment. His work space was about as big as a sailboat galley. "You put the dough in here," he said, as he fed a softball-size hunk of his flour-and-shortening mixture into a heavy-duty mechanical roller called a sheeter. In a split second, the machine spit out the dough on the other side, flattened like a piece of printer paper, round and ready for the pie plate.

"I could make 657 pies in a day, too, if I had one of these," I remarked to Janice.

"I'm making ten today," Kent said, unaware of my sarcasm.

I had mixed feelings about all the mechanical aids. I believed that pie should be not just homemade but *handmade*. To use a machine meant losing the physical, visceral and, yes, spiritual connection to your creation. We live in a world where we are already so disconnected from our food and where it comes from, that when it came to pie, I found myself clinging to the old ways, the lower tech the better. Even though it couldn't be proven, I liked to think people who ate the handmade pies could taste the difference from the machine-made ones, that they could feel the love and the human touch that went into making it.

Technology-assisted or not, clearly Kent was passionate about his pies.

We hung around (and taped him) as he assembled the pies, piling in sliced apples and sugar. He was moving around with such an air of happiness, he was practically whistling. It struck me as an interesting role reversal that he was so at home in the kitchen, while his sister had found her niche running the family produce stand across the street.

We rejoined Theresa and Alison, who were still sitting in the booth working on their tenth cup of coffee. Alison talked about her battle with cancer. "Apples cured me," she insisted. "You know that expression, 'An apple a day?' The pectin in the apple removes toxins from your body, but you have to eat the peel. I started eating apples every day and the cancer was gone."

I was about to make some quip about how I wished apples could also cure grief, but luckily I was interrupted by apple pie. Kent arrived at the table, holding one of his finished pies, now crusty and steaming and wafting its seductive scent under our noses. He presented it to his mother for inspection and Theresa examined it thoroughly, as if the pie had to pass her quality-control check. She peered closer, her eyebrows pulled together, her eyes focused on the pool of filling that had bubbled up on one side. The top was evenly browned, the crust edges were intact. (Kent didn't make a fluted rim; his was flat and uncrimped.) Janice turned her camera on the pie, and managed to get Theresa on tape, finally giving the pie her approval. She was a tough old boss. Mary had never scrutinized my pies like this, in spite of our demanding Malibu customers.

The moment we had been anticipating for four hours had finally arrived. We were served the pie. Drowning in a pool of Kent's special caramel sauce and buried under two huge scoops of vanilla ice cream, there was a slice of pie on the plate somewhere. With soup spoons, Janice and I shoveled bite after bite into our mouths, faster and faster in a race against the melting ice cream, until we were so stuffed we moaned with pain instead of pleasure.

After our pie-eating orgy, Alison took us over to her fruit stand, Mom's Country Orchards, for a tour. Surrounded by fields of bare fruit trees, the single-story wooden building was painted brown with green trim and decorated with sunflowers and hand-painted placards advertising the availability of honey, cider and, naturally, apples. In contrast to the warmth of the restaurant, we fought the chill of the cold rain we picked up in the empty parking lot until long after we were inside the produce stand. Alison introduced us to her son, Jake. "He's the third generation in our family of apple growers," she said, patting him on the shoulder of his Carhartt jacket.

"Nice to meet you," said the husky, blond-bearded guy, who then went back to what he had been doing before we arrived, stacking crates of apples on the concrete floor.

Alison proceeded to explain the many varieties of (cancer-curing) apples they grow and sell up in Oak Glen. I normally use Granny Smith in my pies, occasionally supplementing these with Royal Gala or Braeburn. But Alison, expanding our pie horizons, showed us apples we'd never heard of like Black Twig, Bellflower, Arkansas Black, and too many others to remember without the help of her wall chart. I was shivering too much to care at this point. Plus, I was uncomfortably full from Kent's pie. I wanted to go back inside the RV, turn on the heater and take a nap in my down nest in the back.

Before wrapping up the final Law family interview, we had one last objective: buy apples. We needed more apples than we could get at a grocery store because I was going to make fifty pies the next day. It would have been easier to just buy the pies from Kent, but making them by hand was too important. For many reasons.

Alison called out orders to Jake, who disappeared out the side door of the produce stand. He turned up a few minutes later with five cases of apples loaded on his dolly and rolled them out to the RV. As The Beast was already full of my gear, Janice's luggage and Team Terrier's supplies, we were tight on space. We found room for the nearly two hundred pounds of apples by stacking the crates in the shower stall, where some of my clothes were hanging on the inside of the door. Those clothes would smell like apples for weeks afterward. And Janice, who slept next to the shower on the RV's kitchen banquette-turned-bed, would report later that one of her most prominent memories about the shoot was not the people or the pie she ate, but breathing in the scent of these apples as she slept.

"Hey, Janice," I said as we wound our way back down the mountain, leaving the quiet orchards behind and reentering L.A.'s congested freeway chaos. "How would you feel about stopping in Koreatown on the way back to Santa Monica?" I was cold from our last few days of shooting in the rain, and tired from trying to maintain my on-camera presence, while really just wanting to go lie down and read my newest grief book, so perfectly titled *I'm Grieving As Fast As I Can*. I knew a place I could go to get warm and rested: Natura Spa. "We're going right past the spa on our way back to Melissa's."

"Sure, sounds awesome," she answered in her best Jersey Girl accent as "sure" sounded more like "shu-wah." Even when she wasn't trying to be funny, her voice alone humored me. Not only did I love the way she talked—or, as she would say, "twahked"—her always-light and effervescent mood made her such good company. We had become a tight-knit team of two. Four, if you counted the dogs. But Team Terrier had been left behind at Melissa's for this part of the shoot.

I handed her my BlackBerry to look up the number and schedule appointments for the ninety-minute body-scrub-massage combo. "I think we can make it there by five." I was suddenly very alert and energized. I couldn't wait to get out of the RV—and out of my clothes.

I had been to Natura Spa once. I went with Melissa when I stopped in L.A. en route from Terlingua, moving back to Portland. It was early October, only a month and a half after The Day That Changed My Life. Melissa had just learned about this spa from her magazine publisher friend, Trish, who had become a Natura devotee. While Melissa could have gone anytime she wanted, it wasn't until I showed up on her doorstep in my discombobulated, depleted condition, like an earthquake still having aftershocks, that the time seemed right. She whisked me off immediately to Koreatown.

There—in the basement of a department store on Wilshire Boulevard, in a tile-walled shower room, lying naked on a vinyl-covered table surrounded by other naked women lying on tables next to me—is where I found God.

God was a chubby Korean woman dressed in a black lace bra and panties, and she was inflicting a new kind of torture on me. Instead of the emotional pain I was used to, this was purely physical. Her loofah sponge or scrub brush—or steel wool or wire brush or Brillo pad or whatever torture device she was using—bore so deep into my skin I thought I might be bleeding.

And yet, I didn't resist. I let her continue roughing me up, my senses awakened and invigorated as her brush invaded the deepest reaches of my body, scratching places only Marcus had ever touched. Her brush ventured under my armpits, across my breasts, in circular motions on my belly, into my groin and, when she rolled me over like a filet of beef, her brush found its way into the hidden recesses behind my ears and even into my butt crack.

This kind of treatment was not for prudish types. Melissa was squeamish about the flesh-factory atmosphere at first, but I wasn't. I had been conditioned to public nudity in Germany after many visits with Marcus to the coed naked mineral bathhouses, where I had gladly shed my modesty along with my bathing suit in order to soak in the effervescent hot spring pools—my favorite being the Kristall-Therme in Schwangau, in the shadow of King Ludwig's Neuschwanstein Castle. Natura was women-only, mostly Koreans who were going about their own beauty rituals and unconcerned with our white-girl presence, naked or not. We were simply paying and willing victims of the brush.

Lying on my stomach with my head turned to the side, I opened my eye just long enough to compute that the chunks of gummed up eraser covering the previously clean table were actually pieces of the skin that used to cover my body. I knew what it was like to get a sunburn, when afterward I could pull my skin off in sheets—much like the way I peeled an apple. But I had never lost an entire epidermal layer from a spa treatment.

The underwear-clad therapist doused me in a bucket of warm water, rinsing the blackish-grey debris off my body onto the floor and down the drain. She didn't know it—and she couldn't have cared less, judging by the sounds of her noisy Korean chatter with her coworkers—but the skin she had removed was much more than a bunch of dead cells; she had relieved me of a whole layer of death-related grief.

With my new substratum exposed, the Korean woman's touch—or at least the stiff fibers of her sponge—had put me back inside my body. It was as if my soul had been detached, not inhabiting the vessel it was born to, yet I wasn't fully aware of how disconnected I was until this overweight, torture-device-wielding sadist aggravated my nerve endings to the point of waking me up.

But the biggest payoff was not the baby-smooth texture she had given my skin. Nor was it the reduced eye puffiness from the cucumber mask she had slathered on my face. It was something much more important. Eight weeks after my husband died, feeling like I had died with him, I was lying on a table, getting worked over and hosed off by a woman who might as well have been a wrestler. While my naked body was at her mercy, I was struck with an important revelation: *I am going to be okay.* Maybe not right away, but I was aware that I was indeed still alive and that I was capable of feeling something other than numbness.

♥♥♥

Dorothy Rose Pryor of Mommie Helen's Pies had Jesus and her Baptist revivals to feed her faith. Alison Law had cancer-curing apples as her personal miracle. I had my own God, my own restoration of spirit, my own place of worship. And I was about to introduce Janice to it—to baptize her in the mugwort-infused waters of the Jacuzzi, the eucalyptus vapors of the steam room and the spiky scrub brushes of the women in black bras and panties. Pie could wait. We were headed to the spa in Koreatown.

12

Every year on January 23, America celebrates National Pie Day. The date was officially registered in Chase's Calendar of Events by a man named Charlie Papazian, a Boulder, Colorado-based schoolteacher who happened to love pie and thought there should be a day to commemorate his favorite dessert. January 23 was his birthday, but this guy would have nothing to do with frosting and sugary decorations.

"Cake, be damned. I only want birthday pie," he proclaimed.

He was so serious he registered his date of birth as Pie Day. This led him to create an entire organization, which he called the American Pie Council. At first the APC held homespun pie contests in the shadows of the Rocky Mountains' Front Range. Soon, the big, commercial pie makers wanted to get in on the action. They wanted to win the blue ribbons. Since the machine-made versus handmade competition was unbalanced (and the commercial pies couldn't win), they lobbied to create their own category. After much arguing, posturing and finger pointing, the grassroots bakers and the muscle-bound frozen-food brands just couldn't reconcile their different approaches to pie. The corporate muckety-mucks didn't think the APC founders were thinking big enough. They wanted to expand beyond the quaint pie contests and picnics in the park, so they took over the organization, moved it to Chicago, and now the American Pie Council shares office space with a pie-assembly-line manufacturer. That's one side of the story anyway, the one you won't find on the APC website.

All I knew at the time was that January 23 coincided with our pie shoot, and we wanted to—*had to*—include National Pie Day in some way. How we would do it, Janice and I had decided, was to assemble my closest friends, the ones who were helping me with my Grief Survival Training and, together, the day before, bake fifty apple pies—pies that on the actual holiday would be handed out by the slice on the streets of L.A.

I called them Team Marcus, but in a show of their alliance to me, they insisted on calling themselves Team Beth. Whatever. The team included Jane, my British baker friend from Mary's Kitchen, who now ran a high-tea catering business; Nan, who I had just seen in Phoenix and was now in Hollywood producing and starring in a play she wrote; and Melissa. Melissa's mom Carlene was there, too, visiting from Maine. And Thelma, Melissa's full-time Guatemalan housekeeper, offered a hand.

Melissa arranged with her estranged husband to use the kitchen in their old house, where he still lived, two blocks from her new smaller-but-much-cuter house with the swimming pool. Her Viking range would have sufficed, but the ex had a double oven, and quadruple the counter space.

"But you have to be gone by five," he said. Five was an arbitrary time. There was no reason we would have had to leave by then.

He just wanted to set conditions, to prove he was still in control. I would have been fine just baking at Melissa's. We could have made do with her smaller kitchen. But with six bakers and one cameraperson, the extra space was appreciated. (I would thank him later by giving him a pie, to which he would reply, "I don't like apple.")

Sometime before eleven, we unloaded the pie supplies into Melissa's old kitchen and began making a big mess in it. The clock was ticking. Six hours wasn't a lot of time to make fifty pies, especially when you included the one hour of baking time for each batch. Even with all the help, it was going to be a stretch. Nan, Carlene and Thelma took their positions at two counters, peeling 150 pounds of apples, while Jane and I set up our work station at another.

With my hands once again submerged in a soothing bowl of flour and butter, and with Jane working right next to me, memories of our old baking days came flooding back. The easy banter, and her British accent, took me back to a happier time— happier compared to the days since August 19 anyway. Back then, my biggest worry was how to pay the rent on my meager pie baker's salary. Now my concerns were how to stay alive and not succumb to the madness and confusion caused by the existential question Marcus's death had raised: *What is the meaning of life— and why bother sticking it out?*

Once we had enough dough rolled and pie plates prepared, Jane and I sliced apples. We didn't have our age-old argument about whether it was better to use a paring knife or a vegetable peeler— she swears by the veggie peeler—because the apples were already peeled. But we had a new issue.

"Slice them thinner," she instructed me. "They'll bake a lot faster that way."

"Um, excuse me, missy, but who taught you how to make pie?" I was quick to retort. That's right. Me. At Mary's Kitchen, Jane was the baker for everything else but pie. After I quit, I went to her house one evening and passed along the lessons Mary had taught me. She was right, though. The thicker the apple slice, the longer the baking time. And since we were pressed for time, I acquiesced.

We filled the ovens with our first batch of pies, squeezing in eighteen at once. Jane took charge of monitoring the baking progress as I continued to roll dough, assemble pies and crimp crusts.

Without giving me notice, Janice went around the room with her camera, conducting documentary-style interviews. "What was Marcus like?" she asked Jane.

Jane said, "Marcus was a good chap. I only met him once, when he and Beth came up to my house in Malibu for dinner. He was very polite and polished. And he had lived in London, so we had a lot to talk about. What I remember most is how much he loved Beth. You could see by the way he looked at her. She may have complained about him, as we all do about our husbands—they bloody well deserve it—but I could tell they were in love."

I pretended to be busy crimping my crust edges, but I was listening intently.

The next question was for Nan. "What do you wish for Beth as she moves forward in her life?"

Nan's face turned wistful and she said, "I wish for my Pumpkin to stop feeling so guilty about Marcus. She worked hard at her marriage. I've never seen anyone so determined. Marcus was a great guy but he was German, like me, so I know." She laughed, but quickly became serious again. "It will take time for his death to really register. It seems like he's just in Germany and that's why he's not here. I wish I could take Beth's pain away, but she's amazingly resilient and she'll find happiness again. Someday."

The answers were heartfelt, but the psychoanalysis made me uncomfortable—especially when it came to Melissa's Q and A.

"How does Beth seem to you?" Janice asked Melissa, aiming the camera at her face.

"Weird," answered Melissa. "I don't know what's going on with her, but she's been acting very strange lately. I miss my old friend Beth. She is an important person in my life and I don't know if it's something I did, or if it's just that she's so lost in her grief over Marcus. I am trying to be patient, waiting for her to emerge again."

The room was filled with an awkward silence. Not knowing quite how to respond, Janice clicked off the camera.

I knew what Melissa meant. I had been staying at her house and the lack of privacy and blurry boundaries had been wearing on me. I was torn between her insistence that I sleep on the couch, which was very comfortable, and my desire to sleep in the RV, which was not only comfortable, it was my home. To be polite, I slept in the house—because I knew Melissa wanted to take care of me. And I wanted to let her. But her little girls used my bed as their morning playground, jumping all over my down comforter with their dusty bare feet. After they bumped my coffee cup, causing it to spill, I yanked my bedding out from underneath them in a huff.

"We can just wash it," Melissa said as the girls hopped back up on the couch.

"NO! We can't!" I wanted to scream at her, holding my bundle tighter. The comforter and its orange-and-yellow plaid duvet cover was the one Marcus had used during his Portland vacation. It was one of the last things to touch his body before he died. It was my security blanket. And I was never going to wash it again if I could help it.

So yes, Melissa was right. I was being weird. I was lost. I definitely was not my old self. I couldn't control my feelings, couldn't

predict my reactions, couldn't get a handle on life. I was unsteady, even in the company of my best friend and her innocent
preschoolers.

I went over to the oven to check on the pies and pulled out the
top rack, pulling a little too far as the rack tilted down and a pie
slid off. I couldn't stop its trajectory. It flipped and landed upside
down on the oven door with a resounding, "Splat!" Apple filling
oozed off the surface and dripped, along with hunks of crust, onto
the floor.

"Pie down! Pie down!" Melissa shouted from the other side of
the room. Janice picked up her camera again and zoomed in on
the action.

Pie down. That's exactly what I was. Once intact and so delicious, bubbly and full of promise, I had, in an unforeseen and
sudden change of life circumstances, flipped and landed upside
down, splattered on the hardwood floor. But this was no time to
contemplate pie-grief associations as we had an even bigger mess
to clean up now with only minutes left on our five-o'clock deadline. Thelma, who still worked part-time at Melissa's old house,
knew where to find the cleaning supplies, saving our asses from
the wrath of the ex. As for the rest of the unmade pies—there were
still at least a dozen—we took them to Melissa's house, and finished baking them in her shiny new oven.

I told Melissa about the duvet later. "I was wondering why you
reacted so strongly," she said. "Especially when I have a washing
machine. But I understand." She always understood, no matter
how strange or out of character my behavior was.

♥♥♥

We were finally ready to hand out free slices of pie to strangers
on the crazy streets of Los Angeles.

The closest I had come to this was when I had my own Kenya coffee import business at the age of twenty-five. I was living in New York City and on the weekends I dressed up in jodhpurs and pith helmet, offering free samples of brewed coffee. My motive was to sell my highly priced tins of coffee. Now, the only purpose to giving away free pie—and not just stingy samples but whole, generous slices—was to make people happy. And, oh right, to record these happy moments on tape.

The Beast had never been so fully packed. The apple crates in the shower stall had been replaced by a tower of pink bakery boxes, multiple rows stacked all the way to the ceiling. The RV had also never smelled so good. We had taken on other supplies, too—paper plates, plastic forks, napkins, knives, pie servers, serving gloves and a folding table on loan from my parents. We also had signs. I bought foam-backed poster board and stick-on letters to spell out Free Pie and a smaller one that read "Honk If You Love Pie."

After fueling up at Starbucks, we started off the day at the historic Fire Station Number 39 in Van Nuys, in L.A.'s San Fernando Valley. "We" were now Janice, Nan, Melissa, Melissa's boyfriend, Jeff, and me. "We" were not Team Marcus or Team Beth; we were Team Pie.

We called ahead, so the firefighters were expecting us. We parked the RV in front of the vanilla-colored stucco building, so clean and well-kept you could eat pie off the sidewalk in front. Inside, we were met by a group of fourteen hungry men and women who had skipped lunch in anticipation of pie. They were lined up along a bench at their dining table, holding forks and looking as if they would pounce on the pie the same way they would a fire. As Jeff and Melissa sliced up a few pies and Nan handed out plates, one of the firemen pulled out a five-gallon tub of ice cream.

"We have a tradition around here," he explained. "Anytime a rookie has a first—a first car fire, a first cat rescued out of a tree, a first house fire—the rookie has to buy ice cream." He dished up scoops for everyone and finally took one for himself. As he shoveled bites of apple pie into his mouth, the butter crust dissolving together with the ice cream on his tongue, he offered, "But we'll have to change that tradition now. The rookie will have to bring pie."

When they had finished, we got to climb on the fire engine like a bunch of excited third-graders and, afterward, watch the guys slide down the fire pole. They also tried impressing us by climbing back up. As Janice recorded everything, I interviewed the captain about the work he and his team did. He told us stories about men they had lost, about the 911 calls they answered. "People trust us. They open their doors for us when we rush to the scene to help," he said.

His genuine goodness and his desire to help others choked me up so much, I couldn't stop myself from oversharing. "911 was called when my husband died. I know they did everything they could to save him. So please know I, for one, appreciate what you do."

Janice loved this. I could tell by the way she swung her camera around to get my tears on tape. She was a sucker for emotion, the more sentimental the better. Not that she was opportunistic about capturing drama—my drama—to make for sensational reality TV. She was a deep-feeling soul, a real softie under that sports-loving persona. And if she had her way, we'd aim to sell our show to the Hallmark Channel, not the Food Channel.

After the fire station, we moved a few miles down Ventura Boulevard to Sherman Oaks, parallel parking The Beast at a random spot on the busy thoroughfare. Nan set up the folding table for our Great Pie Giveaway, placing pies on it, while I stood on the street, holding up the "Free Pie" sign. No cars were stopping and foot traffic was light, so Nan and I used the downtime to sample the goods.

"You know, I do love apple pie," I said after polishing off my piece in four quick bites.

"And I love you, Pumpkin," Nan replied, still working on her slice.

"I'm glad you're here, Pooh. I couldn't do this without you." I still called her by her childhood nickname, and could sometimes still picture her as my freckled twelve-year-old friend with braces.

"Yes, you could," she said. "You're a lot stronger than you think."

"Well, I'm still glad you're here, honey. Now, if you're not going to finish that, I'll eat it."

We waited and waited for people to walk by. In this city of ten million, where were all the pie-loving people? It was a Saturday. The streets should have been full of shoppers. Well, the streets were full—with people driving to malls in their cars.

We agreed we should move our pie stand, but first we spent twenty minutes deliberating the wide range of locations L.A. had to offer. Who would appreciate free pie more—people in swanky Beverly Hills, seedy Hollywood, pristine Pacific Palisades or funky Venice Beach? Venice won, so we headed to the beach and parked on the trendy Abbot Kinney Boulevard. I had become highly skilled at parallel parking my big rig in city traffic. The small accomplishments added up to big confidence boosters. Until I misjudged the tree branch overhead and cracked the plastic casing around the air-conditioning unit on the RV's roof. Oh, well. *Sorry, Marcus.*

If you bake it, they will come. They came in droves. The next three hours became a blur of pie plates being passed out to one pedestrian after another. Word had traveled down the block as passersby saw the smiling faces of other people carrying plates of pie, and so more people came. Melissa and Jeff couldn't slice fast enough. I kept going back inside the RV to unload more pink boxes, handing pies to Jeff through the side door, while Nan managed sidewalk traffic, trying to keep people moving. The people didn't want to move. They wanted to stay and talk and share pie stories. They wanted to converse with the other people there eating pie, meet each other, form friendships with their pie-loving neighbors. A New Age-type girl who had just moved to Venice from San Francisco was talking to a homeless man whose clothes were as oily as his hair. But they had something in common—they were both eating free pie and enjoying it.

Happiness was growing exponentially all around us. Except that the bottleneck we had created was pissing off the owner of the antique shop we parked in front of. I made it my mission to placate him with pie. Not just a slice. This guy had one of those impenetrable stonewall attitudes that took a whole pie to get through. But I did it. I didn't quite get him to smile, but at least with the help of an apple pie, I convinced him not to call the police.

If he would have just observed what was happening right outside his door, he never would have made such a threat. Besides, even if he did call the cops, we would have just paid them off with pie, and they'd have left happy—hopefully.

I hung back a little, observing rather than engaging in conversation with everyone. It was too overwhelming, too emotional, too Hallmark. Janice was on fire, she was doing great without my help, getting quotes on tape. And none of the pie eaters needed prompting. They were interviewing us.

"Why are you doing this?" they asked. I heard this question and their subsequent ones over and over until it became a predictable cycle.

Nan, Melissa and Jeff took turns answering. They had the routine down pat after the first half hour. "Because it's National Pie Day."

"Is there really a National Pie Day?"

"Yes, it's today."

"Who's sponsoring you?" This one made me shake my head. I enjoy the benefits of capitalism as much as the next guy, but getting people to grasp that good deeds are not always driven by marketing dollars was more difficult than I had realized.

I watched the stunned faces as they got the unexpected answer. "No one is sponsoring us. We are doing this because we want to give something back to the world. We want to make people happy."

Team Pie was making me so proud.

As the forks moved in and out of these strangers' mouths, their hurried, tense expressions on their faces softened. "Mmm, this is really good," they said, their eyes closing to savor the taste. And, "This is as good as my grandmother's pie." But the best comments were, "This makes me want to do something nice for someone else."

One young woman said, "Pie makes people happy. If everyone ate pie all day, the world would be a better place." Then, talking with her mouth full, she added, "After this, I'm going to go home and do the dishes for my roommate."

Another guy, who was eating his apple pie while holding his dog's leash, announced, "Now I'm in a good mood, I'm happy, so I'm going to pick up after my dog." With that, Janice panned her camera down to his short and squatty, brown-and-white bulldog.

Janice let out a laugh from deep within her core, signaling that she was thrilled with this sound bite. "Did you see the size of that *dwawg?*" she chirped after he and his pooch walked away. "We should be giving this guy pie every day."

I loved seeing Janice happy. I loved seeing all these strangers happy. I loved being with my closest friends and seeing them happy. But I couldn't contain all this happiness. I couldn't process it. I knew this day was a crucial step forward in my well-being. It showed me that there was still so much goodness to be found in the world. That glass I used to see as half full had become bone dry. But on National Pie Day, my cup was about to runneth over. I was so grateful to Janice for wanting to do this pie shoot. If not for her, we wouldn't be here on Abbott Kinney Boulevard, standing in the California sunshine, wearing T-shirts in the middle of January, making all these people smile. With pie.

It was a simple formula, like a message straight from the Bible—the Golden Rule with a slight spin: if you want to feel better, do something nice for others. Or, as the Scottish proverb goes: "Shared joy is a double joy; shared sorrow is half a sorrow."

Feeling overwhelmed but strangely buoyant, I ventured into the crowd, stepping into the midst of the Pie Love Fest, and said hello to some people. One was a woman I guessed to be in her late fifties, who was with her husband and another couple. "How do you like the pie?" I asked.

"Oh, it's wonderful," she said. "Thank you so much. Are you the one who lost her husband?" She had obviously given Team Pie more than the standard line of questioning.

"Yes, he died five months ago."

"Thank you for sharing your story. You are so brave to be out here doing this," she said. "My husband was just diagnosed with terminal cancer." She looked in his direction and I followed her eyes over to the tall, handsome, seemingly healthy man in the leather jacket. He was chatting with his friends, and they were all eating pie. This man had just been handed a death sentence—*and he was smiling.* "So it means a lot to me to be standing here," she continued. "I'm so glad I got to meet you, and have a piece of this lovely pie you made. God bless you, sweetheart."

Fuck. It was too much. My emotions were already in overdrive. I couldn't take it anymore. All I managed to say to this dear woman was, "I am so sorry." We exchanged a hug and then I quickly escaped her embrace. I elbowed my way back through the crowd as fast as I could to get into the RV, where I locked myself in the bathroom, curled up on the floor, and let the tears pour out. Yin and yang. Life and death. Happiness and sorrow. I was a damned yo-yo in this push-pull game and my string was about to snap. I stayed in the safety of the windowless bathroom until Nan knocked on the door. "Pumpkin, are you okay?"

"Yeah, I'm all right."

"I have to tell you who I just saw."

I opened the door and she told me the story. "Remember the director of the play I did ten years ago about Tallulah Bankhead?" I nodded, wiping my nose and pulling myself together. How could I forget? Nan had written and starred in one of the best musical theater productions I had ever seen, but her director tried to claim *he* wrote it—so she fired him. "I just saw him. I recognized his voice, so I hid behind the RV. I heard him say 'What? You're giving away free pie?' What a bitter asshole he is. But then he came back ten minutes later and got a slice." She was giddy and breathless, in that just-dodged-a-dangerous-bullet kind of way.

From her point of view, the best part of the story was that she avoided contact with him using The Beast for cover. From mine, the better part was how he scoffed at our altruistic efforts but then changed his mind. Maybe pie could save the world after all.

"There are only a few pink boxes left," Nan said, reaching out her hand to pull me up. "Which means it's almost time to open a bottle of red wine. Come on. Let's give these last pies away and go to my house for cocktail hour."

13

When I was twenty-four, fearless and invincible, I went to Nairobi, Kenya, to work on a coffee farm. I had just gotten fired for the first time—I had been living in Chicago, recruiting students for an outdoor education program, where never before or since have I experienced this degree of nonprofit politics. My disgust and disappointment over the in-fighting was one reason why the words "We have to let you go" were the sweetest sounding ones I had ever heard. But the other reason was that the moment the reality sunk in, a vision of a huge ball of sun setting over the Dark Continent popped into my mind. I had been having this vision since childhood, longing to see the land where "Born Free" was made, and where all those fascinating pictures in *National Geographic* were taken.

"Good," I thought as I was handed the proverbial pink slip. "Now I can finally go to Africa."

Following a series of connections that began with an old boyfriend whose family was in the coffee business, saving up money from three part-time jobs and applying an extra dose of my God-given chutzpah, I landed an invitation to learn the Kenya coffee business firsthand, with the intention that I would apply my knowledge afterward to help promote the country's number one export crop. I worked on the coffee farm for a month before getting a case of acute amoebic dysentery, combined with sunstroke (I had had the genius idea to work on my tan in the high-noon equatorial sun, while everyone else sat in the shade). A wealthy coffee exporter I had met was concerned about my illness. He insisted, "You need to move off that farm if you're going to get better." He scribbled a phone number on a blue page torn from his elegant appointment book and said, "Here, call this woman. She's American and she takes people in all the time."

That woman was Kathy Eldon, a vibrant redhead, whose energy and polka-dot skirts whooshed like a gust of wind across the savannah whenever she entered a room. She invited me to stay for a few days, but within minutes of meeting each other we discovered we were both from Iowa. I ended up staying a whole year. Kathy was a journalist, married to a debonair British businessman, and she convinced me that I shouldn't rush back to the U.S., that I could just start my coffee business in Kenya. Spurred on by her contagious enthusiasm, I designed a zebra-striped tin, contracted with a local roaster, and my Livingstone Provisions brand of coffee was born.

Fast forward twenty-two years later, I no longer sold coffee (that career lasted an impressive three years) and Kathy no longer lived in Nairobi. She had divorced, remarried and now lived in a sprawling, white-washed beach house just north of Santa Monica. And Janice and I were headed there to interview her about pie.

Being from Iowa, pie played a role in Kathy's background. Her Grandma Knapp in Cedar Rapids, who lived to 106, had written a cookbook full of pie recipes. Kathy and I made many pies together over the years. She was the one who always reprimanded me, shouting, "Don't manhandle the dough." Which made her a sort of pie mentor. So it seemed fitting she be part of our pie documentary.

Sadly, the other thing that united us was grief. Her son, Dan Eldon, was a photojournalist killed in Somalia, stoned to death by an angry mob while covering stories of famine and war for Reuters. He was only twenty-two. Kathy swears I helped her deal with her loss. All I remember is that I sent her an essay I wrote about him after he died. In it, I described how I had babysat him and his younger sister, Amy, when I lived with them in Nairobi. Dan, the aspiring artist, had spent his time making short films in the backyard with his G.I. Joes or hibernating in his room, creating elaborate photo collages. I wrote about how, later, when he came to stay with me in L.A., he would dress in an aviator's cap and safari vest to sell African bracelets on the streets of Beverly Hills at night. He almost got arrested, but the police let him go when he told them in his suave Kenyan accent that his airplane was parked around the corner. Sharing and recording memories of him was my gift to her; it was all I had to give.

Likewise, she had been there for me. I remembered her phone call as I sat on my bed in the Portland hotel room the day before Marcus's funeral. I traced my finger along the swirled patterns of the bedspread as she coached me.

"Don't blame yourself," she said. "You mustn't blame yourself. It is not your fault. You really need to believe that." I hadn't told anyone about my guilt, about how I thought it was my fault Marcus died. But she knew. People who have grieved the kind of loss she had always knew.

Kathy didn't waste time blaming herself with the "what ifs" and "whys"—"What if I hadn't let him go to Somalia? Why did I ever agree to move to Africa?" She and her daughter, Amy, got busy and built an entire empire around Dan's legacy. They made an Emmy-award-winning documentary about photojournalists called *Dying to Tell a Story*. They published books, several featuring Dan's art, as well as a grief journal called *Angel Catcher*. They created a foundation called Creative Visions that inspires and funds young people to become "creative activists"—like Dan—to help change the world through media and other creative humanitarian projects. Kathy had taken a bushel of tragedy-bred lemons and made the world's largest lemon meringue pie.

Janice, anxious to get filming, set up her equipment outside on the sundeck. She positioned Kathy and me around the teak table, pinning minimicrophones to our shirts. The ocean sparkled in the background, salty air mixing with the apple pie we ate, as Kathy and I talked and Janice taped. While we tried to keep on topic, aiming for pithy quotes about how pie could help heal the world, we didn't come up with anything that was usable. We were like a big and little sister with a long and difficult shared history too complicated to distill into a three-minute segment for a pie show.

When Janice finally relieved us of our on-camera duties, Kathy changed subjects.

"I'm worried about your eyes," she said. "One of L.A.'s top plastic surgeons lives next door. Let's walk over there and ask him about this."

"Yeah, okay," I shrugged and, leaving Janice behind, followed Kathy obediently to the plastic surgeon's beach house. It was a Sunday morning and he came to the door, wearing plaid flannel pajama bottoms, his face unshaven.

"It's not from crying," he said, pressing on my upper eyelid as we stood in his doorway. "It's fat. Your hyperthyroid caused the eye muscles to thicken. That's what makes your eyes bulge. It's a common symptom of hyperthyroidism. You lost a lot of weight, right? So you also lost fat around your eyes. When you gained the weight back, the thickened eye muscle took up the space where the fat had been, and now the fat has nowhere to go. That's what's causing the puffiness. We could do surgery, but you'd have to wait a year to see how things settle back into place. But, as you age, you need that fat to protect your eyes, so I don't recommend it."

"Thank you so much," I said. "I'll make sure you get some pie before we leave." He may have offered the diagnosis free of charge, but he wouldn't go unpaid. For the man who already had enough money to buy all the houses on the beach, pie was something he would truly appreciate. I wouldn't have gone for the surgery, even if he had insisted on it. But at least I knew that my swollen eyes weren't caused by my constant crying. I could stop getting down on myself for that.

We returned to Kathy's to pack up our gear and say our good-byes. Amy had stopped by after a brunch, so I got to see her and her bulging belly. She was pregnant with her second boy—and this one was going to be named Dan, after her brother. Seeing her maternal glow caused the pang, the one that had hit hardest in the first weeks after Marcus died, to flare up again. Marcus and I had tried to have a baby and had eventually reconciled that it just wasn't going to happen. But now that he was gone, and there was no legacy left behind, the impact of not having kids with him compounded my sadness. I was always quick to remind myself of the flip side of the equation: his death would have left me as a single mother. To see that Amy had a doting husband and a full-time nanny and still had her hands full eased the pang, sending it back into remission.

Over the twenty-some years I had known Kathy, she often preached a Scottish proverb she had learned when growing up in Iowa. "What's for you won't go by you." Every damn thing was going by me now. I didn't know what was left for me.

♥♥♥

Janice and I restocked the RV with coffee and milk for our morning lattes, and whole-grain bread and Nutella for our breakfast, loaded up Team Terrier and headed four hundred miles north to San Francisco.

Lumbering up the long, straight stretch of Interstate 5 under rain-threatening skies, I kept my eyes on the road, stealing glances at Marcus's visa photo every so often. Janice had dubbed Marcus and his mug shot as "Advance Security," assuring me that he was looking out for us and our safety during this TV shoot. With the only incident being the ding I put on the RV roof, Marcus was definitely doing a good job. I jingled our wedding rings to say thank you. Janice didn't notice. She was petting Jack—who, out of all the comfortable places in the RV, refused to sit anywhere else but on her lap. They were both looking out the passenger window, watching the endless expanse of golden grass fields roll by.

Our first San Francisco interview would be with Natalie Galatzer, a twenty-six-year-old who just started a bicycle-delivery pie business. I had learned about her during my pre-production research by stumbling upon a small article about her on the Internet. We were still trying to figure out how we could follow her on her bike route. Aside from solving our logistical puzzle, I was still mulling over the phone conversation I had had with Natalie that morning. She explained how her dad died only ten months earlier, and that she was dedicating her work to him, that even though he was gone, she was still motivated to make him proud.

"Janice, have you noticed the common thread in this shoot, besides pie, I mean?" I asked. "It's like death is following us to every interview. There was the thirtysomething's pie party with Elissa and her two husbands that died of cancer. The first thing Dorothy Rose Pryor told us was how she missed her mother and sister since their passing. The reason the matriarch of Oak Glen moved to California is her first husband died in World War II. Even on National Pie Day, at the fire station, they talked about how they risked their own lives every day to save others—and they didn't always survive. And, of course, there was Kathy Eldon's son... Seriously. What the hell? Wasn't this shoot supposed to take my mind off of that subject?"

Was it me? Was I attracting these stories of death, of loss, of grief? Or was death just a huge part of life that I had always overlooked, because it had never impacted me? Until Marcus, that is, when it hit me like Freightliner semi. It was as if all these people had a hidden life, a loss that wasn't revealed until I started blabbing about my own grief. Given my grief was so fresh and unresolved, it was something I wanted—and needed—to talk about. But others seemed relieved to talk about their losses, too, a chance to share, to connect, to heal—with pie acting as an unwitting catalyst.

"The thing that stands out for me is how we've met people from all different walks of life," Janice replied, "but we all share common threads. There's a bonding that happens around grief because it touches everyone at some point in their lives.

"Your grief is not my grief, but somehow it's a shared experience. Being inside your grief allows me to revisit mine a bit. After my dad died, I came to Santa Monica and stayed with Melissa for a week. Being in the company of a friend who just let me breathe, cry, stay silent or talk when I needed was a time in my life when I felt most deeply listened to. And we all need that for healing. Not someone who is going to talk and soothe but someone who truly hears you."

We drove in silence for a long while after that, lost in our own thoughts and reflections. The only sound was the occasional rattle from the RV's oven when we hit the frequent bumps of California's ragged roads, and Daisy's snoring coming from the bed in the back.

Bike Basket Pies may have been the name of Natalie's business, but when we arrived at her baking facility—kitchen space borrowed from a Thai restaurant during its downtime—we found that her baskets were actually panniers—bright orange, waterproof saddlebags mounted on her rear wheel. Natalie, dressed in a fluorescent yellow rain jacket, looked up at us from her bike with a perky smile and a mop of brown curly hair, looking wild from the wind and dampness. She was loading her wax-paper-wrapped mini pies into the panniers. In spite of the drizzling grey sky, San Franciscans were going to get their morning snacks—the day's flavors included apple kiwi, Shaker orange and mushroom quiche—delivered to their office doors. In the end, we just parked the RV (which took up two parking spaces and, with two meters to feed, required a hunt for extra quarters) and staged a few moving shots with Natalie pedaling toward Janice, who dodged honking cars in the name of good footage.

While in the city, we also visited Mission Pie located, as the name suggests, in the Mission District. The dynamic duo of Karen Heisler and Krystin Rubin teamed up to do something good for the community: make pie. But they don't just make outstanding pastry out of locally grown ingredients, they hire at-risk youth from the local high school, give them their first job and train them in everything from pie dough to customer service. I was so enamored, not only with Mission Pie's do-good efforts but with the warm atmosphere in the pie shop, that Janice teased me after our visit.

"I thought you were auditioning for a job there," she said as we sat down for one last dinner stop at In-N-Out Burger.

"Maybe I was," I replied, letting my mind wander back to their warm and lively kitchen where Krystin and her assistant, Danielle, had been laughing and talking while rolling crust after crust. "Yeah, that was definitely a cool place. The world needs more pie shops like it."

From San Francisco, we returned to L.A.—and drove straight to The Apple Pan. It was the first place I researched and the last thing scheduled for the shoot. And we barely made it. We had arranged with the owners, mother–daughter team Martha Gamble and Sunny Sherman, to arrive at nine, to have time to set up and shoot before the diner opened at eleven. We had parked overnight at a truck stop half way between San Francisco and L.A., I set the alarm for 4:00 a.m., drove in my pajamas and parked the RV outside The Apple Pan at 9:15 a.m. We would have been on time had I not had to change clothes. As it was, Janice saved us a few minutes by walking the dogs while I put on makeup.

Martha, the mother-half, radiated the glamour of an old-time Hollywood star from a Western or maybe *Dallas*. Bright beaming eyes lined with mascara, a big white-toothed smile and dripping in chunky turquoise jewelry, her spunk defied her grey hair, which was pulled back in a girlish ponytail. Her daughter, Sunny, was equally stunning. Sunny's highlighted long hair swept up with curled tendrils framing her face, blush-tinted cheeks and pink-glossed lips and matching denim vest and jeans combined to make the statement, "I'm just heading to the ranch in my new Cadillac," not "I run one of L.A.'s oldest burger and pie joints and you can find me adding up receipts in my tiny, cramped office in the far corner of the hot kitchen."

While we were inside, interviewing them about their family history, how Martha's parents had opened the diner in 1947 and how she had worked there as a waitress (and not as the actress or model I swore she could have been), customers were already lining up outside the door. Some were pulling on the locked door to see if it would open, others were knocking in hopes of getting in before the rush. The staff inside was used to this; they weren't going to cave in to the demands. Finally, as the hands of the clock struck eleven, the door was unlocked, the masses poured in and within two minutes every bar stool was occupied. Burgers were eaten, pie was ordered, coffee cups were filled. It was just another money-making day at The Apple Pan.

Janice interviewed a few customers. The words of one of them, a man in his early forties, who was there with his preteen son, stood out as they encapsulated Apple Pan's formula for success: tradition and nostalgia. "My dad used to bring me here," the man said. "My grandparents used to bring my dad here. And now I bring my son." Funny, there was that circle-of-life thing again, generations of life cycling through, but instead of relating to death it was about pie. "The apple pie here is our favorite," he added. His son nodded enthusiastically, fully in agreement.

Earlier, we had taped the pie baking in the back, where a stainless steel table was loaded with topless berry, chocolate cream and banana cream pies—none of them had received their final layer. A Mexican man with a mustache and a mischievous smile was busy dousing the assembly line, covering each with piles of whipped cream. Another, adjacent room was reserved just for the apple pie. In it, another smiling Hispanic man with happy, glistening eyes, named Jose, was rolling dough. Behind him, I counted twenty-five pies cooling on a rack with twenty more in the oven. Yes, that kind of productivity—along with that steaming cinnamon scent—would make anyone enjoy their job.

The best part of the shoot, as with all of the segments we taped for the show, was that the culmination of our time there led to eating the pie we had watched being made. As if we were pie judges, Jose brought us each a slice of his apple pie and waited for Janice and me to give him our verdict. "My God, this is good," I mumbled as the warm pie filled my mouth. "Thumbs up, Jose." He flashed a huge, relieved smile. Rodrigo, the other baker from behind the scenes, came out with slices of boysenberry and banana cream, one of each for Janice and me. I couldn't have chosen a favorite because they were all equally, phenomenally, heavenly good.

People always ask me how I can eat so much pie and stay so thin. I answer, "For one thing, I don't eat that much pie. But I also exercise." The Apple Pan's pie was so good, however, I wouldn't be able to live nearby and still keep my shape. I would want to eat so much of it that no amount of exercise could burn off the calories I would consume.

After a very long day, we parked in front of Nan's Venice Beach rental house. We had one more job to do before we were finished with the shoot: record the voice-over for the sizzle reel, the two-minute promotional tape we would use to try to sell our show. We sat in Nan's living room, her husband, Steve, across from me, watching and listening, while Nan topped off my glass with a splash of cabernet.

"Let's try it again," Janice said. "Slower this time."

I took a breath, let it out, and recited my lines for the third time. "Pie is comfort. Pie builds community. Pie heals. Pie can change the world. My name is Beth Howard. I'm a pie baker and I've always believed that pie can change the world. Now I have to put my theory to the test as I attempt to heal from the unexpected death of my forty-three-year-old husband. I'm packing up the RV my husband left behind and hitting the American highways in search of the real healing powers of pie. Be it teaching others to make pie, exchanging recipes and tips with other pie bakers and pie lovers, visiting orchards to pick fruit for filling or seeking out the perfect slice, the journey, no matter how bittersweet, is sure to be a delicious one. So grab a fork and join me for the ride."

I pulled back from the microphone, sat back in my armchair and took a swig of wine.

"That was better. Let's do it one more time. Try not to make it sound so forced."

I swallowed my drink, took another breath and leaned into the microphone again. "Pie is comfort. Pie builds community. Pie heals. Pie can change the world."

When I got to the end, Janice took off her headphones and turned off her recorder. "I think we have what we need."

Steve nodded, the ice cubes clinking in his Scotch glass. "I agree. That last one sounded the best."

"Thanks," I said. "Can we please go to dinner now? I'm starving. I haven't eaten since those four pieces of pie I had for breakfast."

♥♥♥

I drove Janice—and all her camera gear and the twenty-seven hours of digital tape we shot—to the Los Angeles airport. We had expressed our gratitude and said our goodbyes the night before, over an expensive dinner with Nan and her husband. So in lieu of tearing up over the end of our Big Pie Adventure, Janice complained the whole way about how much weight she had gained during our two weeks together. "I'm going to have to go on a diet when I get back to Jersey," she claimed.

"First of all," I told her, "you really didn't have that much pie. You only had one bite of coconut cream the entire time. You only had one full slice of pie at The Apple Pan—it was so good, I can't believe you didn't eat more. Especially considering I had four. And you didn't eat any yesterday." Then, I said to her with a teasing grin, "Don't blame pie."

CHAPTER

14

After Janice left and the shoot was over, I had to decide what to do next. It was early February and I had been gone from Portland for two months. The time away and all that concentrated focus on the TV show—combined with Janice's continuous company and laughter—was good for me. To suddenly go back to full-time grieving was not a pleasant option. I didn't have to do it. I could have stayed in motion. I could have gone anywhere in the RV. But I had to get my thyroid checked—er, the place my thyroid used to be. So once again, I let my medical needs direct my decision. I returned to Portland in The Beast with a very full load: Team Terrier, my new "Honk If You Love Pie" and "Free Pie" signs and all of my belongings from the L.A. storage locker. With all of the TV show activity, I had almost forgotten the original reason I made the journey down there—to collect my stuff.

Back in October—on October 26, to be exact—my endocrinologist, Dr. Vanek, had sent me to the basement of the Oregon

Health and Sciences University Hospital. There, in the cavern of the medical castle, a round man resembling a sinister Santa Claus unlocked a lead box. He pulled out a glass vile, handed it to me and ran out of the room. Just before he slammed the door behind him, he said, "Once you open the vile, swallow the pill as fast as you can."

Alone and abandoned, I unscrewed the lid of the glass cylinder and popped the radioactive iodine pill into my mouth. That is how simple it was to kill my thyroid gland. The thyroid is the only gland in the body that absorbs iodine, so making the chemical element radioactive is an efficient, surgery-free way to deal with a misbehaving body part. All I had to do after washing the pill down with a cup of water was wait for the thyroid to die its slow, painless, invisible death.

In a way, saying goodbye to that small-but-important gland in my neck felt like more loss upon loss. I didn't have an intimate relationship with it, it didn't call me and email every day like Marcus did, I had never had sex with it, but there was still something sad about it. The three-day quarantine in my apartment also made for some melancholy moments—even if I didn't want human contact, the idea that I was forbidden from it made the isolation seem like punishment. As if my grief wasn't repellent enough, now I was contaminated. (Apparently my dogs were immune to the radioactive fallout as they were allowed to stay with me.) In the scheme of things, it was no worse than being housebound with a common cold. And compared to losing Marcus, letting go of my thyroid was nothing.

It takes three to four months for the radioactivity to kill the thyroid's active tissue—causing the gland, along with my grapefruit-size goiter, to shrivel up—so my February return to Portland was well timed for my doctor's check up.

I could never seem to remember the exact date I met Marcus—I mean, I remembered meeting him, of course, but was perpetually confused as to whether it was on September 29 or 30. But the reason I couldn't forget October 26 is because while I was swallowing my little pill, my youngest brother, Patrick, in Seattle, was under a knife and scalpel having his left testicle—and the malignant tumor attached to it—removed.

This is why life is not fair: I was childless and newly widowed with no job, no real obligations (financial or otherwise), no mortgage, no car payments—basically, no pressing need to stick around on this planet except to care for my dogs—and after my treatment I received a clean bill of health. My brother was forty-two, married with four kids under the age of sixteen, with a successful career, a family to feed, baseball games to coach, dance recitals to attend, a big lawn to mow—he was greatly needed here—and after his treatment, he received news that the cancer had spread. Vascular invasion, they called it. For the past two months, they proceeded to pump him full of poison chemicals until he was so sick he couldn't leave his house, let alone his bed. If only we had learned about the apple cure sooner; I would have sent him a hundred cases from Alison's Oak Glen orchard.

Patrick's final chemo treatment coincided with my return to Portland. He called me, excited with the news that his doctor had deemed him "clear" enough to remove the easy-access chemo port that had been sewn into his chest. This was cause for celebration, and a good excuse to visit him in Seattle.

I left The Beast behind and packed Team Terrier in the MINI Cooper for the three-and-a-half-hour drive north. I had missed driving my zippy, little car. But the contrast going from the twenty-four-foot-long RV to a six-foot-long sports car was extreme.

My brother's house lies in the eastern suburbs of Seattle in a town with its own lake called Sammamish. I drove to the end of his cul de sac, where the branches of the tall cedar trees wrapped the neighborhood in a safety net, and saw three of his four kids playing outside. Eleni was on her bike, bundled up in a jacket and boots; Zach and Ben were playing basketball in the driveway, dressed in T-shirts and shorts. They came running like puppies when I got out of the car.

"Hi, Aunt Beth," they all said at once, lining up for a quick squeeze.

"Where's Jack?" asked Ben.

"That's a good question." My dogs knew and liked the neighborhood so well they had already escaped from the car and were racing around on the huge lawn. "Oh, there he is. He's already found a stick." And off the trio scampered, to play with the dogs.

Patrick was inside. I let myself in and found him in the kitchen. Except that it wasn't him. It was half of him, or what was left of him. He had wasted away to a bony, gaunt shell, having lost what looked like half of his body weight. And all of his hair. He was bald with no eyebrows. There was not a hint of hair on his face, arms or anywhere. His skin was grey and his eyes were sunken in their sockets. Even Marcus lying in his casket looked healthier than this.

"Hi, Pat. It's good to see you," I said as we hugged. What I was thinking was, "It's good to see you *alive*." I didn't tell him how shocked I was by his appearance, and that from the way he looked, how scared I was that he wouldn't survive. I had seen him since his surgery, sometime around Thanksgiving, when he still looked robust, but I hadn't seen him since his chemo.

"How are you doing?" he asked. Ah, my generous brother, unconcerned with himself, was kind enough to inquire as to my well-being—which, even though I didn't have a life-threatening disease, had been tenuous these past six months.

The question was easier for me to answer this time, and the words came out quickly and genuinely.

"I'm doing a lot better." Compared to him and his situation, I was suddenly aware—and ashamed—I had been very self-involved in my own grief. There were other people in the world suffering far greater tragedy and loss than me. Every single day people were dying for all kinds of reasons, sometimes lots of people at once, sometimes because of horrific accidents or heinous crimes, sometimes because of heart conditions or . . . cancer. I had witnessed the breadth of others' losses during the pie shoot, and now I was staring at death again in the face—of my own flesh and blood.

Before I had beat myself up to a bloody pulp for being a bad and selfish person, Susan's sweet voice interrupted my thoughts: "You have a right to your emotions, and to experience your grief." She had engrained this into me over the course of our many sessions. Before Marcus died, I was capable of feeling sadness, not for myself but for all the cruelty of the world.

"We call that *Weltschmerz*," Marcus had told me once. For as much as I complained about learning his language, I was impressed by how complicated emotions could be summed up in one German word. "World pain," my husband explained. "It's when you feel overwhelmed by thinking about all of life's problems and suffering."

I didn't currently have my usual capacity to take on the emotions for the rest of the world's issues, but I could still show my support and love to my brother.

"Hey, I recognize that shirt," I said. Patrick was wearing Marcus's blue-and-white-striped dress shirt. The stripes went in a diagonal direction, giving it a distinct design. My eyes followed the shirt farther down to the familiar brown wool cuffed trousers. "Oh, and the pants, too." I managed a bittersweet smile. To see him in Marcus's clothes was one thing, to see that the clothes had once fit Patrick perfectly and were now hanging loosely on his body was another. "I'm so glad you're getting good use out of his stuff."

The next morning, Team Terrier and I walked the kids to their school-bus stop. There is no better way to start your day than to watch a wide-eyed, innocent, bright, beautiful, nine-year-old girl skipping down the street with your dogs chasing after her.

After the bus stop, I drove Patrick to downtown Seattle. I dropped him off at his office on my way to do some pie research. I had not forgotten; I had a purpose now. Janice was taking our footage back to her New Jersey studio to edit and I was pressing ahead, looking beyond our original California radius for pie stories, in case we really could sell this show as a series.

With my MINI idling, I watched Patrick—the back of his newly bald head, his trench coat flapping in the wind, his briefcase weighing heavy in his hand—as he disappeared through the doors of the high-rise. As the doors closed behind him, the knife that had been wedged in my heart for the past six months twisted and gouged its way in even deeper. *Please, God, I do not want to lose him, too.*

The Seattle Pie Company sits in the middle of a peninsula in Seattle's northwest neighborhood of Magnolia. The residential area, where rows of tidy houses line manicured streets, is quiet, except for the occasional ship horn announcing the departure of an Alaska-bound fishing boat. Set just slightly apart and alone from the village's cluster of boutiques and main grocery store, the pie company makes a statement of independence and humility, and offers free parking. Its interior, a simple and plain

Scandinavian design, seems to be intentional, so as to let the enormous red display case packed full with whole pies be the focal point.

Pies, row after row of pies, were covered in mountains of crumble topping, giant clumps of brown sugar and butter weighing down thick and juicy beds of raspberries, marionberries, strawberries, apples and combinations thereof. The scent of more pies baking in the shop's oven was so powerful the longshoremen working on the cargo ships a few blocks away could probably get a whiff.

I recognized the woman behind the counter from her picture on their website. Alyssa Lewis, who owned the place with her husband, was even more adorable than her photo. Young and blonde with a welcoming smile and earthy presence, seeing her standing next to those pies made me think I was at a county fair and not in an urban metropolis. The sign above her head proclaimed Voted Seattle's Best Pies', but Alyssa could also have been voted "Seattle's Best-Looking Pie Baker."

I was feeling very low and didn't have the energy to introduce myself or explain my pie show project. So I just ordered a Swedish pancake and took my laptop over to a table by the window to update my blog and wait for my breakfast to arrive.

I tried to write, but I couldn't stop thinking about my brother. He was so brave and positive. He was not like his big sister. While I continued to sob and wail over Marcus, Patrick donned his suit and tie every day (or Marcus's shirts and trousers), each morning packing lunches for himself and all the kids. He was dragging his weakened, chemo-poisoned body to work to earn the money to pay for the house, the soccer/basketball/baseball/swim team fees, the dance lessons, the soon-to-come college tuitions, the health insurance. While I continued to languish in my grief, my brother was busy fighting the greatest battle of his life. And in spite of how sick he looked, he was actually winning.

My brother, the mighty warrior (and former football star), showed me I needed to stop focusing on the negative. I was fixating on the pallor of his skin, the sunken-ness of his eyes, the hairlessness of his body and the fear of death, but what I needed to concentrate on was his spirit—and his bright, optimistic, willful, unstoppable strength.

Likewise, I also needed to quit obsessing about Marcus's death and appreciate the time I had with him—the joy, the adventures, the sex, the motorcycle trips in Italy and France, living abroad, learning about him, experiencing his culture.

Yes, life had thrown a shit pie in my face and I was still trying to wipe its depressive mess off my cheeks. But so what? Everyone in this life gets served their share of shit pie sooner or later, including my brother. It's just that his response to it was different.

"Shit pie?" he had said to the news of his cancer. "No, thanks. I'll take a slice of determination with a scoop of hope on top."

I understood finally. I needed to change my order. In other words, to borrow a line from *When Harry Met Sally,* what I needed to say was, "I'll have what he's having."

I sat so long in the pie shop, burning up so much energy ruminating on life—and how my brother was fending off death—that I hadn't remembered even eating the pancake. I was ready for a piece of marionberry pie. Just imagining the taste of it brightened my outlook a little. These berries grow only in the Pacific Northwest and to eat them in a pie was a special treat. I was not only hungry again, I was inspired. I was so inspired, in fact, I didn't order a piece of pie. I bought two whole pies—one to take back to Portland, and one to deliver to my brother at his office on my way out of town.

I bought two Desserted Island pies, a mix of berries, apples and whatever else they could fit in. It was the kind of pie that has something in it to satisfy everyone's taste and the perfect pie for a Gemini like me who can't make a decision when faced with too many good choices. Apple? Blueberry? Marionberry? Peach? Strawberry? How about all of them?

When I got back to Portland, I cut a slice of the Desserted Island pie. Oh, my. It was sweet, crunchy, fruity and delicious. I texted Patrick after the first bite. *How was the pie?*

He texted me back immediately with a photo of his empty pie plate on his kitchen counter. *Awesome,* he wrote.

I laughed at his response. And then I took another bite. Pie may not cure cancer, but it could cure the blues.

15

Meanwhile, after several weeks back in Portland, doubts about spending so much time and money on the pie TV show set in. I didn't add up the receipts from the RV road trip and the money spent on pie. I didn't want to know. Looking back, it felt irresponsible that I had ever thought something could come of it in the first place. I had tried to sell a TV show once, teaming up with an old boyfriend to write a sitcom pilot. I was broke then, barely able to buy dog food and coffee on my meager and sporadic freelance journalist's income, yet I had invested every spare dime I had into printing color copies of our TV show treatment. We got meetings with senior-level entertainment executives who fueled our hopes that we were about to win the Hollywood lottery, so I let paying journalism gigs slide and kept spending money I didn't have at Kinko's to print more bound copies to send to more TV executives. I finally broke the cycle by breaking up with the boyfriend and moving to San Francisco for the dot com job.

I continued taking my daily hikes with Team Terrier in the forest behind my house. Every afternoon I put on my rain boots, raincoat, fleece tights, hat and gloves, and set forth into the dark woods. Of the forty miles of trails, I had three different regular loops I would take. None was more scenic than another—they all looked the same—steep, tree-lined trails surrounded by over-grown ferns and fallen moss-covered logs—so my trail choice depended only on how long I felt like walking. My energy was gradually returning, so I increased the length and intensity of my hikes as the days went by.

It was during one of my daily walks that I was trudging up the mountain, dogs in tow, fretting over what the hell I was doing with my life—when I heard Marcus's voice. I knew it was his voice, because it was distinct and clear, complete with his British accent, and something he definitely would have said.

"Bloody hell, why do you think I left you this money?" he reproached from the "Other Side." He immediately answered his own question. "So you could pursue your pie endeavors."

I wasn't scared to hear him speak. I had been wishing for it, waiting for it, every day since he died. I had read so many books about the afterlife, including *Hello from Heaven* and *Ghosts Among Us,* that I was annoyed Marcus hadn't visited me. But he finally showed up—to give me a firm kick in the ass.

"Okay, my love, I will," I whispered to the misty air. "Okay, okay. Thank you." I stopped and leaned against a tree to see if he would say anything more. But except for some creaking branches, the woods were once again silent.

With renewed motivation, I spent the following weeks creating a pie website. On the site I included the TV show treatment (this was a welcome and cost-saving change from the days of photo-copying), but also advertising for my pie-baking parties, my pie blog, and left some blank pages for anything else pie-related that might materialize.

The woman who designed my site for me was Tricia Martin, a graphic artist who had created a pie/literary contest called Pietopia, in which contestants wrote short essays about what their life right now would be if it were a pie. After passing the first round of judging, participants had to make the recipe and enter the actual pie in the contest. I didn't enter, but I did become a judge for it. If I had entered, my pie would have been some kind of caramel apple with walnuts—the caramel representing the challenge of wading through the thick, viscous grieving process; the apples for simplicity as I had pared down my life to the most basic ingredients by living in a sparse studio and spending time with only the most nurturing of people; and walnuts for the hard and bitter parts I still endured. Besides, a little protein is always a good idea.

Tricia's contest gave me another idea. The National Pie Championships were taking place in Orlando in April. If I went, I could meet potential sponsors for the pie show. I could volunteer to be a pie judge and scope out more story angles for us to shoot if the show sold. And I could get out from under Portland's permanent rain cloud. I called the American Pie Council, explained my Malibu baking background and that I had a TV show in the works. I was immediately accepted as a judge. Because I mentioned I was using pie as a way to heal from the death of my husband, they asked if I would also give a speech at their Great American Pie Festival. I have no idea why I agreed, but I did.

I was on a roll. Just as Marcus had insisted, the pie endeavors were being pursued. And sometimes they were pursuing me. Rachel, a friend of Marcus's and mine (whose dad was a pastor and resided over Marcus's Portland funeral), was friends with a local newspaper reporter who was looking for human-interest stories. Rachel mentioned me to her. What was so interesting about an unemployed grieving widow with suicidal tendencies holed up in a tree house on the edge of town? Oh, right. Pie. I had taught Rachel how to make pie. She also knew about my L.A. trip in the RV and how I had given away pie on National Pie Day. Rachel's friend—the reporter, Jen Anderson—loved the idea.

Jen was half-Japanese, short and buff, fast-talking and quick-laughing. She was a ball of energy in clogs and carried a big white leather designer handbag. We met for our interview—and of course, for pie—at Random Order Coffee House on Portland's counter-culture strip, Alberta Street. (It was one of the places where I had—unsuccessfully—applied for a pie-baking job, the one with the kitchen the size of a broom closet.) The glass pie case was filled with so many choices that the dilemma delayed our ability to order, thus causing a line of impatient custom-ers behind us to build up. We finally had to ask the cashier for her recommendations. "They're all good," she said. (Portland isn't known for its stellar customer service.) Jen settled on a slice of Shaker lemon and I chose lemon meringue, not because I liked it—it's too sour for my taste—but because I had dreamed about it the night before. Usually I dream about my dog Jack fall-ing off cliffs or getting swept away in raging rivers. But some-times, on occasion, pie makes an appearance in my slumbering subconscious.

We took our pie outside and sat at one of the sidewalk tables. Bundled up against the cool, damp air in our down vests, our cups of coffee steamed as we dug into our pie. I was used to being the journalist, the one who asked the questions and wrote the stories, not the one being written about.

"So what do you think of the pie?" Jen wanted to know.

She knew I was going to be a judge at the National Pie Championships. Her question made me realize I was going to have to get used to having a more finely tuned pie palate, but for now I just wanted to enjoy a piece without scrutinizing it. "It's good," I said. "Not great."

"I've always wanted to open up a pie shop," she continued. "I'd love to have a pie cart."

"A pie cart is a great idea," I replied. Jen could join the exploding trend of gourmet food on wheels, portable shops that popped up in clusters around Portland in abandoned parking lots, usually near bars or downtown offices. "You should just do it."

"I'm too busy. I have two kids, a full-time job and I barely have enough time to exercise. And I don't know how to make pie."

I set my fork down and told her excitedly, "When you come over to my place for the photo shoot next week, I'll teach you."

And I did teach her. Her newspaper didn't allow her to take freebies, so she couldn't accept an official pie lesson, but that didn't stop her from applying her journalism techniques. While her photographer snapped pictures of me making an apple pie in my Aspen Avenue studio, Jen stood by observing. She didn't get a hands-on experience, but she got answers to her umpteen questions.

"You're not measuring the water. How do you know how much to use?"

"I pour in a little at a time and keep adding more until all the dry bits are absorbed. You can't always depend on an exact amount because there are so many variables. If you live in a dry climate, your dough might need extra water. Here in Portland, where it's damp, the flour may already have excess moisture."

"Don't you refrigerate your dough? I read that you're supposed to put it in the fridge for at least thirty minutes."

"No. I don't find it makes any difference. And I find it easier to roll my dough when it's supple."

"What's that scraper thing you're using?" She was referring to the flat metal rectangle I was sliding under my dough to lift it off the rolling surface.

"It's called a bench scraper. I call it a pastry scraper. Some call it a 'Chop n' Scoop.' It's the world's most useful pie making tool. I got this for three dollars at Target."

"Do you ever use a food processor?"

"Never!"

As I worked my ingredients into a big ball, then into two disks and then began to roll, Jen watched my every move—from the size of my lumps of butter in my dough, the dusting of flour on my countertop, to the thickness of my apple slices—and filled page after page of her spiral notebook with pie-making instructions.

That night Jen sent me an email with a picture attached. "I love your approach to pie," she wrote. "How you get people to stop thinking and just do it. Watching you made me instantly want to go home and make a pie. So I did! If I ever get laid off, I might just open that pie cart." I clicked on the photo. It was her first pie, strawberry-rhubarb with a lattice crust. It was perfect—a craggy, brown top crust outlined the shape of the fruit underneath, red berry juice pooled around the edges of the fluted crust. I was impressed. And proud. And I wanted a piece.

A few weeks later, when the article came out, I went down the hill from my house to the newspaper box in front of the cooperative grocery store to pick up a copy, which was free. In the box's window the current issue was displayed and I was taken aback by the color photo that occupied the entire top half of the paper. It was a close up of my hands weaving a lattice crust. That was me—well, my hands and my pie—on the front page of a Portland newspaper.

I wanted to call Marcus and tell him the exciting news about the article. But of course I couldn't. Every victory was hollow knowing that I couldn't share it with him—victories like driving the RV for the first time, shooting a TV show with Janice, getting my pie-making hands on the front page of a newspaper. Weirdly, these victories seemed to be *because* of him. So every time I got good news, instead of calling him I ran into the bathroom, holding myself up on the sink, eventually just letting go and crumbling onto the tile floor in a sobbing heap.

I didn't know how to accept joy. I didn't have the experience a friend had when her dad died—the forgetful "Oh, right, I can't call him, he's dead." I didn't stop thinking about Marcus long enough for that lapse to happen. Sometimes I would call him anyway, let the phone ring, with some secret twisted wish that he might actually pick up. His phone numbers, all nine of them still in my speed dial (three for each country—office, cell, home in Germany, Mexico and Portland), had been disconnected. No trace of his voice was left anywhere. No voice-mail recording. No video tape. Nothing. Just what I could still hear in my head. Or in the woods. The sound of him saying "bloody hell," or "brilliant" instead of the American slang "awesome" still resonated. As did his use of the word *penultimate*. I had never even heard the word before; it was embarrassing to admit, especially as a writer, that his English was more advanced than mine. I missed his vocabulary. I missed his voice. I missed him.

When I finally stopped gawking over the giant photo of my hands and lattice crust, I read Jen's story. My heart swelled with what I would call big-sisterly pride that she had taken my suggestion and run with it. I had encouraged her to take the story focus off me and encompass the growing pie scene in Portland. And she did. She included all the places I had applied for jobs, as well as a new meat pie shop called Pacific Pie Company run by a darling Australian-American couple. Mainly, she conveyed the most important message: pie is about sharing. Pie is not political. Pie can make the world a better place.

CHAPTER

16

When I booked my trip to Orlando for the National Pie Championships, it had seemed like a good idea. I hadn't factored in some
of the details, like how I would be flying out of Portland's airport.
What I had not considered—hadn't even thought to consider—was
that the past five times I had been in Portland's airport were related to Marcus's death.

These memories must be what triggered the grief burst. In a
surprise attack of sadness, I began crying from the moment I entered the Portland airport and didn't stop the entire six-hour
flight to Florida. I had to lock myself in the lavatory four times
and stayed in there each time until someone knocked on the door
to get in. I was familiar with grief bursts—I had experienced my
share—and was equally aware how they snuck up on you like a
mugger, tackled you from behind, beat the shit out of you and
stole your dignity, along with any sense of progress. And they too
often cornered you in public places. Like airplanes.

Exhausted by my extended cross-country crying jag, I landed in Orlando, "The Happiest Place on Earth." I stepped off the plane and into masses of families with young kids wearing Mickey Mouse ears and carrying Winnie the Pooh stuffed animals. Disneyworld. How could I have forgotten? I raced to baggage claim to get away from the onslaught of happiness-infused humanity and, after learning my luggage didn't make the flight and spending forty-five minutes filing a claim for it, I waited over an hour for the shuttle bus to my hotel. By this time I was really steaming. And not from the humidity.

I was the last stop out of six hotel drop-offs and had become so out of my mind with frustration and fatigue I didn't feel I could go straight to my room. I was sharing accommodations with Gina Hyams, the author of "Pie Contest in a Box." I had never met her, I was not in a good mood and didn't want her to think I was going to be a nightmare roommate. So instead of going to the hotel room, I went to the bar. "Just one glass of wine," I told myself. "That will help take the edge off. Then I'll go upstairs." It was already midnight; she was probably asleep anyway.

The bar of the resort hotel was dark and elegant and, thankfully, wasn't crowded. I was the furthest thing from a barfly, so the fewer people the better. I sat at a bar stool, slung my jacket on the back, and then came the moment that changed everything. I didn't order a glass of wine.

"What can I get you?" asked the bartender.

"I'll have a vodka martini, dry with three olives."

For me, there is a wide chasm between wine and hard liquor. Wine is my beverage of choice. Like the French, I believe a daily glass of red wine is good for you. But if I choose a martini, it can mean only one thing: danger. Exhausted, full of rage and still wearing my cloak of grief, I was feeling particularly reckless.

I pulled out my BlackBerry and hit a number on the speed dial.

"Hi, Dad, it's Beth."

"Hi, Boo, what are you up to?"

I'm up to no good, Dad. Just like you taught me. Why do you think I thought of calling you? "I'm in Florida for that pie contest. I'm at the bar and I just ordered a martini."

He broke into laughter. I knew he would, which is why I called him. "Good for you. I'm drinking one, too."

I stayed on the phone with my dad longer than I needed, mostly because I noticed that the drunk man sitting next to me at the bar was watching me closely. A little too closely. He was handsome enough, in that former-high-school-jock kind of way, but I wasn't in the bar to pick up men. I tried sending him some telepathic communication: *Dude, trust me. You don't want to get close to me. I am damaged goods.*

Once I hung up with my dad, I avoided the drunk guy's attempt at conversation by giving him curt, one-word answers to his vapid questions like, "What brings you here?" I didn't want to talk. I wanted to drown my sorrows. I had already slugged down the martini and ordered a second one.

Not only was there a pie contest taking place at the hotel, there was a truck supplier convention. I discovered this when a guy came breezing by in a Red Wings hockey jersey wearing a huge name tag around his neck. He was slender, boyish looking but graying at the temples, and had a twinkle in his eye. By his air of confidence and easy smile, I got the immediate sense he was in sales. Part wanting to be saved from the drunk guy, part under the influence of my second martini, and, okay, maybe I was actively seeking trouble, I grabbed his lanyard as he walked by.

"Truck business? Who do you work for?" I asked, pulling his tag closer to read his name, " . . . John?" Marcus had worked for the truck division of his German automotive manufacturer, so anything truck related got my attention. I didn't recognize the name of this guy's company, but we established in the first ten seconds that he did business with Marcus's group, and knew some of Marcus's colleagues. "Do you know so and so?" I asked, referring to the former CEO of the company.

"Yes, I do a lot of business in Portland. I've met him a few times."

"When I used to drop off my husband at work, I would see him standing outside smoking his cigarettes. Since they banned smoking in the office, he didn't have a choice. Seeing as he's German, I'm sure he didn't like that too much."

And that is all it took. There was a connection. To Marcus. There was alcohol. There was flirting. Another round of drinks was ordered. And the next thing I knew I wasn't sharing a room with Gina; I was sharing a bed with John.

Oh, it wasn't pretty. I felt sorry for the guy. He had no idea who he had invited to his hotel room. From the moment he put his lips on mine and his hands reached to unbutton my blouse, the familiar saline eye secretions began—slowly at first, then, as his kisses became more urgent, so did my tears. Soon, I was a sobbing mess. But we were both wasted enough it didn't stop us.

It had to happen sometime. I had to break the spell Marcus had on me. It might as well have been a stranger who I would never have to see again. Before I had a chance to register what had happened, I passed out.

I woke up in the morning with a raging headache and a desperate need to brush my teeth. I snuck out of the room while—*what was his name again?*—John was still asleep and did the walk of shame, three floors down, to the room I was *supposed* to be staying in.

I swiped my card key and let myself in. I was greeted by a cheerful woman in a matching green polka-dot sweater set and skirt.

"Hi, Gina," I said. "I'm Beth." I winced from both my headache and my self-consciousness.

"I was worried about you," she said. "I was up all night wondering where you were."

"Oh, I'm sorry." I sat down on the bed and told her everything. After I finished my sordid, shameful tale, all she said was, "The front desk called an hour ago. Your luggage arrived. I'm off to get a pedicure. Come find me in the spa when you're ready and we'll grab some breakfast."

I was so relieved by her lack of judgment. But inwardly I was judging myself. I was a grieving widow from a good family, who had flown all the way across the U.S. in the name of pie. I was giving a speech on how pie was helping heal my grief. I was going to judge pies. Pie was wholesome and I was invited to the event because I represented that wholesomeness. How could I claim to be pure and good when I was behaving like a slut? Looking at it from another perspective, however, it was even worse than that. It was a wasted opportunity. I hadn't had sex in eleven months and I was too drunk to remember it. Damn. I should have stuck with the wine.

After taking a long shower, I blow-dried my hair—which is of note because I normally never bother to do anything but pull my wet hair into a ponytail. I put on makeup to disguise my tired eyes, puffier than ever from all the crying, the lack of sleep and the horrendous hangover, and headed down to the lobby.

The elevator doors opened on the first floor and there he was—John. My mouth fell open in surprise, but I quickly recovered, pursed my lips and pretended not to recognize him. He was with another businessman, probably a customer. I had only left John's room an hour and a half earlier, but I looked completely different in the daylight. The night before, when we met in the bar, the only thing my expression portrayed was weariness. But by morning, I had put on my game face—namely my power-red lipstick. I was dressed in my fitted "The World Needs More Pie" T-shirt, a slim jean skirt and platform sandals. In spite of my condition, I looked so All-American perky I might as well have been carrying pom-poms. *Rah! Yay! Pie!* The elevator came to a stop. As we stepped out we made eye contact and nodded politely at one another.

Thirty seconds after exiting the elevator, I got a text from him. *You look gorgeous!* he wrote. *See you at the bar tonight?*

Bar? I was on my way to judge pie. And I hadn't even had a cup of coffee yet. No, I wouldn't be going to the bar later. I had to give a speech the next day. I would be going to bed early. And sleeping. Alone.

I found Gina in the spa. Her nails were still drying. "Key Lime Pie," I said, noting how her toes matched the color of her sweater, "a fitting choice for spring in Florida. I like it."

"You ready to check out the pie scene?" she asked. She looked me over, seeing through my extra layer of under-eye concealer, and added, "Don't worry. I scoped it out already. They have plenty of coffee."

We walked the long, wide hallway of the hotel's convention area. I held my gaze up to keep the dizzying bold patterned carpet from making my headache worse. The doors for each break out room were labeled—Pie Judging, Pie Preparation Area, Pie Display and Truck Suppliers' Lunch. My stomach twisted slightly upon reading that last one.

Outside the Pie Preparation Room, Gina and I got our name tags and judging assignments. With a few minutes to spare before eating pie, we strolled through the ballroom filled with red, white and blue balloons, its perimeter lined with work stations and home-kitchen-size ovens where bakers were in action.

A smiling grandmother in new white tennis shoes at one station opened her oven to check the progress of her lemon-custard pie, which looked as well-groomed as she did. She possessed the confidence of someone who knew she had a chance at a blue ribbon.

A young woman from San Francisco, making the triple-berry recipe she said she got from her dad, was struggling with her lattice crust. "It's my first time entering the contest," she told us. Yes, that was self-evident. I wanted to give her some advice—she could have avoided the crumbling dough by adding less shortening. Forget that aiding her would have been in violation of the rules; I didn't want to hurt her feelings or dash her hopes of winning.

Volunteers in black T-shirts and baseball hats that read in bold, white letters "Pie Police" guarded the center space, where long tables were loaded with so many pies they looked as if they might collapse from the weight of all that fruit filling. Under the bright chandelier light, the combination of whipped cream, red cherry and strawberry, orange pumpkin and peach, fluorescent yellow lemon, chocolate shavings, confetti sprinkles, caramel drizzle, mixed nuts and the American flag toothpicks identifying each pie made for a dazzling Technicolor display. Janice would have loved to tape this for the pie show. There must have been over three-hundred pies, and the sight of all that sugar made my stomach twist again.

For the next five hours, Gina and I ate pie. The judging room was filled with round tables, draped in white tablecloths, with pitchers of water and baskets full of forks, piles of napkins and bowls of soda crackers. Attendants walked around the room handing out judging sheets and pencils. After that, they came around with pie. Pie after pie after pie.

Day One out of the three-day contest was dedicated to the commercial division, frozen brands, grocery-store pie. The pies made by the grandmother, the girl from San Francisco and the others toiling away in the Pie Preparation Room would be judged the following day, in the Amateur Division. I didn't sign up for the commercial judging, and wasn't thrilled with the idea of pumping my body full of preservatives and stabilizers, but I didn't argue. I didn't necessarily care, either. I wanted to experience every aspect of the National Pie Championships. I was here to do research. So I took my seat at the apple-pie-designated table and accepted the responsibility, along with each slice.

The judging sheet was a full-page, printed with instructions and blanks to fill in for scoring. We were to consider each of the following: pre-slice and after-slice appearance, overall taste, flavor of filling, mouth feel (thick, thin, smooth, chunky, creamy, chalky, mushy, runny, dry, sticky, etc.), crust (texture, flaky, firm, mealy, soggy, undercooked, overcooked, tasty flavor, does it complement filling), aftertaste, overall impression (After scrutinizing this pie, how memorable is it? Would you buy this pie? Do you want more of this pie?). Rate each question on a scale of one to nine—one being poor; nine, excellent. They didn't say anything about needing to be good at math to be a pie judge, but with this many criteria and corresponding numbers, I regretted that I didn't bring a calculator.

There were at least six judges at each table, including mine. To my left was Miss Michigan Apple, a twenty-year-old beauty queen wearing a rhinestone crown. People kept coming to our table to have their picture taken with her. To my right was a feisty Asian woman who owned a local chain of doughnut shops. We were not allowed to compare notes verbally, but since the officials didn't say anything about eye contact, I exchanged periodic glances with the doughnut lady. Sometimes we raised an eyebrow, indicating a pie was questionable, other times we made gagging gestures, and only a few times did we waggle our heads discreetly to say, "Thumbs up on this one." Mostly, the pies were overly sweet, drizzled with icing or caramel to disguise their artificial flavoring or lack of character.

Four hundred bites of apple pie later, I needed a tongue scraper to get the cinnamon taste out of my mouth. A stomach pump and blood transfusion would have been nice, too. But I was keeping it in perspective, thanking my lucky stars for not being seated at the cream pie table. (Note to self: next time you're going to judge pie, do not drink four martinis the night before.)

To relieve all that ailed me, I went to the swimming pool. I felt so ill, I gave up after two laps of easy breaststroke and plopped in the hot tub. I closed my eyes and tried to recreate the events of the night before—the flight, the lost luggage, the bar. The last thing I remember was being half-dressed, with John holding me tenderly in his arms as my tears sputtered on his white hockey jersey. Come to think of it, he was actually a really nice guy. "Fuck it," I said. I got out of the water and grabbed my BlackBerry off my towel.

"C u after dinner? What time r u free?" I texted with my wet thumbs.

If there's any faster way to kill the buzz of having alcohol-induced sex with a one-night stand, it's spending a second night with that person sober. I felt nothing. No guilt. No elation. Nothing. Except the headache lingering from my hangover. I lay there like a zombie. He might as well have been humping a rubber doll.

"You're making me do all the work," he commented.

I remained silent. As if I wasn't there. And in my mind I wasn't. I was meditating, the way I used to when riding on the back of Marcus's motorcycle through Europe. Once, when returning from a weekend in France and trying to outrun a thunderstorm, Marcus opened up the throttle to 120 miles per hour. I could gauge the speed by how trucks blurred in my vision as we passed them.

We were moving so fast I couldn't read the writing on their sides. To keep myself calm, I adopted an out-of-body technique, imagining I was somewhere else, somewhere where I was still and safe, like wading in knee-deep tropical ocean waters. I used the same relaxation mind control when getting my teeth drilled in the dentist's chair. And I implemented it again while laying beneath this stranger, this man who was not my husband. I didn't have time to dwell on the aftermath of this decidedly unromantic interlude. I had a schedule to keep. By first light I was back in my own room, where I took another long shower, trying to scrub myself clean. What I needed was an appointment at the Korean spa to remove a few layers of regrettably contaminated skin. No, what I needed was for Marcus to be alive. And since he wasn't, I needed to forgive myself. I also needed apples. For my pie speech.

I walked to the nearby grocery store with my empty suitcase-on-wheels and bought nine pounds of Granny Smiths. With my suitcase loaded with fruit, I returned to my hotel room to read my notes for my talk and to peel the apples I was going to use in my on-stage pie-making demo.

"Good afternoon. I'm Beth Howard," I recited out loud to no one while I slid the knife between the waxy green skin and the fleshy fruit. "I had long considered pie to be one of the greatest comfort foods. I even believed pie had the power to heal. So when my husband, Marcus, died . . . " I could tell the story without notes. It was my story. I knew how it went. But I wasn't sure I could tell it on a stage in front of an audience without falling apart. And anyway, the story wasn't finished. Yes, with the help of my pie quest, I was healing, but I wasn't done baking. My grief pie was still in the oven. You could poke a knife in it and tell it was coming along nicely, but it—*I*—needed more time. Well, too bad. I had committed to giving this speech over a month ago. It was too late to back out.

I hauled my apple-filled suitcase onto the shuttle bus for the fifteen-minute ride to the Disney-designed town of Celebration. That's where The Great American Pie Festival, the sister event to the National Pie Championships, was being held. Open to the public, the Pie Festival was a free, family affair with pie-related activities for kids—pie-eating contests, "Piecasso" pie painting and pie tin art. And, for a small fee, there was an all-you-can-eat pie buffet, a whole block lined with tented booths where the commercial-division kind of pies I had eaten the day before were being given away. I had already had all I could eat of those.

In addition to all that, there was free, live entertainment on the main open-air stage—a comedian telling pie jokes, a singer singing pie songs, a team of baton twirlers, a harmonica player and . . . me.

I made my way through the throngs of people in shorts and visors, and found the main stage. "Are you Beth?" a woman wearing angel wings and a walkie-talkie asked.

"Yes, how did you know?"

"Mary asked me to keep an eye out for you. She said to look for a girl in pigtails."

Huh? Mary worked for Bakers Square, the sponsor of the main stage, and she was in charge of the entertainment. I had met her only in passing the night before, and had never mentioned anything about what I would be wearing, let alone my hairstyle. But yes, I did have my hair in stubby little pigtails.

"Where'd you get those cool wings?" I asked.

"I can get you a pair. Follow me."

I followed her to the Green Room behind the stage where the Pillsbury Doughboy was sitting in front of a fan, guzzling water, while his deflated costume sat in a pile next to his chair, the harmonica player was warming up, and the crew from CBS's *The Early*

Show was loading camera tape. The stagehand rummaged through a box and handed me my own pair of wire-formed, chiffon wings— with Bakers Square logos all over them. I was so excited about flying, I didn't mind the advertising. I glanced over at the Doughboy as I slid the elastic straps around my back. He was so hot his hair was plastered against his head. It could be worse, I thought. At least I didn't have to walk around roasting in an oversized space suit posing for pie-festival photos.

You get what you pay for, as the old adage goes. The audience paid nothing. What they got was, well, not much more. I stood squinting against the broiling Florida sun, in the center of the stage, facing a crowd of about eighty people. A year earlier, my husband was still alive and I was working for a speakers' bureau. Now my husband was dead, and I was on the other side of the podium, wearing angel wings and a checkered apron, telling the world what it was like to live without him.

"And now, I'm going to demonstrate some of the pie-making tips I learned when I worked in Malibu."

I moved back from the front edge of the stage to the table behind me that was set up with my ingredients and tools. The apples I had peeled ahead of time, heaped high in a bowl, had surprisingly not turned brown in the Florida sun. Gina had offered to assist me, acting as a pie student. If Janice was the Fairy Godmother of Grief, Gina was the Fairy Godmother of Pie Demos. She kept me on track as my nervous energy threatened to turn my performance into an unintentional comedy routine. "And what's the wine bottle for?" she asked, pointing out the out-of-place prop on the table.

"Oh, I'm glad you asked. That is an example of improvisation. If you don't have a rolling pin, you can always find something to use. A wine bottle works just as well."

With my forehead shining and my armpits soaking wet, the stagehand gave me the three-minute warning to wrap it up. I wrapped. I took my bow. And finally, thankfully, mercifully, it was over.

I gave myself an A for effort, a D for preparedness, a C-minus for execution and a hundred bonus points toward earning the Spurs Award.

Gina and I stayed in Celebration for the rest of the afternoon, watching people eat pie, and then watching the announcement of winners from the day's pie competition. Back at the main stage, we sat in the audience, listening as the executive director of the American Pie Council, Linda Hoskins, called up pie bakers from all parts of the country and handed them prize money and gift baskets.

Michele Albano of Michele's Pies in Norwalk, Connecticut, ran to the stage to collect more than one ribbon. Her excitement was genuine when she bounced up and down over her wins for Twisted Citrus Blackberry and Classic Italian Tiramisu. Another winner was Linda Hundt of Sweetie-licious Pies in Michigan, who teetered up to the stage in four-inch stilettos, poodle skirt and pearls, adding another of many ribbons for her Tom's Cheery Cherry Cherry Berry pie. And no, that pie name is not a typo.

Riding the shuttle bus back to the hotel, I got a text message from John. *My last night here. Would love to see you.*

My answer was quick and clear. I wrote him back, *Sorry. Can't. Have a safe trip home.*

I let go of my regrets about sleeping with him. I understood the meaning of our encounter in the bigger scheme of life. I needed physical invigoration to be reminded I was still alive, still had a life to live and that I needed to give myself permission to live it. John also gave me some important validation that I had not turned into a hideous, repulsive creature. He had been brave enough to kiss a grieving frog to see if she would turn into a ravishing princess. It didn't happen. I had only just begun rewriting my fairy tale and hadn't figured out a new ending yet.

17

A few days after returning from the pie championships, I packed up The Beast again for another road trip to Los Angeles, my second journey there in three months. I had received a call from one of Hollywood's biggest and most respected reality-television production companies and they were interested in making the pie show. And since the RV featured in the show's concept, I was going to bring it along for the meeting.

The friend who set up the meeting for me—and had shown the TV executives the sizzle reel Janice made from the footage we shot in January—informed me ahead of time, "They don't know if you look pretty enough to be on camera. So make sure you get your hair and makeup done professionally before the meeting."

Putting myself in highly stressful situations was becoming a habit. A speech at the pie festival? Sure, what's a little added pressure on top of a huge heap of debilitating grief. A pitch meeting at an A-list production company? Hey, why not drive a thousand miles, only to put yourself in a position to be scrutinized for your appearance. Even with these bulging, puffy eyes? Sure, go for it. My friend's comment sent me into a new form of meltdown mode. "I'm a writer; I'm not used to being judged by my looks," I cried to Nan, Melissa, Alison and anyone else who would listen. "And if beauty comes from the inside, then believe me, I know just how bad I look these days. No amount of time in a goddamned beauty salon is going to help."

But I wanted to sell the pie show, so I did it. As soon as I arrived in L.A., I went to a hair salon for a cut and highlights. "I want to get my hair lightened," I told the stylist with the skintight jeans and exposed bra straps. She insisted dark roots—lowlights, they were called—were in. Were they? I wouldn't have known. "Well, that's nice. But I didn't come in here to copy Jennifer Aniston or whoever is going dark. I came here to get my hair lightened." I got the feeling this gum-chewing stylist was not only young but inexperienced. How else would I have gotten a walk-in appointment in vanity-driven L.A.? Three hours and three hundred dollars later, I exited with dark brown, asymmetrically cut hair.

I dropped by my parent's house. "It's awful, isn't it?" I asked my mom rhetorically, pulling at the choppy, uneven layers. "And it's not even straight."

My mom didn't argue. "It's not the best cut," she said.

"I'm calling the salon. I'm going to make them redo it. I can't go to the meeting with my hair looking like this."

The salon manager gave me a damage-control appointment for the next day. Which would mean another two or three hours in the chair. I was already hating this whole TV show business and I still hadn't found a makeup artist. When I called my sister, who is an actress, and a few other friends for recommendations, estimates for a professionally painted face came in at three hundred dollars and higher.

I finally ran to Nan's house. She was still there for her play—opening night was in a few days. Her dog, a border collie named Olive, had just been diagnosed with inoperable tumors in her stomach. Nan's anxiety was running higher than mine. So we did what best friends from childhood do in difficult times. We went shopping.

"You really need that pink cashmere sweater with the dog on it, honey," I told her.

"And you have to get that necklace with the big blue daisy," she told me.

And so we spent our money and bought ourselves materialistic tokens of happiness.

"Now, let's go to that Thai massage place across the street," she insisted afterward. "It's only forty bucks for an hour."

We locked arms, swung our shopping bags by our sides, and the world felt a little sunnier and safer—and saner—being with my best friend.

On the morning of my TV meeting, I went to Sephora and used all their tester samples to decorate my face with the prerequisite glamour. I wasn't spending another penny on this damn effort. I was representing a pie show, not "America's Next Top Model." As a clever move, I had baked an apple pie for the meeting, so they weren't going to be looking at me anyway; they were going to be ogling over the *real* beauty in the room. Pie was going to be the star of this show.

The parking lot of the production company's warehouselike building was packed with Porsches and Land Rovers, so I had to park the RV down the block. It would never get seen. So much for all that extra gas money I spent driving The Beast down from

Portland. Still, I loved having my own space and sleeping in my own bed. Team Terrier liked it, too.

I waited in the reception area for a few minutes, nervous but confident that I had done everything in my power to make a good impression. Eventually, my pie and I were ushered into the glass-walled office of the Vice President of Development. The VP's name was Dan. He had an immaculate desk, a scruffy beard, a plaid, flannel shirt and an artist's intensity. He was like that Desserted Island pie from the Seattle Pie Company—a quirky mix of everything that somehow all fit together and tasted surprisingly good. Especially good when our small talk led us to the discovery that we were both from Iowa.

"I'm from Sioux City," he said.

"No way!" I replied.

Before I could make my show pitch, we were interrupted by the company's CEO, a young, slick executive in jeans. "I heard there was pie." His eyes scanned the room until they landed on my pie. Dan called his assistant. When she arrived in the doorway, he asked her, "Will you take this to the kitchen and cut slices for everyone?"

Finally our meeting got under way. Dan was intrigued with my idea, about traveling in the RV and interviewing people around the country about pie, but I wasn't expecting his first question.

"Why pie?" he asked.

That answer was easier than getting my hair cut and colored, which, now that I was in their casual, laid-back office, seemed completely unnecessary. I explained my pie-as-metaphor philosophy, about how pie represents generosity, community, healing and could lead to world peace. I delivered the answer smoothly. So far so good. But then he grilled me on a more challenging topic: the chronology of my life.

As he sat behind his desk, eating forkfuls of apple pie, while my slice just sat there on the desk, untouched, I talked at rapid-fire pace about how I went from the dot com job in San Francisco to the pie-baking job in Malibu, to moving to Germany to marry Marcus, to moving to Portland and then Mexico for Marcus's job. Then I got to the part where Marcus got transferred back to Germany last summer and how I didn't go with him. And tears began leaking out from my eyeballs.

I should have been able to tell my story without crying by this time. Sometimes I could, but not always.

So as I sat there in the VP's office, with my newly lightened and shortened hair, wearing my new pink lipstick—unsuccessfully fighting back my tears—I blathered on to the development executive. "Not going with him will always be one of my greatest regrets. After Marcus moved back to Germany, I never saw him again. Until he was lying in his casket." I sniffled and added with a half laugh, "Good thing I'm wearing my waterproof mascara."

Dan was unfazed. "Why do you want to make this TV show?" he asked.

"So I won't have to get a job that confines me to a cubicle," I said. I could tell by his raised eyebrow that he wasn't buying my flippant sarcasm. I continued, a little too honestly perhaps, explaining, "Because I need to get busy. When we were shooting the pilot, I was so interested in all the people I met, good people, and all because of pie. Plus, the shoot and travel schedule kept me completely engaged. It was the best I felt since Marcus died and gave me a purpose to keep going. I want to recreate that feeling."

Then, clearly trying to sabotage any chance of ever working with this company, I spelled it out for him. "If Marcus hadn't died, I wouldn't be sitting here right now. And I would rather

have Marcus alive than trying to sell you some fucking TV show."
The tears spurted out even faster, making little water stains
on my skirt. The only upshot to this was that I was pitching
a reality-television company. And if grief over losing one's
far-too-young-to-die husband wasn't reality, I didn't know
what was.

I wiped my eyes and continued my nervous chatter. I was running off at the mouth so much it was as if someone slipped truth
serum into my coffee that morning. I couldn't edit myself and my
inappropriate comments. I just kept right on going.

"But then, you see?" I held up my hands to him, moving them
up and down to demonstrate unbalanced weight on two scales.
"TV show or suicide? Okay, TV show."

I don't know why he didn't call 911 right then. Maybe because
the pie was so good.

When the meeting was over and I stuck out my hand to shake
his, he pushed it aside and said, "No. Let me give you a hug." So
I hadn't scared him away after all. Still, if I could have repeated the
meeting, I would have scheduled it for a week when PMS wasn't
looming around the corner. "We want to work with you," he continued. "We'll call you to discuss next steps."

I wasn't the only one to get promising news that day. I called
Nan to tell her about my meeting and she in turn told me the first
reviews of her play, "Jawbone of an Ass," had come in.

"We got 'Pick of the Week' in *LA Weekly*. And even the *Los Angeles
Times* had good things to say." She had worked hard and deserved
the accolades. But the good news was tempered by her dog's fail-
ing health and her own dislike for the plastic beauty of L.A. "One
more month here, then we can go back to New York. I just want
to get Olive back, take her to the cabin upstate, so she can live out
her last days where she is happiest."

Yin and yang. Good news, bad news. Life and death. Six months later, Nan would be both preparing to take her play to the Edinburgh Festival and grieving the death of her dog—a sweet, energetic, athlete of an animal who was like a child to Nan and her husband.

♥♥♥

If I thought that selling this TV show was going to make my grief disappear, I was wrong. The ordeal of the trip had left me exhausted.

"Don't underestimate grief," Susan had cautioned me. "Grief is hard work. Even when you're staring at the wall, you're doing the work." I wasn't staring at many walls these days with the recent flurry of travel. I didn't want to go back to Portland, to its dark skies, endless rain and muddy trails. I wanted to be done with Portland. I wanted to be done grieving. But grief wasn't finished with me yet. I couldn't get the rest I needed in L.A. So I pointed the RV north again. I-5 was becoming so familiar to me, I had every pit stop planned, every Starbucks, every In-N-Out Burger, and the best rest stops for Team Terrier.

Going back to Portland wasn't such a bad thing. Alison had emailed me the news that Sauvie Island Farm U-Pick was open for business.

"Strawberry season has arrived," Alison wrote. "We have some pies to make."

"On my way," I wrote back. Strawberry pie did sound very tasty. And I missed Alison's laugh. Maybe going back to Portland wouldn't be so bad. For a while.

♥♥♥

My mind may have been in manic pie mode, but my body was having nothing to do with that. It went on strike, shutting down all work operations. I spent most of the month of June in bed with bronchitis. When I wasn't coughing, I was sleeping for hours on end. I celebrated my forty-eighth birthday—my first birthday since Marcus died—in a Nyquil-induced stupor.

One year earlier, I had celebrated my birthday in Terlingua, Texas, and had thrown a little party for myself. My dad had flown in from L.A., so naturally we served martinis at the gathering. And pie. Banana cream for him and a fresh strawberry one, just because strawberries were in season. Betty, my landlord, had said, "You don't want to spend your birthday making pie. You should get out and do something fun."

"Making pie is fun," I told her. "It's exactly what I want to be doing on my birthday."

"But it's so hot, especially in the kitchen."

"I don't mind. Pioneers didn't have air conditioning and that never stopped them from making pie." I enjoyed pie making so much I barely noticed that the kitchen in my miner's cabin was at least 110 degrees.

Marcus called me from Germany that afternoon; it was bedtime on his side of the world. "Happy birthday, my love," he said, then sang the birthday song, his voice breathy, softer and even sexier than his normal speaking tone. "Say hi to your dad for me. And tell him I look forward to having one of his martinis next time I see him."

About a dozen new friends showed up that evening, the women dressed in skirts and heels, and the men in clean, crisp shirts instead of the usual shorts and Teva sandals. We drank our cocktails and ate our pie on the porch of my rock shack, the hot wind blowing fine, white Texas dust into our drinks.

I have a picture of me taken at the party. I'm in a cotton paisley sundress, standing proudly in front of the pies I made, hands on my hips, smiling brightly and confidently at the camera. Whenever I look at that photo, I see the person I used to be. *That was my life before,* I think. *Before I asked for the divorce. Before The Phone Call.*

Ten months. That's how long he'd been gone. I had secretly given myself a one-year grace period to grieve. That's how they did it in the old country. Widows were expected to grieve for one year. And wear black. And accept sympathy and assistance from others. It was a tradition that dated back to the ancient Romans. (What a coincidence—the origins of pie also dated back to that time, when pie crust was used as a sort of storage container, like Tupperware, to preserve and transport meat. They called pies "coffins" back then. Oh, the irony.)

Grief didn't work like that in the new world. Or in my world. We didn't even wear black to funerals anymore. And mourn for a whole year? We might mourn five years or ten years, but, God forbid we show anything but a happy face in public. The day after the funeral, you pretended everything was normal. You went back to work. If you had a job, that is. Which I didn't.

I hadn't given up on the Spurs Award. But this grief business was a lot harder than summer camp. I had not just fallen off the horse. I had been bucked, kicked, thrown, flung across the arena. I had been trying to catch that horse ever since. Ten seconds is all it took to get back on when I was eight, but at forty-eight, here I was at ten months and counting. I had been sprinting when I should have paced myself for a marathon. The Europeans were right. A year was needed. At least. Then again, Islam allowed widows only four months and ten days to grieve and Hindus didn't believe in expressing sorrow or excessive mourning for longer than thirteen days. They felt it hindered the departed spirit from moving forward on its journey.

Was I doing it right? Was I grieving the right way? Was my grief over the top or was it appropriate? I had asked Susan in my most recent session, as soon as I got back from L.A.

"Grief is an individual thing. Everyone experiences it differently," she said softly. "Yes, you are doing just fine." If anyone would know, it was her. So I took her word for it.

I had plenty of time to think about all this, especially during my lucid dreaming moments in between fever-ridden naps. From my bed, I spent hours looking through the rain-blurred skylight, mesmerized by the cedar branches swishing back and forth in the wind. I wanted the year to be over. Even though I had two months to go, I was ready to get out of Portland—needed to get out—so I started making plans. Ideas began to germinate from my sick-bed. I would move back to L.A., I decided. But first I would take a month-long road trip to Iowa. Iowa was my home state, a place that might help me feel grounded during the one-year anniversary of Marcus's death. Even better, the Iowa State Fair coincided with that dreaded day.

In my outline for the pie TV series, I had included the Iowa State Fair as a stop on the cross-country route. If anyone had pie, it was Iowa. And if there was any pie contest to rival the National Pie Championships, it was the Iowa State Fair. I would volunteer to be a pie judge.

The more I recovered (that is, the less I coughed), the faster I laced up my running shoes, so to speak. My horse was still out there on the loose.

18

Once I had made up my mind to leave Portland, I had a renewed sense of purpose. All my belongings (and Marcus's) would go into storage and not straight to L.A., as I didn't quite know when or where I would land there. Regardless, my mother was already forwarding advertisements for apartment rentals.

"There's a brand-new building across the street from us," she said. "They have bike storage and they take dogs."

"How much?" I asked.

"Eighteen hundred."

"For a studio," I stated flatly. That it was one room wasn't the issue, doubling my rent while still unemployed was.

"It's brand-new. And they take dogs."

"Yeah, you already said that, Mom. I'm going to wait until I get back from Iowa. I may get there and want to keep going, maybe drive all the way to New York and see Nan." It was enough that I had made the decision to leave Portland. I didn't want to be rushed into any new commitments. L.A. would be there—when I was ready.

After storing my belongings and arranging for my friends from Switzerland to drive the RV to L.A., I met with my endocrinologist, who gave me an A on my health report card and a refill on my prescription for the thyroid-replacement hormone I would have to take every day for the rest of my life.

The big finale in Portland—and ultimate health inspection—was meeting with Susan. I drove one last time to her office across the river, passing the Legacy Emanuel Hospital emergency entrance on my way, which given its prominent location next to the bridge, was unavoidable.

I still pictured taking Marcus to Legacy Emanuel for stitches in his finger. He had broken a glass salad bowl while washing dishes one morning before work. I humored him while we waited for the doctor, telling him funny stories and stroking his arm. Our most tender and loving moments were the ones like these, when we took care of each other. After the hospital, we got lattes and croissants at St. Honore Boulangerie before I dropped him off at work with his splinted finger. Good memory. But the picture turned dark when I envisioned him being rushed to the same hospital in the ambulance on August 19, wheeled into the emergency room on life support, life that would last only another few minutes. Those stitches were the reason the hospital had my name on file as the emergency contact. Bad memory.

I parked in my usual guest spot in the covered garage and walked the fifty feet, past the smokers taking a tobacco break, to the building's main entrance. Susan was waiting, like always, in a chair next to the double security door when I arrived. She ushered me into her ground-level office, which I had come to know so well, the one with the dried flower arrangements and the multiple boxes of tissue within arms' reach no matter if you were sitting on the couch or on one of the straight-back chairs. "How's everything going for you?" she asked in her butterscotch-pudding voice. God, I was going to miss that soothing lilt.

I was moving away with only a vague sense of my plans—judge pies at the Iowa State Fair and then what? I couldn't say for sure. Was I ready to leave my nest? No, I was still crying a lot, still immersed in guilt, still missing my husband, still having an impossible time understanding why he died. Ready or not, I had given myself one year, and that was that. Time was up. I was determined to catapult myself forward and put this grief behind me once and for all. But this was Susan, my savior. She had invested many hours in my well-being and I didn't want her to think she was turning me out into the cold prematurely. So I lied. "Everything is great," I said.

She shot me a sympathetic smile and paused before replying. "I am feeling a sense of urgency from you," she said in her slow, deliberate style.

This is what I loved about my grief counselor. She was good at her job. And she had X-ray vision. She saw right through my bullshit.

I looked up at her and laughed nervously. I had been caught. "Yes, I am aware of that," I admitted. I wanted the grief to go away, immediately. Even if it meant leaving a safe place. All I wanted was to outrun the grief that continued to plague me, to escape its talons. I told her, "I remember sitting in your grief support group eleven months ago, listening to people say they lost their spouse one or two years earlier and thinking *That will not be me. I won't be grieving a year from now and needing some support group.* I was wrong." What had been almost a year since Marcus died felt more like a month. Susan nodded, her eyes so full of compassion she was virtually hugging me with them.

She was quiet again before offering her insights. "You are like a trapeze artist. You have to let go of one swing in order to grab the next one. There is that moment of being airborne in between when you are holding on to nothing, and trusting that the other swing will come toward you. That 'in between' is where you are now, grasping for air."

I listened intently, watching and wondering how she was able, session after session, to deliver her questions and advice with such kindness. Was she this caring with all of her clients? She had revealed that her own grief led her to this kind of work, but she would never cross the professional therapist's line and discuss her experience.

I took her comment well, though it was not a stretch, because I knew she was right. Her assessment actually felt like a compliment, considering the day before someone told me I was like the Tasmanian Devil and that even when I stopped my tornado twirl the angry grimace on my face remained.

She continued, "You are very open and don't hide things. You are impulsive but you have wisdom that overrides your impulsiveness. You make good decisions—when you listen to your own voice inside."

I grabbed a fresh handful of tissues and, sitting there on her corduroy couch, wiped my eyes and blew my nose as she talked.

For the grand finale of her dissertation, she said, "You are still vulnerable, but also very brave. It was an honor having you as a client."

I was really sobbing by that point.

I blew my nose once more and then thanked Susan for her brilliance, for the months of wise counsel and for keeping my life from derailing completely. We exchanged a long, tear-filled hug. Her body was soft, vanilla-scented and enveloped me with comfort.

I was wrong when I said she was like a slice of warm apple pie. She was a whole apple pie made with extra apples, butter and sugar.

That was the end of grief counseling. I was on my own from here.

♥♥♥

As part of my farewell tour, I drove up to Seattle to spend a weekend with my brother and his family. One last drive north on this part of I-5, I maneuvered my MINI through the dark alley of tall pines lining the heavily traveled north-south corridor—in the blinding rain. Trucks sprayed my windshield with sheets of water so heavy my wipers couldn't clear my view fast enough. Equally frightening, I felt my tires lose contact with the pavement as they hydroplaned on the flooded highway surface. The over abundance of moisture was one thing I would not miss when I moved.

I arrived in time for my niece's dance recital, held in the auditorium of the high school across from my brother's house. I pulled up in front of Patrick's house and got the usual greeting from Zach and Ben, who in spite of the rain were playing baseball outdoors without coats. I guess you had to grow up in this climate to be immune to its bone-chilling dampness. Seeing them with the ball and leather mitts reminded me of when Marcus played his first—and only—game of baseball in this yard, with these kids. Zach pitched the ball and on his very first swing of his life Marcus connected the bat with the ball. He hit it hard, but not quite straight, so it hit an upstairs window of the house. Nothing broke, but I couldn't set foot in the yard without the scene replaying itself each time.

Inside, Patrick was in the kitchen, drinking a glass of wine. "Hey, Beth, glad you made it in time. We're about to leave for the recital."

I felt my body relax as I looked him up and down. I hadn't realized how tense I was, how I had been bracing myself to see the face of death again. What I saw was the brother I used to know, the one with hair. His eyebrows had grown back, as well as the hair on his arms and some fuzz on the sides of his head. "Oh, you look great!" I couldn't help but exclaim. "Any updates from your oncologist?"

"Thanks. Yeah, I got a clean bill of health, an 'all clear.'"

"Too bad when your hair grew back it didn't fill in the baldness." I had to tease him. The men in our family all went bald in their twenties and they were always making jokes to each other about it. I was grateful he was better. And that I could still poke fun at him.

We piled into his SUV with my sister-in-law, Vickie, and the four kids for the one-block drive to the school.

The last time I had been to my niece's dance recital was five years earlier, her very first performance when she was four, when she still had baby fat on her little body. At nine, she had become long, lanky and muscular, a graceful athlete with big brown eyes and excellent coordination. Moving in unison with her fellow dancers across the stage, leaping, twirling, bending, she was full of strength, beauty and confidence—and some fine dance moves. Given her position in the front of the ensemble, she was also a leader. And I was an aunt full of pride.

When the youngest dancers came on stage for their turn, I remembered watching Eleni in her first recital, a gasp-inducing pageant of cuteness. I could still hear the collective "Awww" from the audience when the baby ballerinas came on stage.

I remembered my own dance recitals from my own childhood. My sister and I spent our entire elementary school years in ballet, tap, jazz and gymnastics classes. Over time we collected trunks filled with tutus, leotards and sequin- and feather-covered costumes, which we used for subsequent backyard talent shows, well-organized events that included choreographed song and dance (thanks to my sister), and profit-earning ticket sales to the neighborhood kids. I marveled now at our pre-Nintendo-era creativity and industriousness, underscoring the advantage of growing up in a place (Iowa) and time (the Sixties) when TV didn't air twenty-four hours a day.

But here, in this Seattle suburb, forty-four years after my own first dance recital, I studied this new crop of wide-eyed four-year-olds. I observed their innocent faces, watching them take in the enormity of their on-stage debuts. This experience was their first time in front of a big audience, first time wearing makeup and princesslike layers of satin and tulle, first time hearing the seductive sound of applause.

My sister remembers her first time on a stage like this. She told me that the feeling was so powerful, so addictive, it formed her entire future. She knew at that precise moment, hearing all that clapping—just for her—at the age of four, she was going to be an actress. And that's what she did, she became an actress, and a successful one at that.

I sat there and wondered what all these little girls were thinking during their moment in the spotlight. Were they so smitten by this glorious attention that they were going to spend their lives seeking to recreate this stage-loving feeling? What would they grow up to be? Would some of them prove to be such talented dancers they end up in the New York City Ballet? Or would some go the other direction, maybe become strippers? Would they become doctors? CEOs? Pastry chefs? Pie bakers? Would they win scholarships to Harvard? Would they get into drugs and drop out of high school? Would they have children? Would they get cancer? Have their hearts broken? Would they become freelance writers who marry sexy, smart German men, work really hard at the marriage, threaten divorce only to lose their husbands to ruptured aortas and become emotionally debilitated grieving widows? Did they have any idea of what life held for them? To look at their beautiful cherubic faces, it was clear. No. They had no clue. Lucky them. Lucky, lucky them.

But it wasn't my musing and memories that stood out. It was one specific moment, a blink-and-you'll-miss-it kind of thing. My niece had spotted me sitting in the second row, next to her dad, and flashed me the biggest, most magnificent smile that said "Look at me, Aunt Beth. Isn't this cool? I'm so glad you're here."

Glad I'm here? I wouldn't want to be anywhere else in the world. That moment, that smile, made me forget about everything else— even if just for a few blissful minutes.

♥♥♥

As the moving boxes began to stack up in my tree house, so did my anxiety about leaving. The more anxious I became, the more I mulled over Susan's parting comments.

She was wrong. I was not a trapeze artist in a midair leap. I was not in that free-floating, faith-challenging, empty air space. I wasn't flying; I hadn't let go of the first swing yet. My fingers were still clutching the bar in a white-knuckle grip, afraid to release, afraid of falling into the abyss (the one I had spent the year living in and had barely begun to climb out of), afraid of the unknown. The longer I sat staring at the stacks of boxes—not to mention, the piles of clothes, dishes and other belongings that hadn't found their way into boxes yet—the tighter I was clinging to the first swing.

I was clinging to the security of my nest. Moving was stressful enough under the best of circumstances, but to be running away from your self with no future in mind? I was clinging to the familiarity of the city (St. Honore Boulangerie where Marcus and I used to go, the ease of driving on Portland's uncrowded freeways). I was clinging to my friends, like Alison, Joerg and Katrin, and many others. The list was long with amazing, kind, loving people who propped me up during my darkest months. They were people I had hiked with, baked pies with, walked the dogs with, gotten drunk with, gone to movies with, cried with, spent holidays with.

I was clinging to the trees—literally—in the forest behind my house, hugging them all, channeling energy from their roots to keep me from blowing off into the atmosphere with the next breeze. I did the hugging thing only when I was sure no one would see me, though the moss and bark that stuck to my hair and jacket afterward might have been telltale signs that I had been communing a little more closely with nature than the average Forest Park hiker.

I was clinging even harder now that I planted a tree in this forest for Marcus. On his birthday, July 2, I planted a baby redwood sapling at the edge of a meadow where Marcus had spent many hours throwing a stick for Jack to fetch. It was a memorial he would have appreciated more than a grave headstone or a park bench with a plaque.

And I was clinging to Marcus. What would happen when I left the place that reminded me most of him? Would my memory fade? Would I forget him? I didn't want to forget him. I was terrified of forgetting him, worried that I was leaving him behind. What would happen to my connection to him when I severed the ties to the places that kept my feelings for him alive? For example, what would happen when I no longer drove past the hospital where he was taken in the ambulance and pronounced dead?

Exactly. I got it. It was time to leave. But for the first time in my free-spirited, nomadic, restless life, I was truly afraid of moving forward.

I needed to let go of the swing. Even skydiving had been easier than this. But then, the one time I went was a tandem jump and the instructor had pushed me out the door of the airplane. *Pushed* me. Once I was airborne, I had no choice. I couldn't climb back into the plane. I was already in a ten-thousand-foot free fall and the launch pad had already flown away. Surrender was my only option—surrender and enjoy the ride. I did enjoy it, from the initial high-speed descent, so fast my cheeks flapped wildly from the force of air, to the screeching speed reduction when the chute opened—yes, it opened—and we drifted in slow motion like a feather until we touched the ground.

A good shove out the Portland door was what I needed.

I had already committed to letting go, to being open to the few seconds of free fall without another swing to grab, because I knew where I was headed for at least the next four weeks—Iowa.

And I was going to be busy. Since my initial contact with her, Food Superintendent, Arlette Hollister, had assigned me to every pie competition at the Iowa State Fair, all seventeen categories. And she had volunteered me to give a pie-baking demonstration on live TV, to promote the fair.

I packed up Marcus's shrine, most of it for storage, except for a large envelope stuffed with photos to take with me. I only had the MINI, which had about 1/100th of the space of the RV. I sealed his red plaid robe in a plastic bag and laid it in one of the boxes. Same with his orange-and-yellow plaid duvet cover. Almost a year later, I was still trying to preserve his scent.

The last thing to pack was the contents of my refrigerator. I had a blueberry pie in the freezer. I knew just who would be the recipient: Susan, of course. What better way to tell her how deeply, eternally grateful I was than with a homemade, handmade pie? Gratitude in a crust.

♥♥♥

Within the first six blocks of the two-thousand-mile trip, any trepidation I'd had was replaced with excitement, a sense of possibility, a sudden surge of freedom. Extracting myself from Portland really was like skydiving—first the anticipation, the terror, the leap of faith, the surrender, all followed by a peaceful calm—and then, once the adrenaline wore off, the exhaustion. I was heading toward Iowa and pie, a lot of pie, so I already had a guaranteed soft, safe landing.

The next four days and thirty hours of actual driving time were a blur. I didn't have the RV, but I had my tent. After an overnight in L.A. to see Melissa and my parents, I spent my first night on the road camping on the Arizona/Nevada border, at a campsite just far enough off the freeway to be quiet, and just isolated enough to be a little scary. It didn't help that Team Terrier acted as sentry, performing all-night guard duty. But the morning made up for the sleepless night when sunbeams crept inside the tent, nudging me to get up. I took the dogs on a hike among the red rocks and sagebrush, breathing in the delicious dryness, my eyes straining to take in the width of the desert canyons and the sweeping views. I was no longer trapped in the darkness of the rain forest, no longer confined to the Grieving Sanctuary—the cloud of grief was lifting just by making a geographical shift.

The second night I stayed in Boulder, Colorado, at the home of an old friend, Patti, an athletic-clothing designer. She was out of town, so I had her bungalow on the quaint, tree-lined street all to myself. Marcus had stayed here when he drove the RV from Portland to Mexico, but this was my first time in her house. I looked around her living room, taking it all in. Marcus had sat on her brown suede couch, he had walked on her orange-and-green geometric-patterned rug, he had used her shower, he had pulled this same white shower curtain shut to keep the water from splashing out. I had forgotten that he had been here, and now I couldn't walk around her house without imagining him in it. I was obsessed.

Patti was another in the seemingly endless list of people who had experienced loss. She had given birth to triplets, who were all off to a good healthy start, and then, without warning, one of them went to sleep and never woke up. The grief cost her her marriage. But a peek inside the boys' room, seeing their bunk beds piled high with stuffed animals, and toy soldiers and SpongeBob figures littering the floor proved her two five-year-olds were thriving. And from the assortment of photos covering the refrigerator, in which Patti's beaming, bright white smile stood out, she was now thriving, too. Resilience was possible. She was living proof. I was sorry not to see her and her radiant smile in person.

Ancient glaciers had served as nature's rolling pins and done an expert job, because from Boulder onward, the landscape flattened out like rolled pie dough. The expansiveness of the farmland—open, free, unobstructed—allowed the mind and the soul to open up along with it. The hues of corn-husk green, prairie-brown and periwinkle-blue were straight out of a Grant Wood painting. I felt my body relax.

The road signs indicated Iowa was getting closer. Council Bluffs: 80 miles, then 30 miles, then 4 miles, and the next thing I knew I was driving across the Missouri River. An overhead sign halfway across the bridge read "Iowa: A Place to Grow." It did not say "A Place to Grieve." A lump in my throat grew as I landed on the other side of the river. Not that the Nebraska side looked any different than the Iowa side one hundred yards behind me, but it was *Iowa*. It was home. I could almost feel little stubs protruding from the soles of my feet. Roots. I doubt my mom felt this way when she crossed the state line with me in her womb forty-eight years earlier. She had wanted to stay in California, in that ocean-front apartment. But this was not my mother's life and I was not my mother.

There was nothing between Council Bluffs and Des Moines, except for farms—red barns, white wooden farmhouses and fields divided by gravel roads exactly one mile apart. There was so much space here, yet every inch of it was filled with life. Each acre of black topsoil hosted tilled rows of plants, nourishment, crops of corn and soybeans, all growing, ripening, flourishing. Each barn was home to stalls of animals, sows and cows, all fattening up, preparing to feed a nation.

It was everything I had remembered, and then some. I had forgotten about the smell. Not just the earthy scent of fertility, but the strong stench of the pigs. You knew when you were passing a pig farm without seeing it; the odor was so intense you could almost taste the manure in your mouth. At the first whiff, I rolled down the windows to introduce Team Terrier to my home state. As they got hit with their first blast of farm air, their noses twitched, they both tilted their heads back, and seeing as they view manure of any kind as a delicacy, they made loud hungry, sniffing noises.

"Hey, guys," I told them with a laugh. "Welcome to Iowa." We were still a few hours from Des Moines but I was already feeling the Hawkeye state wrap its arms around me in a hug. And I hadn't even had a piece of pie yet.

CHAPTER

19

Meg Courter and her husband and two teenage kids live in the manicured suburb of West Des Moines. Meg and I were friends and fellow cheerleaders in high school and, with the exception of our twenty-fifth class reunion five years earlier (which was the last time I had been in Iowa), I had barely seen her since we graduated. But Meg embodied Iowa hospitality and when she heard I was coming for the state fair, she insisted I stay with her.

"But I'm going to be there for two weeks," I reminded her. "And I have two dogs."

"We have a dog, too. I'm sure it'll be fine."

And it was fine—from the minute I walked in the door of her colonial-style home and stepped into the Arctic air-conditioning.

I unpacked my gear in her guest room, changed into a fresh T-shirt and continued on my pie quest without delay. I drove the ten miles from Meg's, across the state's capital to the east side of town, passing the modest, medium-size high-rises of a burgeoning downtown dominated by the shimmering gold dome of the state capital building. Eventually, I crossed a big set of railroad tracks and arrived on the "other" side of town, where pie was waiting.

The fairgrounds came into view, first recognizable by the looming grandstand, an old brick monstrosity of a stadium. Starting six blocks from the entrance, private homes offered parking on their front lawns. People held up "Park Here" signs, waving them to lure cars—and money. The Iowa State Fair started long before people drove cars to the grounds, and enterprises springing up from the annual event, like front-lawn parking lots, have evolved more than the fair itself.

From the minute I set foot onto the fairgrounds, I was filled with a giddiness I hadn't expected. First of all, I hate crowds. I prefer solitude with occasional but controlled social gatherings. Secondly, I am not a big junk-food eater. But once I showed my all-access judges' wristband at the ticket booth, I had crossed some kind of line, entering a Magical Kingdom of the Midwest, where everything I thought I hated became some kind of psychedelic feel-good drug—and highly addictive.

I had been to the Iowa State Fair when I was about ten. Our family piled in the station wagon and came to see the Osmonds in concert. I don't remember anything about it. So I was essentially a state-fair virgin.

A green-and-yellow John Deere combine caught my eye. You couldn't miss the thing. It was as big as a two-story house and cost about as much. I walked over and stared up at it, its long arms outstretched as if about to harvest corn, its rubber wheels taller than me. Another machine, with a red "corn head" implement that harvests a dozen rows of corn at a time, was so huge each of its twelve torpedo-shaped blades in the front was bigger than a human. The way the blades lined up made the thing look like a menacing, civilization-destroying claw. There was a whole field filled with similar sci-fi-esque machinery, making the place look more like a movie set for *Transformers* than a state-fair exhibit. Visitors were welcome to climb all over them. So I did. On top of a combine, I met a farmer named Tim, who explained how the corn goes into the hopper and gets husked and processed all with this one $250,000 machine.

I was sidetracked further by food. I had learned the hard way at the National Pie Championships that it's best to eat a solid meal that includes protein before tasting all that pie. Not that fast food from a state fair constitutes a solid meal, but when I saw people walking around with their various meals on a stick—pork chops, roasted corn, ice cream bars, fried Twinkies—I was reminded that I needed to eat. I randomly picked one of the hundreds of food stalls and placed my order. Never have I eaten such a delicious corn dog—on a stick!—in my life. The corn bread was so thick it actually resembled, well, corn bread. And the hot dog inside was plump, salty and smoky.

The fair and all its vibrant primary colors was a bustle of activity—namely, farm girls strutting around in denim cutoffs and cowboy boots, families pushing baby strollers, and farmers, like Tim, in their baggy jeans and work boots. A general air of excitement was luring me deeper into its grasp, like a vortex of Americana.

But I was on a schedule. I had my first pie-judging event and I needed to get to my post.

Inside the cavernous metal warehouse structure that is the Elwell Family Food Center, I walked past the aisles of refrigerated and well-lit display cases that would eventually be filled with the winning food items for the public to view. I breezed past the curtained-off sections that served as a secure staging area for the pies, pickles, banana bread, meatballs, jams and other foods that were waiting to be judged. The section was heavily guarded by fair employees. I also caught a glance of the judging area, three separate areas divided by blue velvet curtains, where rows of chairs lined up to face the long tables where judges sat.

I finally found "Arlette's Corner," marked as such by a sign taped above a desk to the cinder-block wall. And there was Arlette herself, an elegant, tall, smiling, grey-haired woman in a denim jumper with sophisticated spectacles resting low on the bridge of her nose. After a warm "hello," she got straight down to business.

"Here's how it works," she explained of the pie judging. "You'll take a seat in one of the chairs at the judges' table. I'll come over and introduce everyone on the panel. I'll pass the microphone down the line so each of the judges can say something about their background. We wheel in the pies on a table and each judge will get to view the whole pie first, then cut their own slice. There are pie servers and utensils on each table."

"How many pies are in each category?" I asked.

"That depends," she said. "People can enter the contest up to fifteen minutes before it starts. Okay, let's get you over there. The chicken-pot-pie contest is about to start."

Over the next eleven days of the fair I would be judging every one of the seventeen pie contests on the schedule. There would be a few days off, meaning on most days I would have more than one contest to judge.

I found a seat at the front table in Judging Area One and watched the flurry of activity around me. A white-haired woman wearing brand-new high-tech running shoes, a smocklike dress and an apron pushed a long table on wheels loaded with pies. Donna, identified by her name badge, maneuvered the table as if she was wheeling a gurney into the emergency room. She must have been in her late eighties, but she had the strength and speed of a thirty-year-old. Arlette's assistant, Shari, laid out forks, pie servers, napkins, wet washcloths and pitchers of water (to cleanse the palate) in front of each of the six judges. She would later bring each of the pies over, one at time, for our scrutiny.

There were two significant differences from the judging format of the National Pie Championships. One was that each judge had a "writer," someone to literally write down your scores, comments, do the math and turn in the judging sheets. I didn't really see the point of this, especially compared to the brain-numbing addition of scores in the national contest's more elaborate point system. But whatever. We were at least allowed to talk and share opinions so it made for some pleasant camaraderie up there in front of the audience. That was the other thing: we were judging in front of an audience. This means that the people whose pie you were judging could observe you as you nibbled, chewed, smacked and, sometimes, spit out their precious contender.

Patt, my writer, had worked at the state-fair food competitions for many years. She took her annual two-week vacation from an accounting firm just to be sitting at this table. She was teaching me the ways of the event. "There are lip readers in the audience," she cautioned me, "so when you make your comments to me to write down, cover your mouth with your hand so they can't see what you're saying."

Really? People take their pies that seriously? But if I thought that was slightly extreme, I was in for a bigger surprise when it came to the judges and their level of seriousness. When each judge had finished tasting the entire lineup, each of the contestants' pies were sent to yet another table behind the blue drapes. The judges got up from their chairs, parted the curtains and disappeared in the back to deliberate on which pies should be placed first, second and third. This meant tasting each pie again—as if we hadn't already tasted enough—and often resulted in as long as twenty additional minutes of heated discussion, debating the pros and cons—and the minutiae—of each and every pie. "This crust was soggy." "That crust was too salty." "This filling was too sweet." "Too tart." "Too runny." "Too dense." "Not State Fair ribbon worthy." "Too hard for anyone to duplicate the recipe." "This one should be first place." "No, this one should be first and that one should be second." And so it went, without regard to the time or keeping things on schedule.

None of the judges were pastry chefs or bakery owners, but many of them held food-science degrees from Iowa State University. And only a few of them were under the age of sixty-five. I'm not a patient person by nature. I also spent time working as a web producer in the lightning-speed Internet industry. So to stand behind the curtain, knowing there was an audience waiting for a winner to be announced, was an exercise in restraint.

After several days of these behind-the-curtain delays, I de-cided it was time to liven things up. We were deliberating the French Silk category. I agreed with the old biddies, this was a close race. The pies were all so good, the pudding so chocolaty, the cream so lightly whipped, I broke my two-bite-maximum rule and indulged until my brain was buzzing from the sugar. I literally felt high. The pie was so intensely delicious that each bite made my eyes roll back in my head with pleasure. Tasting the flavor and feeling the texture melting in my mouth was the pie equivalent of having an orgasm. I had never had such good sex—I mean, pie. While any one of these totems to the chocolate gods could have taken first place, there was one in particular that stood out to me. It was made by Lana Ross, from Indianola. If you have ever judged, or even watched the judging, at the Iowa State Fair, then you would know her name. She was a regular blue-ribbon winner year after year. And having tasted her French silk, I could see why.

"Ladies," I declared to the group behind the curtain, interrupting them from their anal cavity inspections. (They were lifting the glass pie plates off the table to view the bottom crust. They were prodding the filling with their forks. They were taking five extra bites of each pie.) "I think this one should get first place." I pointed to Lana's pie which sat among the twenty other chocolate-cream sirens. No one looked up. So I continued.

"This is a pie I would like to rub all over my body."

No response.

"And have a man lick it off."

Still nothing. Apparently none of these women had ever thought of pie in this way. No one acknowledged my comment. They didn't even bother to give me a disapproving glance.

The way to speed things along, I discovered, was simply to defer to the elders. There was an obvious hierarchy of judges. Since several of the judges had been around for as long as the fair itself—dating back to 1886—certain individuals had seniority and therefore their opinions were expected to hold more weight. So, with a disdainful sigh, I said, "Whatever you think, Eleanor." And that settled it. Lana Ross's French Silk Better-than-Sex pie took second place and a red ribbon. I made a note to ask Lana for the recipe.

The "Oh My, It's Peach Pie" category was a decidedly easier and lighter affair to judge. For one thing, the sponsor, Neal Rhinehart of Marshalltown, Iowa, had set clear contest guidelines. Pies had to be made with a double crust—no crumble toppings, no whipped cream or meringue, just classic peach pie. Yum. He also hand-selected his own judges, inviting his friends and family members to take part, therefore if anyone had seniority on this panel, it was Neal.

I liked Neal, not just because he was a jovial, pie-loving guy, but because another one of his contest guidelines was that all pie would be given away afterward—to the audience. He had even brought his own paper plates and plastic forks. Now *this* was the spirit of pie. What was the point of having people watch you, as a judge, eat bite after bite of some very good pie (and some really bad pie) only to see the unfinished pies wheeled back to the holding area behind the blue iron curtain? It didn't seem very Iowa-like. Pie is meant to be shared. I was going to have to talk to Arlette about this and lobby for some sweeping changes to the food competitions next year.

We chose the peach pie winners quickly. It was easy when you could immediately eliminate the pies that tried to pass off peach JELL-O as pie filling. I had set my own guidelines: if you used packaged pudding mix, you were disqualified from the running. Except for the categories sponsored by companies that made packaged pie crust, a "state fair worthy" pie should be made from scratch.

Working side by side with Neal, I cut slices as fast as I could, while he handed out the plates to the crowd swarming around the table. It was like National Pie Day in L.A. on a microscale, but no less fulfilling. Seeing the smiles of the people as they shoveled peach pie into their mouths would remain one of the highlights of the entire fair for me.

Taking a break from pie, I wandered around the fairgrounds and was reminded that pie was not the only thing being judged at the Iowa State Fair. I wandered over to the cattle barn. The wooden structure, stretching a city block long, was filled with a pungent, grassy scent, and the soothing sounds of cows mooing. (Not the dying cow mooing sound of grief I was capable of, but instead a calm, contented one.) The place was full of people, animal breath, hay and, yes, manure. As I strolled up and down the cow-filled aisles of the barn, watching where I stepped so I didn't soil my new Converse sneakers, I noticed cots and bedrolls set up right inside the animal stalls. The dedication was incredible—the owners of the show cows slept in the barn with their livestock. I've never known a baker to sleep next to their pies, but then after witnessing the intensity of the pie judging, I wouldn't be surprised if some did.

I talked with a man who was washing down his cow with a hose. "Are you getting him ready to show?" I asked.

"No, we just showed him. I'm washing off the hairspray," he replied.

Huh? There were two reasons for the use of this beauty product, I learned, and it depended on the breed and what characteristics were being judged. In one case, it was used to smooth down the cow's hair to accentuate the bone structure and muscles. In the other, it kept the cow's hair fluffed up and made the animal look fatter, impressing the judges. Kind of like how a top crust of a pie can make a pie look like it has more filling than it really does.

The cows got pedicures, too, their hooves filed to perfection and oiled to look extra shiny and healthy. Before the showing and after the post-show shower, the cows also got blow dried. These were some very pampered cows. Who knew?

For showtime, the cows were led from the cattle barn to the arena, where people filled the stands. A lot of people. Apparently cows were more popular than pie. Once inside the arena, the cattle—white cows, brown cows, black-and-white cows, horned cows—waited behind their equivalent of the blue velvet curtain until it was their turn in front of the judges. Judges were predominantly male, and many of them wore cowboy hats. Did they enjoy scrutinizing cows as much as I enjoyed tasting different pies? From their intense expressions, the cow officials took their jobs even more seriously than the pie ladies. And well they should as the prize money was in the quadruple digits.

Instead of sampling one bite at a time, the judging panel observed young people in white jeans and burgundy polo shirts take turns parading their bovine beauties past their table in the center of the arena. White jeans in a dirt and manure-filled stadium didn't seem like a logical wardrobe choice, but it was obviously the mandated uniform. The judges, stone faced and silent, made notes on their clipboards.

Cow judging was not only more serious and more lucrative than pie, it was also much speedier. I stayed long enough to see prizes awarded to a few winners—ribbons presented by young women wearing strappy sundresses, flip-flops and rhinestone-encrusted tiaras. I found the whole thing fascinating, but I was still devoted to pie. And there was still plenty more to taste.

Back at the Elwell Family Food Center, it was time for the Apple Pie category. This contest was sponsored by the American Pie Council, the same organization that holds the National Pie Championships. Donna in her running shoes wheeled out yet another gurney—I mean, table—filled with pies, unloading only about twelve pies for this session. With my stomach swelling from the excess calorie intake, I began to look forward to the categories with fewer pies. (I was already dreading the one later that had over three-hundred entries.) For the apple contest, pie makers had taken the classic apple pie and put their own decorative spin on it. One had a top crust made from cut-out stars covered in white sugar. Another had walnuts and a caramel drizzle on top of the crust. And another had an apple decoration made from red and green sugar.

Apple is the pie I am known for. It's what I make most often, because apples are readily available. It's a pie I can make without a recipe, and pretty much everyone loves apple pie, so I can take it anywhere and always have appreciative recipients. So for the apple pie judging, I heartily dug in, taking generous bites of each. I was not disappointed.

I continued nibbling on forkfuls of apples, sugar and cinnamon, searching for the nuances that might make one stand out above the rest. It was not always easy. Seeing as I have a bias against nutmeg—I find it overpowers every other flavor—those were the first to get ruled out. But I have nothing against butter, so when a few of them left that rich feeling on my tongue, I set them aside as ones to keep in the running. As always, another behind-the-curtain discussion and re-tasting ensued, but the decision came a little quicker. The winner had baked the pie to an ideal golden brown, did not oversweeten the apples, had cooked the apples until they were tender but still had some firmness and substance, and created a delicious flaky crust. (I found many of the state-fair pie crusts to be overly salty.)

It was my turn as a judge to announce the winner. I took the microphone and explained to the handful of people in the folding chairs, and some standing in the back, how we had come to our decision, how we liked the pie's balance between delicate and hearty, fruity and buttery. I reached for the information card attached to the pie, turned it over to read the name, and when I looked up to see the winner I expected to see a grandmother, or a housewife, or a young college girl. But, no. The winner was a fourteen-year-old boy. By the way he came running up to the judges' table to accept his ribbon, he was as surprised as anyone at his win. His hair was in a buzz cut and he had a mouthful of braces that reflected the fluorescent lights of the Food Center.

Trying to hide my incredulousness, I asked him, "How did you learn to make such good pie?"

"From my grandma," he beamed. He took his ribbon and found his mom in the audience who had the grandma on the other end of the cell phone, waiting to hear the news from her pie protégé.

The days ticked by in a busy, pie-gorging blur. I had barely thought about Marcus, or at least not about the anniversary I was dreading, which was in just a few more days. I had made the right, strategic choice in coming to Iowa; the state fair was the Ultimate Distraction Zone. I had just a few more contests to go, enough to make me confess something I had hoped never to say: I was getting tired of eating pie.

CHAPTER

20

The day I was dreading had to come eventually—August 19. It was the day I had planned my entire trip to Iowa around; the avoidance of it was my reason for coming to the state fair. By chance, the nineteenth was one of the few days when no pie contest took place. Chance? Yeah, right. The grief gods were letting me take this game of evasion only so far.

I woke up at 8:03 a.m. The sun was shining, the humidity high, the heat penetrated the fields of growing corn as I lay in bed, snuggling with Team Terrier, one dog's belly under each hand. With my head still on the pillow, I watched the digital clock on the bedside table as the numbers ticked by until they reached 8:36 a.m.—6:36 a.m. Pacific time—the time that exactly one year ago was stamped on Marcus's hospital report. The number was printed right there in black ink, next to the words Pronounced Dead.

I hated knowing the time down to the exact minute. I hated knowing the date, too, as the nineteenth of every month will always remind me of losing Marcus. Most of all, I hated that Marcus was gone.

My one-year grace period of grief was officially over. One whole year. Reaching the one-year mark of Marcus's passing was not like crossing the finish line of a marathon, where all that hard work and strenuous effort was magically, instantly, behind me. No one was handing me a shiny medal or taking a victory shot with my winning time displayed in the background. There was no finish line for grief. What I could see, as I lay there in bed, watching the clock, was that grief was a lifelong marathon, the training would never end. I would just have to continue building up really, really strong muscles over time.

I stayed in bed as the digital numbers moved toward nine o'clock. I was still aware that even without a medal or a souvenir photo or a Spurs Award, I had accomplished something really big in the past twelve months. I had never been in a race like this one. I had wanted to quit—really quit—many times. If not for Susan's counseling, and my two dogs who depended on me, I'm not sure I would have made it through those first few months. But there I was, in Des Moines, Iowa, in the guest room of a high school friend, lying in bed, staring at the clock. I was alive. I was healthy. And I had to figure out how I was going to spend this day.

I got dressed and, after walking the dogs and making coffee, I did something I never do: I went to church. I drove downtown to the St. Ambrose Cathedral. I wasn't seeking religion. I had already tried that. I merely wanted to go somewhere to symbolize my lost love with burning light. And I knew Catholic churches always guaranteed a ready supply of candles.

I left the bright and hot outdoors and entered the quiet church, stopping for a minute to let my eyes adjust to the darkness. I felt the coolness of marble and stone on my skin, and inhaled the incense that evoked a latent memory of attending Sunday mass with my family. I wandered around the back of the cathedral until I found several religious shrines with rows of votive candles burning in front of them. I chose the statue of Mary as Marcus's anniversary shrine. Mary was holding her baby, and babies represented the circle of life. People are born, people live, people die, new people are born. We all fit into this cycle. It's just that some, like Marcus—or one of Patti's triplets or Kathy Eldon's son Dan—died sooner than we could ever dream.

I lit a candle and said a prayer of gratitude. "Thank you for the time I had with Marcus," adding, as if backpedaling on the compliment, "even if it was cut short." I still missed Marcus, still loved him, still grieved him, but I had made the choice to keep living, to thrive and to eat pie.

I wiped a few tears away and reminded myself that Marcus would want me to keep going. And he would like having candles lit in his honor. After watching the candle burn for a few minutes, its flame flickering among the fifty or so other lit candles, I slid a five-dollar bill in the collection box and left.

I received many phone calls during the day. Joerg called from Portland, then Alison, Nan, Melissa and, later, my mom. Each phone call produced a few more tears. I was touched by everyone's kindness—and more than appreciating their care for me, I appreciated their acknowledgment of Marcus. The biggest gift to me was that they remembered him. I didn't want anyone to forget him. I wouldn't let them forget. I was his conduit, the keeper of the Marcus flame. It's the least I could do for him.

I went for a long sweaty walk with the dogs that afternoon, and that evening I went out with Meg and some of her girlfriends for drinks at a bar in the suburbs. I ordered a martini. I wasn't feeling dangerous. I wasn't feeling self-destructive. There was certainly no possibility of a one-night stand on the horizon. I ordered a martini simply because I felt like having one. In between the small talk with the girls, I made a silent toast to Marcus. "Here's to you, my love. I miss you."

And that was my day. Except for watching the clock in the morning, I didn't spend too much time reliving every detail of that harrowing day and the following ones. I had chosen to spend this dark anniversary in a light place. I had driven 1,700 miles to be in Iowa, to be surrounded by old friends and familiar scenery, to be nurtured by the pastoral landscape and its wide-open horizons, to be—in a word—home.

The anniversary wasn't as bad as I expected. It was even slightly anticlimactic. Really. Was all that anticipation for nothing? Or was I starting to heal?

CHAPTER

21

This is what my life had come to: grieving widow uproots herself from the security of her Portland home to travel across country in her MINI Cooper with two dogs and a bin of pie-baking supplies and in the midst of judging pies at the Iowa State Fair ends up at the Des Moines, Iowa, headquarters for *Better Homes and Gardens* magazine to have her photo taken for the November issue. How did I end up *here?*

The *Better Homes and Gardens's* assistant deputy editor, Kelly Kegans, is how. Kelly had found my blog and wanted to mention it in the magazine. She had contacted me when I was still living in Portland and when I realized I was going to be in Iowa a few months later, I let her know. At which point she asked if I would come to their offices and give one of my pie-baking classes. And, as long as I was there, have my photo taken for the magazine.

Yeah, okay.

But when I said yes, I didn't plan on the shoot taking place the day after Marcus's one-year D-day anniversary. My eyes weren't as puffy these past few weeks as I hadn't been crying as often, but I did plenty of sobbing on the anniversary. Every time I got a sympathy call or a condolence email, my eyes welled up again, until they were back to their "new normal" swollen size. Not to mention, I didn't sleep very well after having that martini followed by a few glasses of wine.

It was with these freshly swollen eyes I entered the sleek offices of Meredith Publishing. I signed in at the reception desk and was provided with a trolley for carting my pie supplies down a long corridor to the test kitchen where both the pie class and the photo shoot would take place.

If everything leading up to being here wasn't unfathomable enough, standing in the test kitchen at this legendary publishing company really made me shake my head in disbelief. Immaculate and new, this was the kind of million-dollar designer kitchen you see only in magazines. With the long granite countertops perfect for rolling dough, stainless steel appliances, recessed lighting and an entire wall of windows, it was also a pie maker's dream. But it wasn't the physical kitchen space that impressed me; it was the fact that my mother's banana cream pie recipe originated here. Not in this modern, updated kitchen, of course, but in this building, under this roof. Des Moines, Iowa, was where the red-and-white-checkered cookbook was written and all the recipes in it tested more than fifty years ago. And now I was going to be teaching people who worked here how to make apple pie? Really, life was getting stranger by the minute.

First things first. A makeup artist was on hand to transform my casual, rather ragged appearance into something worthy of a national glossy magazine. Yeah, good luck with that.

Kelly, a fiery red head with curly locks cascading off her shoulders, sat nearby and watched (simultaneously keeping up with her workload by using her iPhone) while Mary-Kate, the professional makeup artist, applied copious amounts of foundation, concealer, eye shadow and blush to my face. This was all unnatural enough for my plain taste, but when Mary-Kate pulled out little containers of tiny fake hair—false eyelashes, to be applied in individual clumps—I had to stop myself from bolting from the chair. I looked over at Kelly, feigning agony, and mouthed the words "What the . . .?!" She laughed—though I detected a trace of empathy.

Mary-Kate said, "Don't worry. You will look perfectly natural in the photos. Even Gayle gets false eyelashes for her picture." The Gayle she was referring to was the magazine's editor-in-chief, Gayle Butler. I had seen Gayle's picture and indeed there was no trace of stagelike makeup or false eyelashes. In fact, she looked fresh-faced and beautiful.

"Okay," I relented. "If Gayle does it, then fine."

After she glued on the lashes, I blinked my eyes rapidly and hummed the "I Dream of Jeannie" theme song. I'm not sure if Mary-Kate appreciated my joke, but she tolerated my intolerance of her craft. In the scheme of things, I could at least admit that getting my hair and makeup done for the magazine shoot wasn't nearly as bad as my stress over having it done for the TV show pitch meeting.

I have always prided myself on how I've lived my life "naturally," as an athlete, camp counselor—and one summer as a wilderness ranger. My sister, the soap-opera star, was always the glamorous one. I rarely wore makeup and, with the exception of hosting the inline-skating show, I didn't seek out media attention. My career was focused on getting *other* people in front of the camera. It was ironic that at a time I looked my worst, I was finding myself more and more frequently with a lens pointed at me or making public appearances. I could only surmise it was a good thing. For one, I was forced to smile. My dad, the dentist, always told me, "It takes twenty-seven less muscles to smile than to frown." I could stand to save energy and do more smiling. Even if I had to be an actress. If I acted happy enough, healed enough, maybe I would convince not just an audience but myself that I was okay.

The plan of the day was to do the photo shoot with me first, then have me give a pie-baking lesson for the *BH&G* editors in the test kitchen. But life—whether in the magazine world or otherwise—rarely goes according to plan. After the makeup was applied and the shine on my forehead doused with an extra brush of powder, the photographer did not show up as scheduled. He was delayed by a high-maintenance super model he was shooting for the cover, some brown-skinned bird who took longer in the oven than expected. The magazine editors began filing into the test kitchen, ready to make pie. So that's what we did. We made pie.

I shouldn't have been wearing the purple long-sleeved sweater I brought for the photo shoot during my pie class—I never make dough with long sleeves—but with no time to change clothes, I jumped right into instruction mode.

"First measure two and a half cups of flour into the bowl, then add a stick of butter," I began. I ran up and down the long kitchen counter, supervising the dough mixing of eight magazine staffers. "This is not bread!" I reminded them. "If you feel the urge to knead, then don't make pie, make cinnamon rolls."

One of the editors, who was known to her fellow staff as "quite the wordsmith," said, "It's like you want to *fluff* the dough."

"Yes, fluff. That's a great word. I'm going to use that from now on," I told her. She nodded and kept . . . well, fluffing.

One "student" was working her dough so hard she was strangling it. I could see the innocent flour and fat struggling to resist her heavy handedness and, like a battered child, build up an irreversible toughness. I gave her a stern reprimand. "Take. Your. Hands. Out. Of. The. Dough. Now." I found out later she was one of the chief bakers in the test kitchen. I said to Kelly later, "Why didn't you tell me? I am so embarrassed."

"I didn't know, either," she said.

I got a stern reprimand of my own when Mary-Kate came over and looked at my face. "Tsk, tsk, tsk. Look at you," she said, shaking her head. I was a melted mess, mascara was running off my eyes, and my face was so sweaty and shiny (from all that supervising and sticking my head in the oven) you could see your reflection in it. She came back with her giant powder brush to touch up my nose and forehead, and then brought over her lint roller to get all the flour off my sweater.

At last the photographer and art director arrived on the scene and the shoot began. They had me peel apples, but when the photographer asked me to look at the camera and not at the apple while holding a knife in my hand and peeling, I once again shot a look at Kelly. "Hey, when I signed that photo-release form, did that also include a release of liability for any injury caused by my paring knife?"

The shoot went fine—I smiled on cue, I peeled ten apples and the pies from the class all turned out looking so picture perfect they were used in the photo shoot. The pies were so pretty, brown and steaming, they should have appeared on the magazine's cover instead of the turkey. Everyone knows pie is the best part of Thanksgiving.

Two days later, I was in the shower at Meg's and looked down at my chest, where I saw what looked like a small-but-dead black bug. After a second glance I realized, no, it was not an insect. It was a false eyelash that had come unglued from my eyelid. The sight of it made me laugh. I almost kept it as a souvenir. Not only was the experience of being in the famous cookbook's kitchen a privilege, I had proof that, with enough makeup, I could still pass for something other than a weary widow.

CHAPTER

22

I didn't know yet where I was going after the state fair. The fair had pumped me up, fueled my spirit with life, but like attending a big trade show or working a sales convention—or skydiving—when the adrenaline high from "being on" inevitably wore off, the burst of energy was replaced with a heavy wave of fatigue.

Regardless, I was determined to make it down to the southeast corner of the state for a tour of my childhood homes in Ottumwa before moving on to my next adventure.

Ottumwa, my birthplace, lies ninety miles southeast of Des Moines. It is not only where I was introduced to life—from birth to bike riding to *The Brady Bunch*—it is where I was introduced to pie. I might have maxed out on pie at the fair, but by God, I wasn't going to leave Iowa without sampling a slice of banana cream from the Canteen Lunch in the Alley.

I pointed my MINI south on Highway 163, and within a mile of leaving the Des Moines city limits, urban life vanished, and was replaced by All Things Rural. The sudden falling away of civilization was a foreign concept after living in the heavily populated sprawl of the West Coast, where one city limit and strip mall merges right into the next. The only thing I would see for the next hour and a half was corn.

Halfway to Ottumwa, I took a quick detour off the highway to a town called Pella, a Dutch settlement famous for its window manufacturer, its springtime tulip festival, wooden shoes and its European bakeries. In the spirit of retracing my childhood haunts, I pulled into Pella's town square and found Jaarsma Bakery, where I had developed a love for Dutch letters, an S-shaped pastry filled with almond paste. Eyeing the pastry display case like a hungry kid, I wanted to buy one of everything—butter cookies, cinnamon bread, apple rings, chocolate-dipped almond sticks and, of course, Dutch letters. But after two weeks of eating all that pie, I was able to exercise restraint and bought only two big S letters—one for an afternoon snack, the other for breakfast. On the other hand, given the dearth of stores or truck stops or anything, for that matter, in this remote corner of the state, I might have been wise to stock up on at least a dozen in case of a roadside breakdown.

I continued on 163 South and noted how the landscape became increasingly hilly. Make no mistake, the hills were still filled with endless rows of corn. But if anyone ever says, "Iowa is flat," then you can be sure they haven't actually been to Iowa. Or ridden their bike here.

The highway makes a long, gradual descent into Ottumwa, the biggest "city" in the region. Ottumwa's population was 20,000 when I grew up there, but has grown to 25,000, supported by a meat-packing plant. (If you've seen the movie *Fast Food Nation*— well, that's all I'm going to say.)

The first thing I thought when I entered the city limits was, *How could this place have grown? It looks dead.*

Not only did it look dead, it felt dead. I drove through the downtown streets and recognized where Younkers department store, Kresge, Woolworths, Bookin Jewelry and the movie theaters all used to be, places of bustling commerce when I was a child. As ten-year-old kids, we could take the city bus downtown and shop by ourselves. Ottumwa had been an ideal—and safe—place for a kid to practice independence. At Younkers, my sister and I had bought our school clothes without our mother, who let us bring home our selections "on approval." At Woolworths, I had shopped with my grandma for my first training bra. At Kresge, we had stocked up on school supplies and candy. At the movie theater, my dad had taken us kids to Wednesday matinees. In the place of all these businesses now was . . . nothing. Just empty, decaying buildings. It was—in one word—depressing.

In the midst of all this decline, I located the Canteen Lunch in the Alley. I had met someone at the state fair who gave me the heads-up so I knew what to look for. The Canteen was still in its original location—at 112 East Second Street—but the city had built a parking garage over the top of it. A parking garage for what? There was no one here, no businesses, no apparent need for a three-story parking structure. But the city had insisted on the location and, in turn, the town insisted back that the Canteen could not be messed with. A petition was signed and the loyal patrons of the old diner won the fight. The compromise was that the Canteen would live under the concrete structure, like a homeless person camping under a bridge.

If the rest of the town seemed deserted, it was because everyone was in the Canteen, eating lunch. I broke into a smile at the sight of the squatty little building, recognizable the way a friend is who you haven't seen for thirty years. Or, in this case, more like thirty-six years. I entered through the screen door and stepped back in time, way back to 1936 it would seem, as the decor had not changed since the place opened. Nor had the smell. The odor was a greasy combo of beef and onions, in spite of the fact the meat was not fried, rather steamed in large metal vats right in front of the customers. Still, the fatty smell clung to your clothes and your hair, reminding you of the delicious Canteen burger you had just enjoyed.

I found an empty bar stool and sat down. Just as I had imagined from my memories, the waitresses all had grey hair.

"What would you like?" one of the old women asked.

"A Canteen," I said excitedly. "With ketchup and mustard."

I looked around and soaked in every detail. The brown wood paneling. The faded framed photos of John F. Kennedy and Lyndon B. Johnson. The map of the U.S. filled with pushpins to mark where the Canteen's patrons had visited from. Clearly, I wasn't the only tourist—or the only former resident who had returned to fulfill some nostalgia. The red-and-white-checkered curtains were still in place. And so was the pie safe, a glassed-in cabinet filled with a variety of pies.

My Canteen was delivered almost immediately. The waitress set the burger down on the counter in front of me, the loose meat and white bun swaddled in a blanket of waxed paper. I took my first bite and felt like I was eight years old again, with my dad sitting next to me. I wished he was sitting next to me now. But I was at least grateful I could say my dad was still around, and that we had enjoyed our own taste of nostalgia at The Apple Pan in L.A. eight and a half months earlier. Had it been that long? Time was passing, and it wasn't all based on how many months Marcus had been gone. It had been filled with something more than just tears and grief—there had been relationships with people who still meant a lot to me.

As I ate I listened to the conversations around me. A couple across the horseshoe-shaped counter was telling another patron about their class reunion. They were visiting from California, they said. California got my attention, but so did their appearance. They looked to be around my parents' age. Because the diner was so tiny and no conversation could be considered private, I boldly asked the woman of the couple when she walked past me on her way to the restroom, "Excuse me. Can I ask how old you are?"

She stopped and straightened her back in surprise. But then she did answer. "Seventy-five," she said. She was still blonde and had sparkling ice-blue eyes, a clear complexion and the spirit of someone much younger.

Seventy-five was my dad's age, so I continued. "Did you know Tom Howard?"

She recoiled, her blue eyes shot open even wider. Looking directly at me, she said, "Tom was my boyfriend. He was my first love." I could see why. She was beautiful, even in her midseventies. "I'm Ruthie," she added, sitting down on the stool next to me.

I was in as much shock as she was. It must have been shock, because I blurted out, "You're Ruthie? I've heard about you. You could have been my mother!"

She laughed, though probably out of embarrassment, and then asked, "How's your dad?"

"He's great. He's retired from dentistry and living in L.A. He spends a lot of time sailing. Let's call him."

I grabbed my cell phone and my dad answered. "Dad? I'm at the Canteen in Ottumwa and I just ran into someone who wants to say hi." I pushed my phone into Ruthie's hand—and prayed that my dad's poor hearing would be good enough to register who was on the line. He heard. It registered. And she stepped outside into the alley to catch up with her lost love.

The grey-haired waitresses had watched the entire episode unfold. "Small world," I said to one of them, still shaking my head. I couldn't concentrate on my burger after that.

When the blonde woman who could have been but was not my mother returned, she said thank you. I showed her a few pictures of my dad I had on my phone—and a few of my mother, too. I gave her my card and a hug when she left. I presumed she returned to California with her husband and that our encounter hadn't given her—or my dad—any ideas about rekindling their romance.

When she left, it was time for that slice of banana cream pie. The diner was so small I didn't see how they could make their pies on the premises, so I asked the waitress, who was clearing away my wax paper and crumbs of loose meat off the counter. "Where do you make your pie?"

"Oh, honey, we don't have anyone to make them anymore," she said. "We buy them from Hy-Vee." Hy-Vee was the local grocery store chain. "Would you like a piece?"

"Uh, no thank you. I'll just take my check." I had gone from the exciting high of meeting Ruthie, only to plunge to the depths of disappointment. No homemade pie? That was what made this place so special. The locals were so determined to save the Canteen from the parking-garage debacle, so why didn't they protest and sign a petition about the pie?

It was Mary's Kitchen all over again, when I went in search of the outstanding pie they were supposedly known for and they didn't have any. Mary's words echoed: "We're too busy to make it." So when the Canteen waitress said they didn't have anyone to make pie, history might have repeated itself. I could have said, like I did in Malibu, "I'll make it for you." I didn't really have any other place to go. What if this was another one of those genie-in-the-bottle moments, an opportunity magically presenting itself? But Ottumwa, Iowa? Meat-packing town where more than half the city center's buildings were labeled with "condemned" tags? No. I don't think so.

I spent the next hour driving around town to find my two old family houses, the first one on Asbury Avenue, on the south side of town. North and south sides were designated by which side of the Des Moines River they occupied. Our one-story, three-bedroom, one-bathroom house was not only still standing, it was freshly painted with a well-groomed garden. I had lived there until I was five and thus I wouldn't have found it—or recognized it—without the help of my GPS. The house was red when we lived in it—and full of water bugs that scurried for cover when you turned on the light in the middle of the night. My mom hated that house. But to see it now, bright white with flowers planted in the front yard, it looked immaculate and bug-free. Though I guess it still only had one bathroom, which had been a hardship for my parents with four kids under the age of six.

The fifth child in our family, Patrick, was born after we moved into a 5,000-square-foot house on the north side of town. I drove the few miles to East Golf Avenue and noted how small everything looked—the houses that had appeared so large to a child looked quaint, almost miniature. Or maybe I had lived in L.A. too long where mansions abounded and had skewed my perspective. This place, this street that bordered a golf course, was quiet, still safe and offered a lot of room to play; I could see why I had had a happy, carefree childhood.

I parked in front of the split-level brick and wood three-story house designed by my Grandpa Lyle, who was an architect. My mom gave him input in the plans—she made sure there were ample bathrooms—four—and an entire lower level designated as a soundproof playroom. I sat there in my MINI for a while, envisioning days gone by of playing football with our Old English sheepdog and holding talent shows in the backyard, until a well-dressed man came out to see what I was doing. He was Indian—from India—and when he approached my car window, I explained. "I grew up here. My grandpa built this house."

"I had a feeling that was why you were parked here for so long."

I wanted to tell him everything, about how we baked cookies on the long Formica table in the family room, how we held Christmas pageants in front of the fireplace and my sister and I dressed up as angels, how we didn't have furniture in the living room for the first few years, how my mom took karate classes and when showing us what she learned she flipped my dad onto his back. How we walked across the street to the golf course after dinner and hit balls on the front nine. But he didn't appear curious about me having lived in what was now *his* house. And he didn't offer me a tour. So out of courtesy, I left.

My grandparents had lived a mile away in an old Victorian house that always smelled of mothballs and green beans and bacon boiled in the pressure cooker. It was still there, on North Court Avenue, still burgundy and yellow with sunflowers blooming in the side yard. My grandpa had made homemade wine in the cellar and my grandma grew rhubarb in the back garden. If only I had appreciated rhubarb back then and the fabulous pies you could make from the celerylike red-and-green stalks. It was now one of my favorite pies.

Before leaving town, I drove past my elementary school (Horace Mann), the cemetery to see if the dog stone monument was still there (it was), and drove past my dad's dental office (also designed by my grandpa). I took pictures of each place with my phone and emailed them to my family, who promptly emailed back, "I remember that place! Thanks for sending. I can't believe you're there." I couldn't believe it, either.

I had seen enough. My curiosity was satisfied, my belly still full with that Canteen burger, and I still needed to travel twenty five miles to the next town over. I was headed to Fairfield (pop. 13,000), home of the Maharishi University for Transcendental Meditation, for an interview with a local radio station. No, I wasn't going to talk about mantras or levitation. I was going to discuss what it was like being a pie judge at the state fair.

Driving back out the way I came in, I wasn't sad to leave. In fact, my sentiments were clear. The last thing that went through my mind as I pulled back onto the highway was *I don't think I'll ever be coming back here.*

CHAPTER

23

Sometimes you come to a fork in the road where you are forced to make a decision about which way to go, and the direction you choose can forever change your life.

When I met Marcus in 2001, I was on a road trip from California to Oregon. I was taking a break from my pie-baking job in Malibu, exploring the possibility of moving to Bend. Sixty miles south of Bend, I saw a big brown national monument sign that read "Crater Lake National Park, 10 Miles." Should I take the detour and have a look at the volcanic lake or keep going to Bend?

I spent the next 9.99 miles deliberating whether or not to stop. I had never been to the park, but I also wanted to keep moving forward. When the fork appeared, it was as if some spiritual force grabbed my steering wheel and spun me into the park.

After paying the twenty-dollar entrance fee, I pulled into the first parking lot marked Scenic Overlook and there it was—a vision of pristine blue water nestled in an amphitheater of snow-capped mountains. All was silent except for the pine-scented breeze and my own voice that whispered, "Thank you, God, for preserving this peaceful place."

When I returned to my car, an SUV whipped into the parking lot, screeched to a halt and a woman jumped out screaming, "Beth! Beth!" I held my body in a defensive stance, until I realized it was my friend Kim from L.A.

"What are you doing here?" I squealed as we hopped up and down, hugging each other.

"I'm here to see my client in Sun River. We're sneaking in a side trip so Laz and Gabe can see the lake," she explained, pointing to her husband and one-year-old son in the car. "We're going to watch the sunset, then have dinner in the Lodge. Come with us. Get in."

After the sun dipped below the jagged ridgeline, leaving a chill in its wake at 7,100-feet-elevation, we drove to the Lodge. We hurried inside to warm up by the fire blazing in the lobby's six-foot-tall stone fireplace, where other weekend travelers dressed in plaid flannel and fleece already occupied the oversize, Mission-style leather chairs and sofas. We found empty chairs—outside. A long row of wicker rockers, each supplied with its own wool blanket, lined the veranda overlooking the moon rising over the now-black basin.

"Merlot?" Kim asked when she saw a cocktail waitress in a down jacket taking orders.

"Definitely," I answered, pulling the scratchy blanket tighter around my neck. As we reminisced about the days we used to work together in Hawaii, I was aware of a dark-haired man hovering near our chairs; he could have been eavesdropping or just searching the inky sky for shooting stars.

By the time we finished our wine, Laz had found us seats in the lobby inside. We ordered French Onion soup from the bar menu and talked way past the baby's bedtime.

Meanwhile, in some other corner of the lobby lounge, a gay waiter was asking the dark-haired man if he needed a place to stay. "No, just the check, please," he replied, avoiding eye contact, his credit card already in his hand.

"Here, hold Gabe while we go to the restroom," Kim instructed, and thrust her bundle of joy into my arms.

For the next five minutes I stood in the middle of the reception area, twirling, bouncing and—unaware anyone was watching—enjoying my motherhood fantasy. In reality, I was a road-weary car camper, who at thirty-nine had recently been dumped by the latest in a recent string of unsuccessful boyfriends. My blond hair was in a messy ponytail and I was dressed in an Ecuadorian wool sweater—orange with a giant daisy on the front and back—jeans and trail running shoes.

"Who's a good baby?" I cooed to Gabe, holding him up to the ceiling as he smiled down at me.

"This is a beautiful place, isn't it?" the dark-haired man ventured, his voice confident with a hint of a British accent mixed with something else, something European.

I turned to look at him. "Yes, it is," I replied. He had a shadow of a goatee and warm, inquisitive green eyes. "Are you staying here?" I asked, shifting Gabe to the other hip.

"No, I tried to get a room but they're sold out." He was wearing a funky combination of a traditional Austrian boiled-wool sweater with big silver coin buttons, surfer-style cropped jeans and brown leather hiking boots that laced on the sides, and he had a book by Thomas Mann tucked under his arm.

"I know," I said. "I tried, too. It's getting a little cold for camping."

"You're camping? I wish I had my camping gear," he replied. "I would love to sleep by the lake."

"I'd love to sleep with *you* by the lake," I wanted to say, but instead I asked, "Where are you from?" to keep the conversation with this sexy stranger going.

"Germany," he replied.

"Where in Germany?"

"I was born in Bremen, but raised in the South."

"Bremen. That's where they import coffee for Europe," I remarked.

His eyes widened. "I caahn't believe you know where that is," he said, his British accent making his words so soft and seductive. I loved how he talked. "I've been heah for three munths," he continued, "and find that most Americans don't know their geography very well."

I was surprised myself for remembering this tiny fact; I hadn't thought of it since I worked on that Kenya coffee farm fourteen years earlier. "And what brought you here?"

He ran his hand through his brown hair. "An assignment in Portland with my company," he answered just as Kim appeared.

"We need to get going," she announced.

"Hi, Kim," I said, quickly passing her the baby. I looked back to my new acquaintance. "This is ... "

"Marcus," he said.

"Nice to meet you, Marcus," Kim said, adding playfully, "I leave her alone for a few minutes and, what do you know, she meets a hunk."

He turned back to me. "And you are ... ?"

"Beth."

"By the way, Kim," he said, "you have a very nice baby." He looked back at me with a knowing smile.

Laz joined us and we all walked out to the parking lot together. The night had turned colder, our breath visible underneath the dim street lights. "Kim is giving me a ride back to my car," I told Marcus. "I'm sorry, I have to go."

We just stood there, eyeing each other, immobilized by a pull of energy. With Kim and Laz observing, there was nothing more we could say—or do. But, damn it, I didn't want to spend the rest of my life wondering if there could have been something more between us, if he was "the one" instead of the one who got away. In my unbarred, soul-searching state, I figured, "What the hell," and handed him my card.

"If you want to stay in touch, here's how to find me."

And that was it—the fifteen minutes and the fork in the road that changed my life.

So there I was, leaving the surprise encounter with my dad's first girlfriend and the disappointment of the Canteen's store-bought pie, and on my way to Fairfield. The date was August 25, 2010—approximately nine years since meeting Marcus at Crater Lake, seven years since marrying him and one year since burying him. I was speeding east on the spiffy new four-lane Highway 34, singing along to my Marshall Tucker Band CD (a throwback to my high school days), enjoying the open landscape, the puffy white clouds, the lack of billboards, and admiring how tall all that corn was growing.

It was in this free-floating, mindless state, when I came upon another fork in the road.

One of those familiar brown national monument signs came into view. It read "American Gothic House, 6 Miles." *What? The house from the classic painting of the old couple holding the pitchfork?*

I had grown up less than fifteen miles from this famous place and never knew it was here? So much for learning my Iowa history.

Unlike my Crater Lake decision, my direction was immediate and certain this time. I didn't spend the next miles vacillating about whether or not to make the detour. I had several hours to spare and I wanted to see this house. I slowed down, turned right and took the two-lane highway, winding through more farmland, to the tiny town of Eldon.

Following the rest of the signs that marked the way, I steered my MINI through the sleepy, residential streets of Eldon, passing two bait shops, an appliance store, a tiny public library, a grain elevator and a city center approximately a half block long. I turned into the last street, passing the Living Hope Church with its white siding and blue neon cross, traveling along a block lined with a mix of well-kept and well-worn homes. There was a certain humble aesthetic about the architecture—so simple and unpretentious that some of the houses weren't even houses, they were double-wide trailers. The tidy properties indicated that some Eldon folk were hardworking and conscientious. But there were also plenty of rusty cars and junk piled in a few yards, which showed some residents had a different kind of mindset.

At the end of the long block, the road turned left and I entered the clearing of trees that separated the tourist destination from the town. Across from the visitors' parking, sitting back from the road and slightly in the distance, I recognized it at once—the American Gothic House. Just like in the painting, it was the white, old-fashioned, adorable cottage with the churchlike second-story window beneath the peaked roof. It had a front porch and was surrounded by a giant grass lawn dotted with oak and pine trees and picnic tables. The place was just begging to have someone bake pie in it.

I was smitten in the way I was when I met Marcus at Crater Lake. And *smitten,* as I had learned, could be a dangerous, life-changing word.

I parked in front of the shiny new visitor center and, upon entering the lobby, I was greeted by an oversize reproduction of Grant Wood's *American Gothic* painting, and then by a volunteer, Carleen, an elegant blonde in jeans, who offered to take my picture in front of the house. She suggested I first dress up in one of the free costumes. There was a rack of bib overalls, black suit jackets and calico pinafore dresses adorned with cameo pins at the collar. All costumes came in a range of sizes. Plus, there was a bucket full of pitchforks, so tourists could replicate the couple in the painting precisely.

I dressed up as the woman by tying one of the calico smocks over the top of my shorts and T-shirt. I also grabbed a pitchfork. We walked outside to the concrete circle in front of the house that marked the place to stand and I struck the pose—solo.

Afterward I walked through the museum, marveling at the display of all the painting's clever parodies, from Newman's Own packaging to Miss Piggy and Kermit, Barbie and Ken, Garfield and countless other magazine-cover interpretations depicting the *American Gothic* couple.

It was here in the museum I learned that the couple in the painting was not a couple, but rather Grant Wood's sister Nan and his dentist from Cedar Rapids, representing a labor-weary farmer and his spinster daughter. The pair had never modeled in front of the house, nor had they ever posed together. Wood had painted all three elements separately. Except the sister and dentist did finally stand side by side—for a photograph—in 1942, twelve years after they appeared in the painting. Their photo was on display in the lobby of the visitor center. Nan posed for another photograph, finally recreating her famous portrait in front of the little white cottage, when the house was named a National Historic Site in 1981.

Considering I didn't even know the house was so near my birthplace, it should have come as no surprise I knew none of these details about the painting, including the fact it was created in 1930 and that, no, it was not a work by Norman Rockwell.

Grant Wood had come to Eldon—which back then was a thriving railroad town, sitting at the crossroads of two cross-country lines— for an art show hosted by his friend John Sharp's mother. During his visit, John drove Grant around town and when they drove past the little white house, Grant said, "Stop the car! I want to sketch this." He made a small pencil drawing, capturing the details of the unusual window—though if he had driven by today, he more likely would have just snapped a photo with his cell phone—and went back to his studio in Cedar Rapids to create the masterpiece. The occupants had seen him outside, drawing their home in his sketch pad. They were so flattered by the attention they cleaned house and washed all the curtains in anticipation of his return. But he never did come back to Eldon.

Instead, he entered the painting in an art contest held by the Art Institute of Chicago, where it garnered third place, won prize money of $300 and sold for $300 to the Art Institute (where it remains on display today and is now worth millions). But Wood's work didn't receive all accolades. The portrait of the sullen father-daughter duo also took a whole lot of flak from Midwesterners for how he had stereotyped them with this seemingly negative portrayal.

I went into the adjoining gift shop, where the museum curator, Molly Moser was unpacking a box of T-shirts. Molly was a young, bright-eyed woman with long brown hair, glasses and rosebud lips that rivaled Angelina Jolie's. I had brushed up on my Grant Wood history, and then turned my focus to the curator, quizzing her on her background. What was this cute, brainy girl doing in this remote corner of the earth? She had just graduated from the University of Iowa, where she had studied art, museum studies and business. Running the American Gothic House Center was her first job out of college, and she used her free time to paint. Once she explained it, it made sense.

Included in the museum display was a list of the house's previous owners and, in more recent years, its renters. A schoolteacher had lived in the American Gothic House only two years earlier. That meant the house was modernized. I immediately began picturing myself living in it, this adorable white-washed cottage surrounded by acres of open, grassy space. With my curiosity piqued as to why the house was sitting empty, my questions to Molly began. "I read through the timeline of the house's history," I started. "Is the house for rent? How much? Who is the landlord? What is his number? Would he allow dogs? Can I see it? CAN I SEE IT NOW? PLEASE?"

"Well, I do have to do my monthly inspection, so I suppose I could let you come with me," she offered, though cautiously. The house was not open to the public. You could only stand in front of it, pitchfork in hand. My explanation that I was in Iowa to be a pie judge at the Iowa State Fair and was subsequently visiting my childhood homes might have given her reason to believe I was a safe bet. Or her rationale might have been that I was salivating so much over the house she was only trying to avoid my drool getting on her shirt. Molly knew I wasn't going to leave until I gathered as much information as I could. So she let me in.

It was yet another fork in the road, a path Molly offered, and one I hungrily chose.

Before I could compute the repercussions of making this choice, I was inside the landmark house. The interior wasn't quite as charming as the outside—the wood plank floors creaked and their wide cracks were filled with dust. The short but deep bathtub was full of cobwebs and dead flies and covered in a layer of mildew. The lifeless kitchen had cheap 1970s appliances, including an overhead light with a coiled fluorescent bulb and a dingy linoleum floor. I wasn't deterred. I could see past the layers of its abandoned state to its full potential.

We climbed a narrow, twisting staircase to the upstairs, where the low attic ceiling sloped at extreme angles. This house was not built for tall people. The second floor consisted of two small adjoining rooms and whatever charm the downstairs lacked was redeemed upstairs—and then some. The room at the top of the stairs was the smaller of the two and had a Gothic window that mirrored the front one. Outside the back window was a view of the big green lawn punctuated by a clothesline and a forest set farther back. I could picture it already: *this place could be my writer's retreat—and this is where my writing desk will go.*

We moved into the second room, the bedroom, where I stood looking out from behind the world-famous window. I pulled the lace curtain aside to get a better view of the lawn, the visitor center and the people posing for photos in the concrete circle. Could I really see myself living here? Strange as it would be to live in Iowa again, yes. Not just in Iowa, but in a tourist attraction in rural Iowa? Yes. Yes, I could. I felt that certainty in my belly, the same way I did when I met Marcus and had felt that pull to him. I knew it was right—even if I couldn't explain it logically. And I would definitely have some explaining to do.

I could still remember the protests from my mother when I told her I was moving to Germany to marry Marcus. "German men are chauvinistic and domineering. You don't want to live in Germany."

It was the first time I stood up to her and even at the age of forty it took some coaching from my sister before I got up the courage to make my declaration of independence. "I'm sorry you don't approve, but I love him and I'm going to marry him."

She wouldn't be happy about me moving back to Iowa, especially since she had already been apartment hunting for me in L.A.—in her neighborhood. I could hear the new protests already. Not just from her, but from every one of my West Coast friends. "You don't want to live in Iowa. What will you do in the winter?"

My brain was calculating so fast, I already knew what I would do in the winter. I would drive back to L.A. with the dogs and stay in the RV, which I had left with my brother who was currently getting good use out of The Beast for his weekend surf trips. As for living in Iowa in general, I had been happy living in the Texas frontier town of Terlingua, whose population was 200, so Eldon, which was five times bigger, might even seem overcrowded.

After I thanked Molly for the tour, I was on my cell phone calling the landlord, the administrator of the State Historical Society of Iowa. I asked him—*begged* him—to rent the house to me. I told him I would be coming back to Des Moines so we could meet in person and I would write him a check immediately. I happened to mention that I was staying with Meg, my friend from high school. When I told him her last name he said, "I know Meg. We served on the board of a foundation together. Well, in that case, the house is yours."

With this one phone call, life as I knew it ended. Again.

CHAPTER

24

The moving truck arrived from Portland with all of our furniture—I still couldn't claim it as just mine—on September 20. I was so caught up in the chaos of unloading I didn't realize until two days later that the date was the seventh anniversary of our German wedding, when Marcus and I walked down the aisle of the thousand-year-old church in the Black Forest. Out of our three weddings, this was the date we chose to celebrate. Even as I hung my wedding dress in the upstairs closet of my new house, I still hadn't remembered.

The only date I remembered without fail was the nineteenth. Every month when that number showed up on the calendar, I marked how long it had been since Marcus died. At first I counted time in days, then weeks, months, then one year, and now one year and one month.

While the movers carried box after box inside the house, the mayor of Eldon, Shirley Stacey, stopped by to drop off a slice of her homemade peach pie. It was such a large piece I planned to share it with Molly at the visitor center next door. But once I dug my fork into it, tasting the ripe peaches, their juice thickened perfectly with tapioca, the buttery crust flaking off onto the plate, I couldn't stop. I devoured what must have been a quarter of a pie. Molly would never know.

I first met Mayor Shirley two weeks earlier when I went down to City Hall to get the water and garbage accounts put into my name. I was standing at the glass window of City Clerk Carrie Teninty's desk, talking to her about cutting my grass and helping me give the Gothic House a much-needed scouring. Eldon, I could already see, was a town of multitaskers, real doers. Carrie had been caring for the two-acre lawn of the American Gothic House for several years, driving her John Deere tractor over from her house on Friday afternoons. In between that, raising two kids along with their menagerie of pets, and working full-time at City Hall, she was also willing to give up a whole weekend to help me scrub the scum out of the bathtub, the mold out of the refrigerator and the cobwebs out of the corners.

While Carrie and I made cleaning plans, her nine-year-old towheaded daughter, Chloe, was behind the window talking to a woman I assumed was her grandmother. The woman had heard me come in and walked around to the front of the window. A full-bodied blonde wearing a bright orange T-shirt that read "City of Eldon," she held out her hand with manicured red nails to shake mine. "I'm Shirley, the mayor of Eldon," she said. "I've got a pie shop picked out for you to rent. It's right across the street."

I am not joking. Word had traveled quickly that a pie baker was moving into the American Gothic House and Shirley, in her determination to make improvements to her hometown, already had plans for me. "Nice to meet you, too," I responded, laughing. "You don't waste any time, do you?" I had been in Eldon all of forty-eight hours, I was sleeping on an air mattress I borrowed from Meg in Des Moines because my furniture hadn't yet arrived, but what the hell. Why not go look at some Eldon real estate? A potential pie shop? "Sure, I'll take a look," I told her.

We walked across the main artery that ran through town—also known as Main Street, Elm Street and Highway 16, depending on if you were a tourist, a resident or a truck driver. My prospective pie shop—sandwiched between the Eldon post office and the historic McHaffey Opera House, which was undergoing an interminable restoration project—had previously served as a tearoom. But once we got inside, it was obvious the tearoom had occupied the space ten or more years in the past. Currently it was being used as a dumping ground for the owner's ex-girlfriend's junk—a tattered, flea-infested sofa, stacks of dusty suitcases, boxes of yellowed books, lamps with torn shades. I couldn't understand why anyone would buy a building on the main drag and use it as a storage unit when the town is ripe for development.

In spite of the appeal of the pounded tin tiles on the ceiling and the huge bay window, my ability to see the potential in the place, the way I had immediately seen past the grime in the American Gothic House, was not working. And anyway, I needed to scrub my own home; I didn't have the energy to take on someone else's cleaning project on top of it. This was more than a cleaning project; it needed complete gutting. No matter how bad I might want to open a pie shop—or should I say, no matter how bad the mayor wanted me to open a pie shop—this was not a space where I could envision spending my days.

"The rent is one dollar a month," she said.

"One dollar a month? Are you kidding me? That is tempting, but I'm sorry. I can't take this on. It would be far too labor intensive and expensive to make this place work."

"But Eldon needs you."

"Yes, I can see that." Eldon was a struggling, threadbare village, worn out and tattered like a favorite old quilt. It was probably polished and pretty in its earlier days with its row of red-and-brown brick townhouses, but it was dying a slow death in the wake of the railroad industry's departure twenty years prior. The town boasted six sites listed on the National Register of Historic Places—including the library, the opera house and, of course, the American Gothic House—but without a hotel, a motel, let alone a grocery store or any shops besides the Opera House's thrift store, it couldn't attract the commerce needed to resuscitate its economy.

Shirley, as the newly elected mayor, was working hard to infuse new life into the town, lobbying for new businesses and medical facilities, grant money and even publicity. If she thought it could help Eldon, she wrote the letters, made the phone calls, went to the meetings, served on the boards, put in the extra hours and didn't rest until she got what she wanted—what Eldon needed. I could see the tornado force I was up against; she was a funnel cloud of determination tearing across the plains. How could I say no to someone who was trying to make the world—or at least her tiny rural town, where I now lived—a better place?

As I stood there, overwhelmed by the building's state of disrepair, I came up with another, better idea. I knew what I would do. "Don't worry, Shirley. I'm going to sell pies. But just not downtown. I'm going to open a pie stand at the American Gothic House. That's where all the tourists come, but there are no refreshments available. They can visit the museum, have their picture taken and then they can have a reason to stay longer. They can buy a slice of pie and sit at the picnic tables to eat it."

Opening a pie stand was a good compromise for someone of my mercurial nature. It wouldn't take a lot of money, certainly not a bank loan, and I could limit my business hours to the weekends. I told my sister about the store for rent on Main Street. "It's one dollar a month, but I would have to put a lot of money into it, plus buy all the equipment."

"Marcus would want you to use his money to invest in a pie shop," she insisted.

I had already thought about that in Portland and couldn't pull the trigger. And now that I was in Iowa, it seemed prudent to get more settled into my new place before putting down an outlay of cash or make long-term commitments. But beyond that, my house was the cutest—and soon-to-be cleanest—building in town, my dogs were there happily free to roam in the yard, and it's where I wanted to spend my time. My kitchen was small, but I could manage. I had made pies in the RV, so I knew space wasn't the biggest concern. And I've always liked working from home. I could make pie in my pajamas. So pie stand it was.

Behind the faded facade of this southeastern Iowa town, hidden beneath what I had first seen as decline and decay, was a community spirit shining brightly. What I learned in my first weeks in Eldon was how the appearance didn't matter; the people did. Like with historic ruins in Europe that exuded an artistic beauty in the weathered brick and peeling paint, there was a rich culture inhabiting within. And that culture was turning up at my back door every day.

Besides Mayor Shirley welcoming me with her homemade peach pie (which I still salivate over whenever I think about it) and encouraging me to open a pie shop, Priscilla Coffman turned up with two lawn chairs for me to use until my furniture arrived. Priscilla was a poet and retired schoolteacher who served as the current chairman of the visitor center. Then there was Patti Durflinger, a special-education teacher with a big-city haircut and tailored clothes, who came by to welcome me with a gift basket the size of a grain bin, filled with brownies, hand lotion, candles, kitchen towels and more. Her parents, Bill and Joanne Maynard, dropped off a bouquet of roses from their garden. Allen and Rosie Morrison delivered an even bigger bouquet, an arrangement of daisies from the garden store across the highway. And then there was Bob and Iola, my eighty-year-old neighbors to the rear, who were celebrating their sixtieth wedding anniversary this year. They walked over with a loaf of zucchini bread. Don and Shirley Eakins, who lived one house closer to me, came by too with offerings of help whenever I needed. Oh, and I *would* need it in winter and spring as Don owned a snowblower, a garden tiller and a heavy-duty truck to tow my MINI out of the mud.

Every morning another neighbor, Linda Durflinger (Patti's sister-in-law), walked the bike path that cuts in front of my house. The first time the short, feisty woman introduced herself, she said, "You'll never remember my last name."

"Yes, I will," I assured her. "Durflinger was the name of my husband's boss in Germany." Linda didn't know I had lived in Germany. She may not have even been aware that Iowa sits smack in the middle of America's German belt and that hers wasn't the only surname of Germanic descent in town. Other neighbors, the Allmans and Snyders, and even my grandma on my dad's side—the one from Ottumwa, whose maiden name was Rater—had Teutonic roots.

Linda, a retired high school secretary and now a city-council member, was partly responsible for initiating the idea for the American Gothic House Center. She had rallied the townsfolk to raise money to build the visitor center and museum to support the famous house, as there was previously nothing but a signpost and a muddy parking lot. They collected over $63,000 by holding bake sales. Basically, they created this beautiful, well-built facility with handicapped-equipped everything, a paved parking lot and landscaping with wildflowers and grasses to recreate the native Iowan prairie—all by selling pie. Amazing. My instincts were right. I had landed in the right place.

In Eldon, I was witnessing hospitality, generosity and community pride like I had never experienced before. Anywhere. These people were nothing like the father and daughter depicted in the *American Gothic* painting. They were not stern-faced and stoic. No. They were always smiling.

♥♥♥

Word soon spread beyond Eldon that a pie baker had taken up residence in the American Gothic House. A week after my furniture arrived, I got a call from Kyle Munson, a columnist for the *Des Moines Register,* Iowa's main newspaper.

Could he drive down from Des Moines the next day and interview me, he wanted to know. Apparently it was statewide-worthy news that the historic house had finally been rented.

"Sure, okay," I said. "Will you be here in time for lunch? Because I was invited to City Hall for ham balls and you can come with me." I was about to experience one of many firsts in my initiation to rural life and figured Kyle might as well join in.

Ham balls, contrary to what the name implies, are like meatballs, only they are made with ground pork, ground beef, some mysterious thing called ham loaf, Campbell's tomato soup, graham crackers and a whole lot of brown sugar. And as I would learn, they are delicious but because of their bulk they must be eaten in moderation.

The lunch at City Hall, attended by the mayor, Carrie the City Clerk, the public works crew of three (which included Carrie's husband, Tony), Kyle Munson and me, was served promptly at noon. They call it "dinner," not lunch, a colloquial distinction that had already caused me confusion when I originally marked my calendar for 5:00 p.m., the favored Midwest evening meal time, which in these parts is known as "supper." This dinner was another fine example of Mayor Shirley's country cooking. We scooped out her homemade ham balls from the Crock-Pot, piled scalloped potatoes and cooked carrots (drowning in margarine) on our plates and helped ourselves to puffy white bread rolls. We polished off the feast with the homemade apple pie I had brought. Reminiscent of a Thanksgiving-induced food coma, my stomach was so full, so stuffed, so heavy, that I could barely answer Kyle's questions when we sat down to do the interview afterward. And I could barely eat for two days.

On Monday, October 11, when Kyle's article came out—on the front page of the newspaper, no less, with a photo of me—it was titled, American Gothic House Meets America's Pie Lady. America's Pie Lady? I found this a little too grandiose for my taste. I wouldn't, *couldn't* claim to be Eldon, Iowa's, Pie Lady, let alone the whole nation's. Whatever. It was a refreshing change from my lingering status as Grieving Widow. But not only had Kyle, with the swish of his pen, anointed me with a new identity—an identity which, like it or not, took hold—he had declared to the world, or at least to all of Iowa, that I would be selling pie. I was suddenly and officially committed. I needed to get busy.

I drove to Des Moines, where I went on a shopping spree. After dropping $300 on supplies I loaded up my covered wagon, I mean, my MINI Cooper, and made the two-hour trek back to Eldon. The whole drive back, I wondered a) how many apple pies I should make, b) how much I should charge for pie slices, whole pies and the Starbucks French Roast that I would serve by the cup

(there would be no weak diner coffee served with my pie!), and
c) if I had lost my mind by moving to a remote corner of Iowa
and starting a pie business. For one thing, many people in this
town of 928 already make damn good pie. And several residents,
like Arlene Kildow and Janice Chickering, are legendary, blue-
ribbon-winning pie bakers. (I had finally sampled Arlene's coconut cream pie when Kyle and I went to lunch at City Hall. With
its mile-high toasted meringue, thick and creamy pudding and
generous amount of coconut, it was, in a word, perfect.) They
certainly didn't need me, some highfalutin West Coast pie baker-
to-the-stars, to get quality pie in these parts. Besides, I would
have to sell quite a few pieces of pie to recoup my $300 invest-
ment. I also had to consider that with winter coming, meaning
fewer tourists as pie customers, I could be in the red until next
summer.

What Kyle Munson didn't mention in his article was my business plan—or lack thereof. Kyle had asked me how much a slice
of pie was going to cost. That was a good question.

I had squirmed, shrugged my shoulders, looked down at my
feet, I had done everything but answer him. Then turning my gaze
high up on the kitchen wall, I said, "My problem is this." I pointed
to my huge foam board sign, decorated with a red-and-white-
checkered tablecloth border, emblazoned with the huge letters
that read "Free Pie." It was the sign from the TV shoot that had
found a new home as a wall decoration in my kitchen. "I don't
think I'll ever make a good businessperson, because I like giving
pie away. If you came to my pie stand, feeling down, I would say,
'Oh, it looks like you could use a piece of pie to cheer you up. Here
you go. No charge.' Not a great business strategy."

But seeing as the numbers in my savings account had dwindled
in direct proportion to the number of months since I had been

employed, I wasn't going to allow myself any guilt over charging three dollars a slice. Anyway, since Marcus died, my guilt account was already full.

Guilt can be a good way to gauge your moral compass, like a warning signal when something is off balance. Guilt can force you to ask yourself "What part of this situation am I responsible for? Am I acting in the best, most upstanding way possible? Am I behaving like a good, caring person?" But apart from using it to get that initial bearing, guilt—as I was still learning—doesn't serve any other useful purpose. At the end of the day, one needs to be mindful of one's own needs without constant self-incrimination.

Since Marcus died, I hadn't allowed myself to feel guilty over letting go of certain friendships that felt negative, for turning down invitations to dinner parties or for treating myself to the occasional massage in spite of having no income. Being a widow gave me a legitimate excuse for being selfish—er, I mean, for practicing self-kindness. I figured those were good steps, even if just baby ones, toward kicking guilt to the curb. But fourteen months after Marcus's death, after a year of grief counseling and working hard at forgiving myself, guilt still reared its ugly, energy-draining, unproductive head. That asking people to pay for my labor-intensive, high-quality baked goods made me feel guilty underscored just how susceptible I was to this human condition.

In spite of the uncertainty, I refused to give in to guilt or doubt or any other self-defeating notions. The wheels of my pie stand had already been set in motion. Front-page articles had been published. Money had been spent. I was going to make—and sell—pie.

Besides my investment in the hard goods, I needed a Home Baking License from the Wapello County health department. This required filling out a one-page form, writing a check for thirty bucks and having a health inspector visit my kitchen, ensuring

I was practicing good hygiene. Considering I had just moved in and, with Carrie's help, had scrubbed the place to the bone, I not only passed inspection, I exceeded the standards.

Finally, after everything else was in place, I required ingredients. The nearest grocery store was twenty minutes away—in my old childhood hometown of Ottumwa. The place I thought I'd never return to after my nostalgic trip to the Canteen Lunch in the Alley. Right. Just like when I graduated early from high school at seventeen and vowed I was never coming back to Iowa to live. Oh, boy.

Aldi is a German-owned discount grocery store chain in both Germany and the U.S. (Aldi U.S. has 1,000 stores in 29 states. And, a little-known fact, Aldi also owns Trader Joe's.) Marcus introduced me to Aldi in Stuttgart when we were still dating and I had found their prices were beyond cheap. After we got married and I moved to Germany, I made almost daily trips to Aldi. I was as in love with Aldi as I was with my husband, so much so that Marcus's grandma, Oma Inge, used to tease me.

"Du hast Aldi Fieber," she would say. Aldi Fever.

Yes, it was true. I was delirious over the organic produce, the variety of dairy products, spicy sausages, fresh roses and the German specialty foods (like Maultaschen, Spätzle and Rote Grütze), and—my favorite—the weekly, rotating offerings of nonfood items like Turkish bath towels, bicycle gear, sheepskin slippers, raincoats, DVD players, juicer machines, flannel sheets, pajamas, running tights, ski gloves and so on. All high quality for very low prices. If there was anything I loved in life, it was a good bargain.

So when I moved into the American Gothic House and discovered the closest place to do my grocery shopping was—why, yes!—Aldi in Ottumwa, fifteen miles away, I was thrilled. Until I walked in the door.

Not only did the Aldi in Ottumwa, Iowa, look similar to the Aldi in Stuttgart, Germany, it carried many of the same brands. I made it two steps down the first aisle when I saw the chocolate display with the Moser Roth label. That's the same chocolate we bought in Germany, same name, same box, same everything. Then, because it was a German store after all, there was a display of sauerkraut, red cabbage, pretzels and even Spätzle (egg noodles). I laughed at the sight—and at myself. I had not liked living in Germany, and yet now I was practically doing cartwheels over finding German food—and the rock-bottom prices—in rural Iowa.

I wanted to call Marcus at work and tell him where I was and what I was putting in my shopping cart. He would love to hear this and would tease me about my change of heart toward anything related to Germany. For a moment I actually thought I could call him. But in the split second I forgot, I also remembered again. I lost my breath, along with my composure, as reality struck like a hay baler barreling over my chest. "I can't call him. He's dead." It was the first time that lapse had happened to me.

I stood there in that first aisle, tears streaming down my face. What a strange site I must have been to the other Ottumwa shoppers. "Why is this girl crying about chocolate? Or is she crying over the egg noodles?" they must have wondered.

I managed to wheel my cart over to the produce section and my mood was buoyed by the apple selection. I could get Granny Smith apples for about fifty cents a pound. I filled my basket with sixty pounds worth. Enough for twenty pies. I bought bags of flour and sugar, tubs of the store-brand shortening and butter—pounds and pounds of butter.

When I got to the checkout, I wished I could tell the clerk—or anyone in the store who would listen—my story. My story about how I had been married to Marcus and had shopped at Aldi in Germany. How shopping here was a powerful connection between my past and present. How I was born here in Ottumwa, had lived all over the world, and now, as if by some divine intervention, I was back. Would this clerk know that Aldi's first U.S. store was right here in Southeast Iowa? Would she even care? Would she or any of the other shoppers appreciate the ability to buy these wonderful European goods here in rural America?

As the cashier pulled my purchases off her conveyor belt, I wanted to tell someone how Marcus taught me that sauerkraut is full of vitamins, and how he pronounced *vitamins* the British way, with a soft *i*, and how he could make something as mouth-puckering as sauerkraut sound delicious and sexy. But gushing my jumble of thoughts to her would have only confused her and embarrassed me further, so I left as quickly as I could.

Like everything associated with grief, this was just another step in the conditioning process. The first anything was the hardest. I had made it through an entire one-year cycle: the first holidays, birthdays and anniversaries. I had made it through my first trip to Aldi. I had made it far enough and long enough that I could see my progress. I was adapting. I was surviving. I was crying less and living more. I was building a new life. And I was shopping for pie ingredients for my new business.

♥♥♥

In Ottumwa, Aldi wasn't the only connection to my past. When I needed to get my thyroid prescription refilled, I found myself at the South Side Drug on Ottumwa's Church Street. The pharmacy is one block down from my dad's first dental office, which is still there, across the street from St. Patrick's Church, where I was baptized. My Grandpa Lyle, an architect, had designed both the church and my dad's office. As kids, after getting our teeth cleaned by our dad, we would walk to the South Side Drug for milkshakes from the drug store's soda fountain.

South Side Drug is, like Canteen Lunch in the Alley, old and unchanged. And, unlike many of Ottumwa's other buildings, well preserved. In fact, not only is the soda fountain still intact—along with its seemingly fixed 1960s prices (milkshakes made with hand-scooped ice cream are only $1.75!)—the people working there are the same. One older woman working behind the counter said, "I remember you from when you were this tall," holding her hand down to the level of her knees. "I still have that crown your dad put in for me thirty-five years ago."

I shook my head at the incredulity of it, of this living history. It was hard to imagine my life that long ago. It was a good reminder that my life hadn't always been about grief. It had been about riding my purple Schwinn Hollywood up and down East Golf Avenue, feeling the wind in my face. It had been about learning dance routines and dressing up in tutus to perform those dances on stage. About daring each other to jump off the high dive at the swimming pool. About shoveling snow off the golf course pond so we could ice skate. It had been about cross-country family road trips to Disneyland in the station wagon back when we could sprawl out on sleeping bags and not be restricted by seat belts.

Life had held such promise of adventure. Of career. Of love. And I had gone out and found it, experienced it fully. I was lucky to have parents who gave me the freedom to leave home, parents who gave me the foundation on which I continued to build. I went to a college in Washington State (as far from Iowa as one can go and still be in the U.S.), and kept venturing farther and farther out from there, to Europe and Africa and Asia. And now . . . strangely, unexpectedly back to Iowa.

Grant Wood was quoted as saying, "I had to go to France to appreciate Iowa." Yes, I got it. I felt the sentiment completely, especially as I continued discovering roots that I had no idea were still there, and still so important to me. Roots I had never fully appreciated. Until now.

I met Steve Siegel, who, because he is a board member for the American Gothic House Center, comes to meetings next door to my house every month. When he introduced himself, he told me, "I live in your grandparents' house on North Court. I bought it from them thirty-one years ago."

"You knew my grandparents?" I thought my heart had burst—in a good way. I pictured them still alive and active, before they got cancer, accepting a check from Steve for the sale of their beloved old house. I had a flashback to sliding down the wooden banister, looking through my grandpa's collection of painted rocks and trying to snoop in my grandma's pantry, which she called the "Off Limits Closet." I wondered what Steve and his wife kept in that closet now. And if the house still smelled of mothballs and green beans.

"I worked with Genny down at Ottumwa City Hall when she was City Clerk," he continued. "My wife and I will have you over for dinner sometime."

"I would love that," I said.

And then, of course, there was Canteen Lunch in the Alley. After my lunch there that hot summer afternoon following the state fair, I thought I'd never see the place again. Now I was eating there whenever I could coordinate my grocery shopping trips to Aldi with the Canteen's hours and my hunger pangs. And while I loved their loose-meat burgers, it wasn't always the Canteen's food I was specifically hungry for. I was feeding a hunger for my past, for my innocence, for the simplicity of those childhood years. Which is to say, I was eating at the Canteen regularly. I quickly became recognized and whenever I would come in, the women behind the counter would say, smiling, "Oh, it's the Pie Lady. How are things in Eldon?" Their friendliness was a contrast to my first trip back to the Canteen in August, when I had tried to make conversation and was greeted by an air of gruffness and suspicion. I didn't take it personally. I had been a stranger in town then; I was a local now. I liked being remembered for who I was as a child. But even more important, I was being welcomed for who I had become, for who I am now. And that felt good. Really, really good.

CHAPTER

25

Like some kind of divine joke, the opening day of my pie stand coincided with a funeral held in front of my house.

I could run, but I couldn't hide. From grief, I mean. At eight o'clock on a mid-October Saturday morning, I saw Brenda Kremer, owner of Kremer Funeral Home in Eldon, walk up the path to my house with two men in tow. All of them were carrying folding chairs. I knew why. I was informed a few days earlier there would be a funeral service for Helen Glasson in front of the American Gothic House. Helen was the granddaughter of Gideon and Mary Jones, the owners of the house at the time Grant Wood created the famous painting that, subsequently, made the house famous. Helen was passionate about preserving Eldon's history—not just her grandparents' house but also the McHaffey Opera House— and had also spearheaded the creation of the American Gothic House Center. But by the time the ribbon-cutting ceremony for the Center was held three years ago, her Alzheimer's had advanced to the point where she was able to attend the celebration but, sadly, was not aware of why she was there. She eventually succumbed to the disease. And now her life was going to be commemorated.

Given my new residency of the house, it had seemed fitting that I pay my respects. But I need not have bothered debating whether or not I should attend the funeral. As always, the answer came on its own.

Sometime between the time Brenda and her crew finished setting up the chairs, the flower arrangements and the CD player, and the time the funeral attendees arrived, I took a stroll out front. This was not a good idea. The sight of the flower arrangements reminded me of Marcus's funerals. That, combined with an instrumental version of "Morning Has Broken" by Cat Stevens on the CD player, undid me. I ran back inside the house, locked the door behind me and collapsed on the sofa in a fit of tears.

I had been so busy since leaving Portland the first of August—driving cross-country, judging pies at the Iowa State Fair, touring my childhood stomping grounds, moving into my new house and starting a pie business—that I'd almost forgotten what grief felt like. But there it was. Flooding back. Oh yes, I remembered it well. Grieving was like riding a bike. You never forget how to do it. Because it never goes away.

No, I would not be going to the funeral. They wouldn't want the distraction of a sobbing mess like me in their midst.

In the height of my bawling session, I thought of Brenda Kremer. Brenda had lost her husband less than two years ago to pancreatic cancer. (Cancer sucks.) But here she was, organizing not just this funeral, but having taken over her late husband's business, Brenda organized every funeral in Eldon. "How could she do it?" I wondered. How could she heal when she was constantly reminded of loss? That soul-wrenching, heart-shattering loss that leaves one permanently wounded and lost, going through life feeling like a leaking vessel, or missing a vital limb. I vowed to ask her. When the time was right. That time would surely not be the day of Helen Glasson's funeral.

I eventually uncurled from the fetal position and extracted myself from the couch to call Melissa, telling her how the proximity of this funeral had triggered a grief burst.

"You always talk about how pie heals," she said. "Why don't you get busy and do something that makes you feel better? Go make some pie."

She had a valid point. Especially as it was the opening day of my Pitchfork Pie Stand and I was scheduled to set up my table outside after the funeral. That I actually needed to be reminded to get busy baking showed just how deep I could still sink when it came to grief. Of course making pie always made me feel better, but it could also be a little like jogging. If I wasn't already in the mood, I had to muster an extra dose of motivation to get started. Once I got going, I was fine. After the initial resistance, be it with pie baking or running, I would inevitably settle into my spiritual trance—I would get in the zone.

I hung up the phone, dried my eyes, rolled up my sleeves (and not just figuratively), to make ten more apple pies for my launch, to add to the ten I had made the previous day. The sight of the ten pies alone should have been enough to cheer me up. I had stabbed vent holes in each of them. Without giving it much thought, I simply carved the shape of a pitchfork. It was an obvious symbol of the American Gothic House, easy to create, and allowed for just the right ventilation for the steaming fruit. I looked down at my little emblem, a symbol that, like a horse's brand, could be my trademark, and the name popped into my head: Pitchfork Pie Stand.

But before I began baking—and carving more pitchforks—I lit a candle in the living room. For Helen. It was my way of participating. In the only way I was capable at the time.

I pulled the kitchen curtain shut so the funeral attendees wouldn't be distracted by my movements in the kitchen—and I wouldn't have the constant reminder of all that sadness—and eventually lost myself in the creative, meditative process of pie. The steady and familiar rhythms of kneading, rolling, peeling, slicing, crimping worked their soothing magic on me, and pretty soon I found my balance again.

When the funeral was over, I carried my fresh-baked pies out to my folding table, set up to the side of the house on the lawn. The sight of the bountiful homemade goods lifted my spirits further. I had watched many of my students beam with a sense of accomplishment from their finished pies. And even after making thousands of pies in my lifetime, I was not immune to the joy of the accomplishment. I was so proud of my twenty baked beauties on display, I had forgotten all about the funeral and my earlier eruption. But I was also slightly nervous. What if no one came to buy them?

I needn't have worried. I sold out of my pie inventory in less than two hours. What I hadn't expected is that my customers didn't want just a slice; they wanted whole pies to take with them. In that short span of time, people from all over the U.S.—tourists who came just to have their picture taken in front of the American Gothic House—came up to my makeshift pie shop. When they learned I lived inside the icon the barrage of questions began. "People can live in the house? Really? How long have you lived there? What brought you here?"

I learned very quickly that I was going to have to dodge the questions or come up with a pat answer or both. I whittled my long, complicated explanation down to one quick and easy sentence: "I'm from here." It was true. And as I said it, I could feel the little sprouts under my feet grow a little more, seeking to plant themselves deeper into the ground.

Some of my first customers included the grandchildren of Helen Glasson, a sophisticated, articulate bunch who had moved away to major Midwest cities and reassembled in Eldon for the funeral. I offered to let them go inside of the house, their great-grandparents' house that they hadn't seen since they were little kids.

"Please excuse the disaster in the kitchen," I called after them as they stepped through the front door. "I didn't have a chance to clean up my pie-baking mess. But feel free to look around. Take your time." It seemed fitting. With the exception of my furniture and clothes inside—and the fact I paid the rent—the house felt like it belonged more to them than to me. The Glasson Family was grateful for the tour.

"Thank you so much," they gushed. "We love how you have it decorated. So modern." And I was grateful for them buying pie afterward. It was mutually beneficial, a salve on a day with a somber beginning.

But the day wasn't over yet. A little later I spotted Brenda Kremer walking up the path toward the house again. This time she wasn't in her Sunday best. She had changed into jeans and was surveying the grounds to make sure everything had been cleaned up after the service. I stepped out of the house to meet her. I put my arm around her shoulder and walked with her up the sidewalk and said, "I am amazed by your courage. I don't know how you do it. Just seeing the flowers tore me apart."

We had been introduced only once and never really had a conversation before. And yet I felt her body relax under my arm with the relief of finally broaching the subject.

"I heard about your husband, too," she said. "We should talk sometime."

"I would really like that," I replied.

For the next two months, from October to December, my focus was solely on building my pie stand business. Having stocked up on my equipment and supplies, I turned my attention to making some home improvements. I painted the oak cabinets red to cheer up the otherwise bland kitchen, adding iron drawer pulls to make the space look more 1880s instead of 1980s. I nailed a Peg-Board (purchased for fifty cents from the McHaffey Opera House Thrift Store) to the wall to hang aprons. I assembled a rolling rack to store my five rolling pins, stack of large plastic mixing bowls and all of my other pie supplies (like pastry brushes, bench scraper, lattice cutter and cookbooks) liberated at last from their travel bin. Over the window of the back door, I hung a red-and-white-checkered curtain, sewn by my neighbor, Rosie, out of a remnant I bought for two bucks at Wal-Mart. Rosie added a white eyelet ruffle, which was a fitting touch. I asked my landlord for a new oven and he said yes. I tried to keep the old one, too, so I could double my pie output. But the house was not wired for that much voltage, so the old oven was carted away. My wooden butcher-block table became the centerpiece of the kitchen. Its space served triple use for rolling dough, then pie assembly and, finally, pie cooling.

Local Eldonites were excited about the new activity in the neighborhood and wanted to get involved. Various neighbors and new friends all came by at various times to help peel apples by the bushel. Priscilla (who had loaned me the lawn chairs a month earlier) introduced me to the miracle tool, the apple peeler/corer/slicer. An ancient-looking cast iron contraption that adheres to the countertop with a suction cup, you place an apple on the prongs, turn the hand crank, and the apple spins around and around until it comes through a metal bar on the other end completely—as the name suggests—peeled, cored and sliced. This was not only a time saver, it was a way to avoid blisters and tired hands from too much time with a paring knife.

In between all the visitors—both the helpers and customers— I spent many hours alone in my kitchen. I listened to my iPod, swapping the cello music from my wedding for slightly more upbeat Jackson Browne and John Mayer—which represented an incremental step forward in my grief recovery, so I liked to think. I built up my forearm muscles while kneading bowl after bowl of dough. I was selling up to thirty pies every weekend, which means I was rolling sixty separate pie crusts at a time.

Surely the American Gothic House had never experienced such a prolific production of baked goods within its walls. Surely the American Gothic House had never had such a healing effect on one of its residents, either. In those late-autumn days, as winter approached, all I did was bake. With each push of the rolling pin and each pie that came browned and bubbling out of the oven, my soul was soothed and my heart mended a little more.

CHAPTER

26

March 19, 2011, Eldon, Iowa—19 months since Marcus's death

My morning starts the same way every day. I open my eyes to the soft light penetrating through the three layers of opaque curtains on the famous Gothic window. I roll over to my right, rouse Daisy from her snoring sleep and pull her closer to me. Jack sleeps on the other end of the second floor, on Marcus's red leather Stressless chair, next to the back Gothic window. My writing desk ended up downstairs, and while placing the leather chair upstairs was intended to be a reading nook for me, Jack claimed it for his squirrel patrol instead. He perks up at the sound of Daisy's grunting. She makes purring-type noises when I stroke her behind the ears and Jack wants his share of snuggling, too, so he joins us in the bed as we greet the day in a group hug of dog hair and down pillows.

The bed is the "amazing memory foam mattress." To get it upstairs, the movers hauled it up over the roof of the back porch and in through the rear Gothic window. (The front Gothic window is sealed shut, but the back one swings open on a hinge.) The king-size mattress takes up the entire bedroom and rests directly on the floor. It couldn't be on a bed frame anyway because the slanted ceiling reaches down so low, to have the mattress raised any higher would mean you couldn't sit up in bed. Some visitors have called my bedroom set up "glorified camping." I call it "just right."

Before I get out of bed, I check my iPhone for messages. I no longer have the BlackBerry in the red rubber case, but I do still get an occasional call from an "Unknown" number. While there might be a perceptible twinge when I see that reminder of the medical examiner's call on the screen, I can predict it will be one of two people who I actually want to hear from—Susan, my grief counselor from Portland with whom I still check in every few months, or Jonathan, my entertainment lawyer in L.A. who is still hoping the pie TV show sells. While I look forward to calls from both of them, I try to keep the ones from Jonathan short because he bills for his time and even with the deep Team Pie discount he gives me, it's still expensive. After several yes-no cycles thinking the show had been sold, only to have my hopes dashed yet again, I have let go of the outcome for getting the TV series on the air. It was the making of the pie show that was the gift. It gave me purpose when I needed it and set me on a positive, new path. It was about the journey, not the destination. It led me to some wonderful new people in my life, some very delicious pie and, without realizing it at the time, it led me back to Iowa, and ultimately to this house I now call my home.

I go downstairs, ducking my head as I round the bend on the tight, narrow staircase, and fire up my espresso machine. I use the time before the coffee drips to open the front door. The dogs know it's their cue and they're ready, certain that this time they really will catch the squirrel that's been taunting them all week. While they race off in the yard, I go back to the kitchen to steam the milk for my latte. When it's ready, I put on my long, puffy coat over the top of my pajamas, slide on my tall rubber boots purchased from Tractor Supply Company and go outside to join Team Terrier.

I didn't spend the winter in California as I had expected to. My coat, which I bought for $8.99 at Goodwill, kept me so warm I never felt cold. And the house? It was also warm and surprisingly well insulated. It was so cozy, especially with the colorful Christmas lights I hung on the back porch, I couldn't bring myself to leave.

The tourists aren't here yet. It's early spring and the threat of snow keeps them away. If the roads aren't icy, a few might stop by for a photo later in the afternoon. It's a rare day, even in sub-zero temperatures, that the American Gothic House doesn't get at least one visitor. The house, looking dreary and dull against Iowa's winter-thaw backdrop of gloomy, gray skies and leafless trees, still surprisingly sees a trickle of traffic at this time of year, people showing up like drips from a faucet leaking so slowly it's not worth calling the plumber. The visitor center next door is open year-round, but during the cold months there are days when I am the only human being its administrator Molly sees. During the week, if I've woken up late, anytime after 8:30 a.m., Molly will already be at work and I'll stop by to say hi—in my pajamas, hair uncombed, carrying my mug of coffee.

Molly sees me more often in my bathrobe than in proper clothes, and the times I do bother to get dressed I just slip my bib overalls on over the top of my pajamas. My life is uncomplicated that way. It's not like I am letting myself go. I live in a rural place with no reason to wear the many cute wool skirts, silk blouses and the Armani suit that fill my upstairs closet. And in the cold weather my concerns have more to do with staying warm than looking stylish. I do bathe, almost every night, in my half-length iron bathtub. The tub is so short I have to lay in it at an angle with my legs up the wall in a yoga pose in order to submerge my torso.

I no longer wear my wedding ring or Marcus's. I can't say exactly when and why I stopped wearing them. Maybe it was just that my skin was pruning underneath all that thick gold and steel. One day I took them off to let my finger dry out and that one rest day led to another and another. Instead of the wedding bands, I wear Marcus's chunky silver ring that looks like a cross between primitive African art and a motorcycle part, made by the same German jewelry designer who created our wedding rings. I often rub my fingers on it as if it's a worry stone or, when I'm feeling vulnerable, as a way to channel some of Marcus's warrior-like strength.

It took nineteen months, but I finally washed Marcus's red plaid bathrobe, the one I used like a security blanket when it still held his scent. I could no longer tell whose scent was on it—it merely smelled stale, like it needed washing. Badly. And as long as I was putting the robe into the washing machine, I added his orange-and-yellow plaid duvet cover along with it. I poured in the soap and shut the lid and felt a pang of regret and shame that I had snapped at Melissa's innocent kids for playing on it. I took my spring-cleaning actions one step further and packed away most of Marcus's pictures—the most visible ones on my refrigerator door and the ones in the living room. These steps were like prying my fingers loose from my grip on the past. If I wanted to make room for new life, I needed to stop clinging to my old one. It was simply time to let go. I had discovered my inner trapeze artist. I was no longer afraid of the empty space in between the swings. I was preparing to grab the new swing, whenever it might come to me.

I don't believe it's a coincidence that this urge to move forward coincided with the onset of spring. Spring is the season of fertility. Farmers are tilling their fields, getting ready to plant new seeds. After a dark and quiet winter of hibernating, allowing time for the vestiges of grief to fall away, I too am ready to plant new seeds. I am also waiting for the rhubarb to ripen so I can make pie. I have already inspected the progress of the budding red-and-green stalks in the garden of Bob, my eighty-year-old neighbor, who is quite a good pie baker himself.

I still wrestle with the question of whether or not there's life after death. Is it just a matter of lights out, it's over? I was on a Grand Canyon river trip when I was thirty. After a five-hour, toenail-blackening hike to the bottom of the canyon to meet our raft and three days into our trip, we got enough distance from city life to settle into the rhythm of the river. As we floated downstream, I studied the striated rock walls of the canyon, carved out over millennia, and had a revelation that stuck with me ever since: our human species is going to be just another layer in the rock one day. We will eventually die out like every other species before us. Morose as it sounds, I found a strange yet overwhelming sense of peace at the thought.

But since Marcus died, I've questioned the meaning of life and what happens afterward in ways I never have before. I hope my layer-in-the-rock theory isn't completely accurate. Physically, we may end up as just another colored stripe in the Grand Canyon wall, but spiritually, I like to think there is something more. I like to believe that Marcus's soul is alive and well, learning, growing, traveling, listening, watching, protecting, helping, loving.

It's 10:30 a.m. Central time, I'm just back from walking my dogs. I mostly walk these days, but I have started running again. Exercise was too difficult emotionally for a long time. Instead of endorphins released, a workout would tap into the residual grief, allowing it to escape from the safety of its deep well of storage, and I would end up doubled over in tears in the middle of a run or bike ride. Believe me, this is not convenient when you're several miles from home. Grief is a heavy load to carry. My cells will always hold a memory of the pain I felt that first year. I will not forget what it feels like to touch the void. But now when I run, instead of doubling over in sorrow, I feel strength returning to my heart. Jogging on the long, gravel country roads, finding my old stride, shows me my Lance Armstrong potential is still there. The heart, after all, is a muscle and mine just needs some conditioning. The healing power of pie has taken me this far. Now it's time to add some fitness and some oxygen to the mix.

Whether walking or running, sadness never accompanies me when I'm out with my dogs. It's the opposite. They make me laugh as they sprint after an elusive critter, or pounce on a mole hole, thinking they are masters of their rural universe. Jack inevitably identifies a perfect stick, often a tree limb or log ten times the size of his little body, and he stands over it, barking, until he gets my attention. "Come throw this for me, Mom," he shouts.

"Are you crazy?" I reply. "This one is too big for you." But he persists. He is stubborn—like Marcus—and barks until I relent and break the branch until it's manageable enough for me to toss for him. I give it my best softball pitch and he comes bounding back, stick in mouth, victorious, the tautness of his compact, muscular frame conveying his pride. His hair blows back as he runs, his black nose turns up and I smile at the vision of him until my smile gives way to complete, gut-level laughter.

Daisy is every bit as funny and, having logged several American addresses since being rescued from Mexico, has taken a liking to

Midwestern living. Since we moved to Iowa, she has blossomed, expressing her gratitude and approval for our new landscape. Independent, adventurous and much braver than her German stepbrother (we got Jack as a puppy in Germany), Daisy leaves the security of the trail or the bike path and takes her own meandering, yet parallel way. I keep an eye out for glimpses of her curly, blond Mohawk and pear-shaped physique as she moves in and out of the prairie grass, the trees and the creek bed. She always rejoins us, her big brown eyes glistening as she sprints with joy toward our reunion. To see her run is the highlight of my day. Her gait is unusual and could be best described as a waddle, and her coat makes her look heavier than she is ("It's all fur," I say defensively when people suggest she needs to go on a diet). One cannot watch this odd, kinky-haired creature gallop without cracking up at the sight of her.

Sometimes we walk on the bike path and turn up the next road over to go see the neighbor's horses. They have seven of them. If I have leftover apple cores, I take them with me as treats. The horses are picky though, they don't like the peelings. I don't blame them as the Granny Smith skin is tough and waxy. I pet their noses and run my fingers through their manes and promise myself I am going to ask their owner if I can ride them when the weather gets warmer. I haven't forgotten—I still have a Spurs Award to win.

Our favorite walk is in the neighbor's soybean field, previously owned by Hollywood celebrities Tom Arnold and Roseanne Barr before they split up. (Word around Eldon has it that Roseanne did not take well to country living.) It could strike me as an ironic touchstone to my life in L.A., but there are so many more interesting, less stressful things to think about than overcrowded L.A.—and television. And for the record, I still don't have a TV.

The American Gothic House is wired for cable, but my high-speed Internet provides enough contact with the outside world for me.

Following the tractor tracks that provide a makeshift trail, we climb the hill until we get a view of the Des Moines River along with the rooftops of distant farmhouses and sunsets of the deepest pink hues over the plowed pastures. During these outings we almost always see deer, huge majestic mammals with white tails so long and bushy they seem to belong to cats. The deer, in groups of six or eight or sometimes twelve, bound away and Team Terrier watches in awe, wondering what kind of large squirrels they have just missed chasing.

For as much as making pie soothes my soul, I find my greatest solace in nature. Just as the Grand Canyon gave me that feeling of peace about the meaning of life, when I am walking in the soybean field, the world just seems to make more sense. My rubber farm boots firmly connecting with the ground, the views of the fields all the way to the horizon, flocks of geese flying overhead, the sound of nothing but prairie grass rustling in the wind, the cool air and sun on my face, breathing in the earthy scent of wet hay and moist soil—my surroundings serve as a spiritual connective tissue. Pie connects me with people, but nature connects me with God and with myself.

I find myself laughing a lot more these days. And crying a lot less. The grief bursts still come, but they most often correspond with my menstrual cycle, when my hormones surge and act as a truth serum, heightening any suppressed emotion, causing an occasional need to purge. I understand it. And I can track it on the calendar. Therefore, I am able to manage my lingering sadness.

At night I walk the dogs—without fear of rattlesnakes or tarantulas like in Terlingua—in a loop around the visitor center parking lot and the city's public works facility, which consists of two metal-sided barns overflowing with heavy equipment. I leave the lights on in the American Gothic House and can look back at the glow coming from its windows—as if the house is keeping an eye on us during our walk, welcoming us back into its warmth when we return. I never get tired of the sight of it. The cottage looks as cute and huggable to me after six months as it did the first time I laid eyes on it. I look at the place lovingly, grateful I can call it home. It feels like home, a place I will live for a long time. I tell my dad he won't have to get a new address book anytime soon.

Each night I look up at the sky—dark, sometimes cloudy, sometimes clear with the brightest, twinkling stars—and I talk to Marcus. I always greet him first. "Hi, my love." Then I add, "I miss you" or ask "How are you? I hope you are okay." Sometimes I ask for his help and guidance, other times I just make comments about the dogs. "They love it here. I wish you could see them. I'm taking good care of them, I promise." And I might add, "I'm taking good care of myself, too."

I know now that I did not kill my husband. I've had it drilled in my head too many times by too many experts (and endless Internet searches) that a ruptured aorta can only be caused mechanically, physically. It cannot be caused by emotion or stress—or by filing for divorce. Marcus had a heart condition. A bicuspid aortic valve. He was born with it. I will always live with the sadness that he is gone. But it wasn't my fault. I did not kill him.

I also have gone back and read the last emails Marcus wrote to me in the days and weeks before his death—I indulge in them and look through all his pictures about once a month. I can read his letters with more clarity now, without the "It's my fault" filter. He did want the divorce. He was sad about it, yes, but like me, he was tired of our struggle. He wrote to me on August 10, 2009, nine days before he died:

Don't worry, I am okay. I think you know me.
I take comfort in knowing we fought hard for this.
We didn't squander it away. I had no idea how to
make our personalities fit into a marriage without
changing what and who you are—and I love who
you are. Yes, the thought of filing the paperwork is
strange. There's tremendous sadness when I look
back on our good moments and realize that this
seems to be over. I know that there will be a time
when I look back on those moments and they will
fill me with happiness, because they are so special and no one can take them away from us. Our
good moments were really special, you have to
admit that! You probably have no idea how much
tenderness and appreciation I feel when thinking about you, but also a quiet anger when I think
about our marriage. Once all this administrative
stuff is out of the way, I can again enjoy who you
are without needing to make us fit into a marriage.
That's what keeps me going. This current phase
is not pleasant, far from it, but beyond it lies the
opportunity for us to respect and appreciate and
enjoy each other.

Love,
Marcus

I often wonder what my life would be like now if Marcus hadn't
died. Would I have found my way back to Iowa? Or would I have
found my way back to my husband? He was—and always will be—
my husband. Many of my friends who had seen us through our

temporary separations, our near-divorce, said, "You two would have gotten back together." I always liked hearing this, I still think it's possible and I constantly tell Marcus so. Wherever he may be, convinced he can hear me, I say to him—er, to the earth's atmosphere, "We're going to be together again. I know we are. We're going to find each other. And we're going to get it right next time."

Until then, I sometimes feel like I am biding my time. As much as I appear to be embracing my new beginnings, to have found a healthy new home in Iowa, and to have found a purpose through pie, sometimes there is a sense that all of this is just temporary. And it is. Plain and simple: life is temporary. None of us knows how long we'll be here. My dad was right when he said, "We all die someday." (Though I still say he could have timed his comment better than during Marcus's funeral.) I live with the notion that life is short, there's not much time. Whatever it is you want to do, do it now. Don't wait.

I'm not waiting. I'm writing with a sense of urgency. Summer is coming and, along with the warm days, the tourists will return. They'll be picnicking on the lawn, groups arriving by the busload will be posing for pictures, kids will scamper on my front porch, and in spite of the polite little "Private Residence" signs I've hung in the windows, many of them will be peering in through the lace curtains. They'll be hungry for pie. And they won't just want pie, they'll expect it. The Pitchfork Pie Stand will be open soon. So I write faster and faster.

My time pressure—self-inflicted, to use Marcus's word—also comes from the idea I've carried with me since my husband died: my grief was so profound—some had even called it over the top— that it made me wish for death. In the months following Marcus's passing I had wanted so intensely for my life to end—so I could go find him. With that kind of powerful thinking I have worried

I might actually manifest a deadly disease. I wonder if I will get cancer. Or if I already have it. That headache I get once a month might be a brain tumor. That pimple thing on my forehead is surely melanoma. That side ache I feel every so often could be a malignant cyst. Whatever it is, doctors will tell me I have only three months to live. Oh, I can really get myself worked up. But as soon as I become aware of them, I swat those negative paranoid thoughts aside, the way I do with the bees when they swarm around my pies on the table outside.

I'm still alive, I still have my health, I still keep living. I am breathing, walking my dogs, making pies, making new friends and making new memories in the American Gothic House. Eventually, over time, I will have another story to tell. I will write a new one, hopefully one that includes new love, one in which I can finally have my happy ending.

I may not have Marcus, but I still have hope.

I thank pie. If my mom had never made my dad that banana cream pie, I never would have been born. If I had never been born, I never would have learned to make pie, never would have had that job in Malibu and thus never would have taken that road trip to Oregon where I met Marcus. If I had never met Marcus, I never would have spent seven and a half years with him, a time too short but one I feel very grateful and blessed to have had.

If not for pie, I never would have gone to the Iowa State Fair to be a pie judge or taken that road trip to Ottumwa after the fair to visit my birthplace and eat lunch at the Canteen. If I had never taken that road trip, I never would have been on my way to the radio station in Fairfield. And if I had never gone to Fairfield, I never would have seen the highway sign for the American Gothic House. If I had never met Marcus due to a similar fork in the road, I never would have bothered to stop at the tourist attraction and thus never would have discovered the famous house was for rent, that it was affordable, that it was perfect for me.

If I hadn't moved back to Iowa, into the American Gothic House, I never would have discovered how kind and hospitable my neighbors could be, how it feels to be warmly welcomed into a community where I'm fed ham balls, farm-fresh eggs and the mayor's own peach pie. I never would have known how healing it would be to return to my roots, how breathing in the scent of fertile soil and grass and snow would make me feel grounded, how the openness of the landscape would open my heart again.

If not for pie, I never would have started the Pitchfork Pie Stand, making my handmade pies in my historic kitchen and selling them to tourists on the weekends, finding the balance between solitude and socializing.

If not for pie, I never would have survived the grief and guilt from Marcus's death, I never would have set forth on my pie quest and built the strength to forgive myself, or found the faith and the grace to keep living.

If not for pie, I never would have made peace with myself.

I'm glad my mom made my dad that banana cream pie. I love pie.

BETH'S PIE CRUST
(Makes a double crust)

2½ cups flour (but have at least 3 and ½ cups on hand, as you'll need extra flour to roll dough and to thicken filling)

½ cup butter

½ cup vegetable shortening

Dash of salt

Ice water (fill one cup, but use only enough to moisten dough)

In a large bowl, work the butter and shortening into the flour with your hands until you see marble-size lumps form. Pour in ice water a little at a time, sort of "fluffing" the flour to mix in liquid. When the dough feels moist, do a "squeeze test" and if it holds together you're done. Your dough should feel tacky, but not wet. (Do not overwork the dough! It takes very little time and you'll be tempted to keep touching it, but don't!) Divide the dough in 2 balls. Form each ball into a disk shape. Roll flat and thin to fit your pie dish. Sprinkle flour under and on top of your dough to keep it from sticking to your rolling surface. Trim excess dough around the edges with scissors so that it is about 1 inch wider than the dish edge.

mary spellman's apple pie

(Made by Beth at Malibu Kitchen…and at the Pitchfork Pie Stand)

CRUST:

1   double crust (see Beth's Pie Crust recipe on page 301)

FILLING:

7   large Granny Smith* apples (depending on size
    of apple and size of pie dish)

¾   cup sugar

4   tbsp flour

    Dash of salt

2   tsp cinnamon (or more, depending on how much
    you like)

1   tbsp butter (to put on top of apples before
    covering with top crust)

1   beaten egg (to brush top crust before putting
    in oven)

(*It's also okay to use a combination of apples, try Braeburn and Royal Gala. Do not use Fuji or Red Delicious—they lack tartness. Also note, the approximate rule of thumb is three pounds of fruit per pie.)

Lay the prepared bottom crust into the pie dish. Slice half of the peeled apples directly into the pie, arranging and pressing them into the dish to remove extra space between slices. Cover with half of your other ingredients (sugar, flour, cinnamon, salt), then slice the remaining apples and cover with second half of ingredients. Add dollop of butter. Cover with top crust and crimp edges, then brush with the beaten egg (this gives the pie a nice golden brown shine). Use a knife to poke vent holes in the top crust (get creative here with a unique pattern if you want). Bake at 425° for 20 minutes. Turn oven down to 375° and bake for another 30 to 40 minutes or so, until juice bubbles. Poke with a knife to make sure apples have softened. Do not overbake or apples will turn mushy.

Marie Howard's Banana Cream Pie
(The one that prompted her marriage proposal; the pie that is the reason I was born)

CRUST:

1   blind-baked single-crust pie shell (half of Beth's Pie Crust recipe on page 301)*

FILLING:

¾   cup sugar

¼   cup cornstarch

¼   tsp salt

3   cups whole milk

5   eggs (separate yolks and whites, saving whites for meringue)

3   tbsp butter

1   tbsp vanilla

4   sliced bananas

(*Blind baking is when you pre-bake a pie crust, which is what you use for a cream pie where the pudding is already cooked. Using half Beth's double-crust recipe above, line a pie plate with dough and crimp the edges. Prick the bottom of the pie crust with a fork. This keeps the dough from puffing up during baking. Line the pie plate with foil or parchment paper and fill with a few cups of rice or beans—or pie weights if you have them. The weight keeps the dough from shrinking. Bake at 425° for 20 minutes, remove foil and weights and bake another 5 minutes or until it's light brown.)

Whisk dry ingredients together in heavy saucepan, then gradually whisk in milk. Stirring constantly, cook until thick and bubbling. Once it bubbles, continue cooking for another 2 minutes. Remove from heat. In a separate bowl, add about a cup of the hot filling to the beaten egg yolks, then add this egg mixture to the pan of pudding. Constantly stirring, bring to a gentle boil and cook for another 2 minutes. Remove from heat and stir in butter and vanilla. Fill bottom of blind-baked pie shell with sliced bananas. Pour hot pudding on top, then make meringue as directed on the next page.

MERINGUE:

- 5 egg whites
- 1 tsp vanilla
- ½ tsp cream of tartar
- ½ cup sugar

In a clean mixing bowl, beat egg whites, vanilla and cream of tartar at high speed for several minutes. Gradually add sugar, just a little at a time. Continue beating on high speed until stiff peaks form. Spread meringue over warm pudding until it covers the entire pie, sealing the crust edge. With the back of a large spoon, dab at the meringue, lifting the spoon high as you pull back to create curlicue effect. Bake at 425° for 7 to 8 minutes, until meringue looks toasted. Watch carefully so as not to burn!

Lana Ross's Better-than-sex French Silk Pie

(Second-place winner at Iowa State Fair, 2010)

CRUST *(Lana's recipe is for a blind-baked single crust)*:

1 cup flour
½ tsp salt
⅓ cup lard
  scant ⅓ cup water

Prepare crust by cutting the lard into the flour and salt. Gradually add water until all is moist. Roll out and place in a 9 or 10-inch pie pan. Blind bake for 15 to 20 minutes, then let cool.

FILLING:

1 cup butter
1½ cups extra fine sugar
4 ounces unsweetened chocolate, melted
4 eggs
1 tsp vanilla

TOPPING:

2 cups whipping cream
4 tbsp powdered sugar
1 tbsp vanilla

Beat butter and sugar until light and fluffy. Blend in chocolate and vanilla. Add eggs, one at a time, beating at medium speed for 5 minutes after each addition. Pour into cooled pie shell. Chill at least 4 hours. Whip the cream, sugar and vanilla until thick. Pipe onto cooled pie. Garnish with chocolate shavings.

SHIRLEY STACEY'S PEACH PIE
(Served as my housewarming treat by the Mayor of Eldon, Iowa)

CRUST:

1   double-crust (see Beth's Pie Crust recipe on page 301)

FILLING:

6 to 8 ripe peaches (peeled and sliced into pie crust)

1 to 1 ½ cups sugar

2   tbsp flour

¼   cup tapioca (small pearl)

small amount of cinnamon

1   beaten egg

Mix sugar, flour, tapioca and cinnamon and sprinkle over peaches. Dot with butter. Add second (top) crust and brush with egg. Sprinkle top crust with sugar and cinnamon, if you like. Bake at 425° until crust is set (about 20 minutes). Reduce heat to 350° and bake until peaches are done (about 1 hour total baking time). Insert fork in the middle. If peaches don't cling to fork, they're done.

ArLene KILDOW'S COCONUT CREAM PIE

(Eldon, Iowa's, finest and first-place winner of Wapello County Fair, 2011)

CRUST:

1   blind-baked single-crust pie shell (half of Beth's Pie Crust recipe on page 301)

FILLING:

½   cup sugar

3   tbsp cornstarch

3   cups half-and-half cream

4   egg yolks

1   cup coconut

1   tsp vanilla

1   tsp coconut flavoring

1   tbsp butter

In a sauce pan, combine sugar and cornstarch. Stir in half-and-half and egg yolks. Cook over stove until thick, then add coconut. Remove from heat and stir in vanilla, coconut flavoring and butter. Pour pudding into prebaked pie shell and prepare meringue.

MERINGUE:

4   egg whites

½   cup sugar

1   tbsp cornstarch

Beat egg whites until peaks form, then add sugar and cornstarch. Spoon meringue on top of warm pudding. Sprinkle coconut on top, then bake at 350° until egg whites turn brown (10 to 15 minutes).

ACKNOWLEDGMENTS

It takes a lot of people to tell a story. It takes a tremendous amount of support to recover from grief. These are the people, who, during the past two years, helped me through the most unimaginable darkness. Some of them are featured in the book, some read my early drafts, some knew Marcus, some were just really great inspiration or influence, some made me laugh, some even made me pie. Regardless of their direct involvement in *Making Piece,* these are the people who have touched my life and who deserve my public gratitude. This book would not exist without them.

Deidre Knight (my literary agent, a goddess and Steel Magnolia), Ann Leslie Tuttle (my compassionate and enthusiastic editor) and the staff at Harlequin Nonfiction.

Team Marcus (and the first three numbers in my speed dial): Nan Schmid, Melissa Forman and Alison Kauffman.

My grief counselor and godsend: Susan Hodnot (How did I get so lucky?!).

My family: my parents, Tom and Marie Howard; my sister, Anne (thanks not only for reading my manuscript, but for the supersoft pajamas, the "Daisy" perfume and Bach Flower Essence "grief drops"—that care package really cheered me up); my brothers, Tim, Michael, Patrick; Patrick's family; and my aunt Sue and uncle Mike Finn.

In Terlingua: John Alexander, Cynthia Hood, Mimi Webb Miller, Betty Moore and Ralph Moore (three weeks of dog sitting while I was at Marcus's funerals earns you a lifetime supply of Guinness and guitar strings, Ralph).

In Portland: Frank Bird, Arlene Burns, Bennett Burns and Andrew Rowe, Janine Canella, Colleen Coleman, Saumya Comer, Liz Heaney, Don Hofer, Stacy James, Thomas Lehman, Donn Lindstrom, Sylvia Linington, Megan McMorris, Marty Rudolph and Heather Wade. *Ein besonderes Dankeschön* to the Portland/ Freightliner gang, in particular: Dayna and Gerald Freitag; Julia Hofmann, Joerg, Katrin and Nolan Liebermann; and Lyndsay, Andreas and Heidi Presthofer and Rachel Wecker.

In and around Eldon, Iowa: Priscilla Coffman; Meg and Jeff Courter and family; Linda Durflinger; Patti Durflinger (who delivered dinners to my back door to keep me writing); Don and Shirley Eakins; Cari Garrett; Brenda Kremer; LeAnn Lemberger; Allen and Rosie Morrison; Molly Moser (who holds the distinction of being the very first reader of my book and my salvation for getting through my first Iowa winter in thirty years and whose painting inspired my book title); Shirley and Gene Stacey; Carrie, Chloe and Tony Teninty; Bob and Iola Thomas; Jerome Thompson; and the ladies at Canteen Lunch in the Alley (Yvonne Warrick, Linda Grace and the rest of the crew).

TV Shoot in California: Janice Molinari (my coproducer—thank you for your laughter, your singing, your vision for the pie show and for giving me a purpose when I desperately needed one). Sunny Sherman and Martha Gamble of The Apple Pan, Natalie Galatzer of Bike Basket Pies, Bill Miller of Malibu Kitchen, Karen Heisler and Krystin Rubin of Mission Pie, Dorothy Pryor of Mommie Helen's, the Law family of Oak Glen, Carlene Baime, The Doscher Family, Kathy Eldon and Amy Eldon Turteltaub, Prudence Fenton and

Allee Willis, Susanne Flother and Anthony Scott, Elissa Harris, Jeff Mark, Thelma Orellena, Elana Pianko, Shanti Sosienski and Jane Windsor.

Pie People: Kathleen Beebout, Gina Hyams, Arlene Kildow, John Lehndorff, Tricia Martin (also my ace web designer), Mary Pint (the original "Pie Lady"), Lana Ross, Mary Spellman (my pie mentor, to whom I'm forever grateful), Mary Deatrick and Linda Hoskins of the American Pie Council, and Arlette Hollister, Patt Kerr and the food crew of the Iowa State Fair.

Friends, colleagues, readers, advisors and general hand-holders: Christine Buckley, John and Laura Climaco, Susan Comolli, Barbara DeMarco-Barrett, Julia Gajcak, Maggie Galloway, Angela Hynes, Steve Johnson, Jim Keppler, Ann Krcik, Dana Long, Patti Nilsen, Alayne Reesberg, Maria Ricapito, Jean Sagendorph, Andrew Salomon, Sue Sesko and Jonathan Wight.

My blog followers (who encouraged me to keep writing about my grief publicly): Chris Bauer, Sigrid Holland, Jeff "Prop" O'Brien, Kelly Sedlinger and Paul Szendrey.

Journalists (the people who discovered my story and wanted to share it): Jennifer Anderson (*Portland Tribune*), Mike Borland (WHO-TV), Steve Boss and James Moore (KRUU-FM), John Gaps III, Kyle Munson and Tom Perry (*Des Moines Register*), Lianne Hansen and Jacki Lyden (NPR), Kelly Kegans (*Better Homes and Gardens*), Katherine Lagomarsino (*Spirit* magazine), Ron Lutz (*Our Iowa*), Trevor Meers (*Midwest Living*), Meghan Rabbitt (*Natural Health*) and Peter Tubbs (Better TV).

Pie makers and pie lovers everywhere: you all help make the world a better place.

And last, but certainly not least: Banana Cream Pie.

Beth M. Howard is a journalist, blogger and pie baker. Her articles have appeared in *Elle, Shape, Travel + Leisure* and *Natural Health*, among many other publications. In 2001, at the height of the dot com boom, she quit a lucrative web producing job in San Francisco to bake "pies for the stars" at a gourmet deli in Malibu, California. Her popular blog, The World Needs More Pie, which she launched in 2007, regularly receives national press that has included *Better Homes and Gardens,* the *New York Times* and NPR's *Weekend Edition*. Beth lives in Eldon, Iowa, in the famous American Gothic House.